"... Marvelous Miami,
the town with one
thousand souls and
the survey of the
place yet to be
completed. The
coming Metropolis
of South Florida."

Miami Metropolis, 15 May 1896

University Press of Florida

Gainesville   Tallahassee   Tampa   Boca Raton   Pensacola   Orlando   Miami   Jacksonville

BUILDING MARVELOUS MIAMI

Nicholas N. Patricios

Copyright 1994 by the Board of Regents
of the State of Florida
Printed in the United States of America
on acid-free paper
All rights reserved
98 97 96 95 94 5 4 3 2 1

Library of Congress
Cataloging-in-Publication Data

Patricios, Nicholas N.
Building marvelous Miami /
Nicholas N. Patricios.
p.   cm.
Includes bibliographical references and
index.
ISBN 0-8130-1299-6
1. Architecture—Florida—Miami.
2. Architecture, Tropical—Florida—
Miami.   3. Miami (Fla.)—Buildings,
structures, etc.   I. Title.
NA735.M398P38   1994
720'.9759'381—dc20   94-7650

Cover photo by Marc Morganstine.
Half-title photo, Miami skyline at night
(1932), and photo facing contents page,
Everglades drainage canal at Tamiami
Trail (1927), both courtesy of Miami-
Dade Public Library, Romer Collection.
Frontispiece photo, aerial view of
downtown Miami in the 1970s, courtesy
of Archives and Special Collections,
University of Miami.

The University Press of Florida is the
scholarly publishing agency for the State
University System of Florida, comprised
of Florida A & M University, Florida
Atlantic University, Florida International
University, Florida State University,
University of Central Florida, University
of Florida, University of North Florida,
University of South Florida, and
University of West Florida.

University Press of Florida
15 Northwest 15th Street
Gainesville, FL 32611

To Emily and Leon

for their ceaseless support and encouragement, and

To Lana

future architect, for her graphic and literary contributions to this book

Contents

Tables and Illustrations

Preface

BUILDING MARVELOUS MIAMI presents the urban history and architecture of Greater Miami, with a comprehensive description of the founding, development, and growth of the area and a wealth of information on its architectural heritage and tradition. The name *Miami* in the title refers to Greater Miami, an urban composite of varied-size municipalities and a large unincorporated area. The linear-shaped city is compressed between the Atlantic Ocean to the east and the swamp of the Everglades to the west.

Part I outlines the urban history of Greater Miami. From the settlement's origins as a Native American camp, its evolution is traced over the centuries. Development first took the form of Spanish missions, then an American fort, and in the nineteenth century an area of pioneer settler homesteads. In the twentieth century Greater Miami crystallized into a mosaic of towns and cities. Now, late in the century, it has emerged as an international city. Distinctive individual communities make up the character of this city. Miami, Miami Beach, Coral Gables, Coconut Grove, and various towns, cities, and districts in North and South Dade give the metropolis its unique attributes. Greater Miami's urban history is not complete without descriptions of the factors of growth, the framework for land development, and the political, economic, and social backdrop of the development and growth of the city.

All these facets of its urban history form a context for the city's architecture. Part II begins with a description of Miami's significant styles of architecture, setting the stage for written depictions and photographs of its architectural gems. Street addresses are given in most cases, so that readers can locate and visit these splendid buildings. Naturally, addresses are not given for the modern private buildings, to protect the privacy of the occupants, but information is given for historic residences that are part of the public realm. The descriptions help the reader to grasp the visual image of each community. Greater Miami's architecture is represented, for example, in the notable historic-style residences in old Miami, hotel and apartment buildings in Miami Beach, houses and foreign-style villages in Coral Gables, and single-family residences in Coconut Grove, Miami Shores, South Miami, and other areas of South Dade. Besides the striking private buildings, most of these communities also have treasured public buildings, such as commercial edifices, schools, churches, and government buildings. Including all the award-winning buildings, from the 1940s to the early 1990s, gives the city's modern architecture historical perspective. Contemporary architects thereby take their place in Miami's history of city building. An epilogue on the aftermath of Hurricane Andrew and the damage done to the significant buildings in its path makes the book timely and useful.

Building Marvelous Miami provides both area residents and visitors with absorbing facts about a city possessed of multiple dimensions. It is also a compact overview of the urban history and architecture of a remarkable place. Extensive notes provide valuable sources for those who wish to delve further.

Greater Miami is marvelous because it grew from a settlement of scattered homesteads into a twentieth-century global city in a remarkably short time. It is marvelous for the physical growth that occurred during the land boom of 1921–26. It is marvelous for its diversified population and the way the city has absorbed wave after wave of immigrants and refugees. It is marvelous for the internationally oriented economy that has developed. It is marvelous for its metropolitan government, one of only a handful in North America. It is marvelous for its range of distinctive communities, each distinguished by buildings of varied architectural styles. It is marvelous for its fine examples of the vernacular, Mediterranean, Moderne, International Modern, and Progressive styles of architecture. But Greater Miami is more than the sum of its parts. It is a tropical city full of fascination and excitement that will enthrall residents and visitors alike.

Biscayne Bay and Florida are paradoxes. The bay and the peninsula were among the first places discovered in North America by Europeans, at the beginning of the sixteenth century. Yet they were one of the last to be developed, toward the end of the nineteenth century. The history of the city of Greater Miami, which developed around Biscayne Bay, is a prime example of the growth of a city through the classic stages of urban evolution. The settlement grew from a fort into an agricultural homestead, a trading post, a single city, a metropolis or an association of cities and towns, and finally, a cosmopolis or global city. What is remarkable about the evolution of the settlement is that it went from a trading store place to an international city in a little less than 150 years.

The five chapters of Part I, taken together, present an urban history of Greater Miami. Chapters 1 and 2 trace the building of the city through its stages of urban growth and differentiation into individual communities. Chapters 3 to 5 describe the various influences on this development. Overall, Part I forms the milieu for the depiction of the architectural images of the city. The images take the form of written and photographic portraits of the notable historic- and modern-style buildings of the different communities. These descriptions will be found in Part II.

Part I

Emergence of
Greater Miami as an
International City

chapter 1

Camp to Cosmopolis

FROM the sixteenth to the eighteenth century, little occurred in the Miami area; only American Indian camps and settlements and Spanish missions and forts were developed. After that, the history of the area can be divided into periods that are distinguished, chronologically, by the formation of homesteads by pioneers and early settlers (1836–1895), the establishment of cities and towns (1896–1956), and the transformation of Greater Miami into a metropolis (1957–1977), followed by its emergence as a cosmopolis (1978–present). The beginning of each period is identified by a landmark event—the creation of Dade County in 1836, the incorporation of the first city, Miami, in 1896, the establishment of metropolitan government in 1957, and the introduction of international banking in 1978, which signaled the arrival of Greater Miami as a global city.

Camps, Missions, and Forts

American Indian Camps. Florida was inhabited by hunters sometime before 10,000–12,000 B.C.[1] Around 5000 B.C. the first semipermanent Indian settlements began to appear in the large river valleys of the St. Johns and the Withlacoochee. About 1000 B.C., there was an influx of new people into Florida and settlements expanded into previously unoccupied areas.[2] Flat-bottomed cooking vessels developed in the St. Johns region at that time have been found as far south as the area that is today Miami.

Around 500 B.C., the Indians of South Florida were divided into three major geographical regions. The first group, the Tequesta Indians, lived along the coast from what is today Pompano Beach to the Cape Sable area. They resided in small villages at the mouth of estuaries (as they relied heavily on marine products for food) or in camps on small hammocks within or on the edge of the Everglades.[3] The second group, prehistoric ancestors of the Calusa Indians, inhabited the coast and the offshore barrier islands from Cape Sable north to Charlotte Harbor. The third group lived in villages along or close to the shore of Lake Okeechobee. A small fourth group, composed of the Ais and the Jeaga, occupied the coastal and Indian River region from Cape Canaveral to the St. Lucie River.

Indian dwellings consisted of a seven- or eight-foot-square platform made of small logs. The platform was built on posts a foot or two above the ground for protection against snakes and other animals. A low roof of palmetto thatch sheltered the platform, which was open on the sides (Figure 1). The Tequesta first buried their dead in piles called middens, and later separately in mounds. Burial mounds began to be introduced into Florida as a whole after about 100 B.C. A Tequesta Indian mound, found at the mouth of the Miami River in 1896, which measured 100 feet long and 75 feet wide, and about 20 feet high, was leveled by John Sewell to make way for the veranda of Flagler's Royal Palm Hotel.[4] Fifty to sixty skulls were removed. The Indian town of Tequesta at the mouth of the Miami River was mentioned by its ancient name by Herrera after his visit to the settlement on Sunday, 2 July 1513. Tequesta was also shown on the Freducci map of 1514–1515.[5]

In the two and one-half centuries after the visit of Ponce de León in 1513, most of the aboriginal Indians had disappeared. They were victims of European-introduced diseases, warfare, and slave catchers. Some had migrated out of the area. When the Spanish left Florida in 1763, the last of the Indians, fewer than two hundred, left with them. Other Indians began to move into Florida to escape the whites in Georgia and Alabama early in the eighteenth century. In the nineteenth century they began to push toward South Florida as the war for their removal continued. The last major movement of Indians into Florida took place after the end of the Creek War in Alabama Territory in 1814. Newcomers lived in separate villages as small bands with no central authority to coordinate their activities. These Indians began to be called Seminolies or Seminoles ("wild people") to identify them as seceders or runaways from the Creek Federation.[6] Seminoles were not truly a tribe.

The First Seminole War began in 1818 with the invasion of Spanish Florida by General Andrew Jackson. Refuge provided to Indians raiding the Southern states and to slaves running away from Southern plantations hastened the War. The Second Seminole War (1835–1842) was the climax of the constant demand by white

1. Seminole thatched chickee.

settlers for Indians to be removed from Florida. Indians meanwhile mistrusted actions to get them to move west of the Mississippi River. With Andrew Jackson's inauguration as President in 1829, the proposal for the general removal of all Indians in the eastern United States to the West received new official support. The Indian Removal Act became law on 28 May 1830. From about five thousand in number, only some two hundred Indians remained after their forced removal from Florida to Oklahoma over many years. A consequence of the War was that the interior was explored and mapped for the first time. Also, the army laid out a network of trails and roads and constructed many forts that became the nuclei of settlements.

Spanish Missions and Forts. Juan Ponce de León reached the coast of Florida on 2 April 1513, naming the land after *Pascua Florida,* the Feast of Flowers at Easter time. He is given credit for the European discovery of Florida, although he may not have been the first to find the peninsula. There may have been previous visits by John and Sebastian Cabot in 1497 and 1498. Also, Florida appeared on the Alberto Cantino map of 1502 and others in 1508 and 1511. On his way southward, Ponce de León passed Cape Canaveral and Biscayne Bay, on 13 May. He then sailed down the Florida Keys (which he named Los Martires) to the Tortugas and then northward up the west coast of Florida. On his return from the west coast, he stopped at Biscayne Bay on 3 July. The entry in his journal for the place read "Chequescha."[7]

French actions along the south Atlantic coast spurred Philip II of Spain to settle Florida despite the severe losses already suffered by the Ponce de León, Narvaez, de Soto, de Luna, and Villafane expeditions. Pedro Menéndez de Avilés was sent out with settlement in mind. He reached the coast of Florida at a point that is today near Cape Canaveral on 28 August 1565. He proceeded northward to found the first permanent Spanish settlement in Florida, Saint Augustine, named for the day on which he reached Florida, the festival of San Augustin. Menéndez's intention was to found another six settlements on the Atlantic and Gulf coasts of Florida. The sites at Santa Lucia and Biscayne Bay were eventually abandoned in the face of relentless hostility from the local Indians. After he died in 1588, only the settlement at Saint Augustine and the garrison at San Mateo (Jacksonville) endured.

In 1567, Brother Francisco Villareal established the Jesuit Mission of Tequesta, the first white settlement in what is today Dade County.[8] After a clash between the small garrison of Spanish soldiers and the Indians, the site was abandoned. In Florida, Spanish missions were a multipurpose frontier institution. Although the primary objective of the missions was to Christianize, or "civilize," the Indians, they were also agents of the state and served economic and political purposes as well. In 1743, the Spanish attempted to build another mission at Tequesta. This time they built a substantial fort that was named Pueblo de Santa Maria de Loreto. Besides the soldiers, there were two Franciscan priests, Father Joseph Xavier Alaña and Father Joseph Maria Mónaco. Five longhouses that held about one hundred and eighty people made up the Indian village, which was located on the north bank of the Miami River. This village was apparently seasonal, used only in the summer months. Eventually the Spanish abandoned the settlement owing to the hostility of the Indians.

The first Spanish occupation lasted from 1513 to 1763. The source of title to 2,735 acres in what is today modern Miami was made during the second occupation of Florida by Spain, from 1784 to 1821.[9] Land grants were made by the Spanish to Pedro Fornells in 1790, 175 acres on "Key Biscayno," and 640 acres each to Polly Lewis (1805), James Hagan (1810), Mrs. Hagan, mother of James (1810), and Jonathan Lewis (1813). The Hagan name was also spelled Egan.

There was also the grant made by the Spanish Council in Havana to Don Juan Xavier de Arrambide on 4 December 1813.[10] The grant was about ninety thousand acres from New River (Fort Lauderdale) to Key Largo. Arrambide settled two miles north of the Miami River but Indian attacks forced him to abandon his settlement after several years. On 1 December 1817, he sold 80,000 acres to Archibald Clark for $20,000. In the early 1830s, the U.S. Supreme Court ruled that the Arrambide donation was invalid as the provincial council in Havana had no authority to make large land grants. The land reverted to the federal domain.

To date there is no satisfactory explanation how the place name "Miami" (meaning "Sweetwater," according to local legend) became associated with the river or Biscayne Bay. What is known is that the name was first used during the second Spanish occupation. There are also various theories on how Biscayne Bay received its name: one supposition is that the name is derived from the designation *Viscaino Bay,* which appeared on a Spanish map of 1765, and another, from the Spanish province *Biscaya.*

British Grants. The British occupied Florida from 1763 to 1784. In 1764, William Gerard De Brahm was appointed surveyor-general of East Florida. In February 1765, he initiated a survey and mapping of the entire east coast of Florida, a task that took six years. The first grant of 20,000 acres, located in a section that extended from the Miami River to somewhere near Shoal Point, was bestowed on Samuel Touchett in 1766. In 1770, the second grant was made to the Earl of Dartmouth, William Legge, allotting him 40,000 acres south of the Touchett grant at a point about three-quarters of a mile north of Black Point. On his land the Earl had planned to establish a community; he had set aside 6,000 acres for a town for the Cape Florida Society to be established on a site approximately southwest of the present area of Cutler. The third grant, awarded in 1774, was to John Augustus Ernst, who received a 20,000–acre tract extending between the Miami River and Arch Creek. None of the grants was settled, however, and the lands later reverted to Spain, then eventually to the United States.

Neither De Brahm nor another surveyor, Bernard Romans, mentions Indian settlements in the Biscayne Bay area. Perhaps this was because the settlements may have been transitory camps only. In the second half of the eighteenth century, Biscayne Bay was essentially deserted. The Indians who had lived along the shore for centuries had disappeared sometime before the British occupation in 1763 in the wake of warfare, political changes, and disease. In 1770, Romans, who was mapping the Touchett grant, marked the Miami River as Rio Rattones. Romans noted a clearing on the north bank of the river, at its mouth. He described the clearing on the survey map as the "old field of Pueblo Ratton Town,"[11] as it continued to be called for many years afterwards. Touchett intended to raise indigo, sugar, and rice on his tract. Situated south of the Miami River, it would have included all of present-day Coconut Grove and the area down to Gables Estates and would have extended to a point somewhere near Ludlam Road.[12]

American Plantations and Forts. In 1821, along the south Florida coast, there were as many as five hundred Bahamian "wreckers"— seamen who salvaged the remains of the many ships that went aground on the many reefs. The wreckers almost had the area to themselves. They were known to frequent the "Punch Bowl" (Coconut Grove) for fresh water. At this natural spring, about one mile south of the Miami River, there was also the ten- to twelve- foot "Key Biscayne Bluff." Today its remains are known as the Silver Bluff on South Bayshore Drive.

Key West was made the port of entry for all wreckers in 1828 to enable the United States to control and tax the emerging respectable and licensed profession of wrecking. A United States District Court was established, and all wreckers were required to obtain a license and to bring salvage to Key West for adjudication. Key West was soon inhabited by "Conchs" and became the largest city in Florida, attaining a population of 12,750 by 1876.[13] The Conchs were descendants of the many Loyalists who emigrated from the United States to the Bahama Islands in 1783. There they eventually became seamen, then wreckers. The Conchs also settled elsewhere in South Florida, including the Keys. Captain Jacob Housman, ". . . a bold wrecker and autocratic proprietor," established a settlement on Indian Key, an eleven-acre island midway between Key West and Key Biscayne, in the 1830s.[14] He succeeded in turning the island into a port of entry in competition with Key West. Indian Key's original name was Mantanzas, "Place of Murder," in memory of an Indian massacre of some four hundred shipwrecked Frenchmen there in the late 1600s.[15] After Chekaika's raid on 7 August 1840, Indian Key was never rebuilt.

On 22 February 1821, President James Monroe proclaimed the Adams-Onís treaty ceding Florida from Spain to the United States. General Andrew Jackson was appointed the military governor of the new territory. At that time Florida had fewer inhabitants than at any previous period. Over a year later, on 30 March 1822, Congress created a civil territorial government that provided steps for eventual statehood as population increased. The territorial government created the new county of Monroe. It consisted of all of south Florida from Charlotte Harbor on the west coast to the Hillsborough inlet on the east coast. Key West was designated the county seat with a customs house.

On 8 May 1822, Congress provided for the establishment of

When the United States took over the territory of Florida, Congress considered the newly acquired peninsula "too sickly and sterile" to merit the expense of land surveys and sales. The area of South Florida was described by a prospective buyer of 24,000 acres of land as "Cape Florida or Key Largo named Monroe's Presque Isle."

Jean Taylor, *The Villages of South Dade*, 1.

2. Cape Florida Lighthouse, Key Biscayne. Built in 1825, rebuilt in 1846.

adjudication boards. These boards were to confirm the land grants made by the Spanish government. Congress also decreed that all large claims were to be made before December 1829. The five land grants in the Miami area were confirmed by 1825, well before this deadline. The names Hagan, Lewis, and Davis thus became the first titleholders to United States land in the Biscayne Bay area.[16] James Hagan claimed 640 acres on the north side of the Miami River. Rebecca Hagan claimed 640 acres on the south side of the river. Polly Lewis claimed land south of Rebecca Hagan, and Jonathan Lewis south of Polly Lewis. Mary Ann Davis claimed 175 acres (about half the island) on "Key Buskun." She had bought the land from the heirs of Pedro Fornells on 12 July 1824. William G. Davis, husband of Mary, sold three acres for $225 to the government for a lighthouse. In 1839 he laid out a town on the south end of the island and sold lots to several persons. Venancio Sanchez bought the remaining half of the island in 1840 from the owners, who lived in Havana.

In 1825, the Cape Florida Light, a sixty-five-foot-high lighthouse, was the first permanent structure in the Biscayne Bay area to be built (Figure 2). The lighthouse began to operate in December of the same year. A fort became the second structure. At the beginning of the Second Seminole War (1835), Commodore Alexander James Dallas of the U.S. Navy forces in the West Indies was requested by the army to help them. He established a naval station at the mouth of the Miami River. When buildings were constructed in 1838, the installation was named Fort Dallas. On 5 February 1839, the Army took over the fort when the Navy withdrew to Key Biscayne. Fort Dallas was occupied by the Army until 1 February 1842.[17] The Fort was reoccupied from 20 October 1849 to December 1850 and again from 3 January 1855 until 28 May 1858, when it was finally abandoned. During the 1850s, the fort was the nucleus of a small community.

All the Hagan and Lewis lands on either side of the Miami River were bought by Richard Fitzpatrick, a leading citizen of Key West. He purchased the James Hagan Donation of six hundred forty acres for $400 in 1830. By 1832 he had acquired the Polly Lewis Donation for $500, the Jonathan Lewis Donation for $300, and the Rebecca Hagan Donation for $640—a total of four square miles for $1,840.[18] He had his slaves clear three miles of jungle along the river to plant cotton, limes, and sugar cane. Before Richard Fitzpatrick's arrival, yeoman farmers made up much of the population of Florida. They had small plantations with fruits and vegetables, some livestock, and a house and workshop. His goal, however, was to establish the plantation system prevalent in the Southern states to bring South Florida into the mainstream economic system. He concentrated on sugar cane and used slaves for labor. His example was not followed, probably because the outbreak of the Seminole War deterred other planters from immigrating to South Florida. The area thus never became a plantation-based society. Other reasons for this were the unsuitability of the climate and soil and the sparse population.[19] Fitzpatrick's hopes were dashed when his homesite was destroyed by Indians, and in 1836 he abandoned the plantation.

Homesteads, 1836–1895

Creation of Dade County, 1836. Jacob Housman was apparently the organizer of a petition to found a new county to be independent from Key West.[20] Fifty-seven residents of the northern part of Monroe County had signed the petition. The original name proposed in the Bill was Pinckney County, but this was changed to Dade when the Bill was passed. The new county was named for Major Francis Langhorne Dade, who had been killed by Indians in Sumpter County in December 1835. Dade County was created out of Monroe County by an act of the Territorial Legislative Council on 28 January 1836 and approved by the Governor on 4 February 1837. Richard Fitzpatrick, a member from Monroe County, was president of the Council. His efforts in having the act passed have led to his designation as Father of Dade County.

The territorial act described the limits of the new county of Dade as commencing "at the West end of Bahia Honda Key [the Key is west of today's Seven Mile Bridge], and running in a direct line to Cape Sable on the mainland; thence in a direct line to Lake Macaco [Lake Okeechobee]—thence on a direct line to the head of the North-Prong or Branch of Potomac, commonly known as Hillsborough River [Hillsborough Canal], and down said River to the Sea [Deerfield Beach] . . . ."[21]

Radical changes to the boundaries of Dade County were made by an Act of 1866.[22] Indian Key was left out. The southern boundary was established and remained unchanged up to the present. The northern boundary was moved from the Hillsborough River northwards to the St. Lucie River to include Lake Worth (Palm Beach) and Jupiter. Lake Macaco was now called Lake Okeechobee (Seminole for "Big Water"), a name that first appeared on a map of December 1841–January 1842. Further corrections were made in legislation passed in 1874 to eliminate certain indefinite descriptions of the boundaries in the 1866 Act. The vast area of the county was reduced when Palm Beach County was carved out in 1909. Dade County's current boundary was established when the Legislature created Broward County in 1913.

Until a permanent seat for the County could be established, the act of 1837 envisioned Indian Key and Cape Florida (Biscayne Bay) as alternate locations for the County Seat. In the new county, Indian Key was the most important settlement, whose inhabitants depended on the business of marine salvage or wrecking on the Florida Reefs. Initially, Indian Key remained the county seat because it had a settlement. It was considered safer than the mainland as there was protection in a naval and army station at nearby Tea Table Key. The county seat was transferred to Miami in 1876, moved to Juno in 1888, and finally returned to Miami permanently in 1899.[23]

Pioneers and Homesteaders. After the departure of Richard Fitzpatrick, many pioneers and homesteaders began to establish themselves in the Biscayne Bay area, able to buy land at last because of the completion of the long-awaited land survey. The first American survey in South Florida had been certified by Robert Butler, surveyor general, one year after Florida became a state in 1845. Pioneers were scattered in three broad localities—in an area north and just south of the Miami River, in the Coconut Grove area, and in the Cutler-Perrine district.

"As the Seminole Wars went against the Indians, a band moved deep into South Florida and became the fiercest of all elements of the Seminoles. . . . those Indians were probably a band of Miccosukee who had separated from the main body of the tribe.

"The Miccosukee did not legally become a tribe in the eyes of the Government until 1962. Before then, the Indians who lived on reservations in Broward County and those who lived along the Tamiami Trail were seen as one and the same: Seminoles.

"The separation [between Miccosukee and Seminoles] occurred because the Miccosukee did not agree with the legal accommodations the Seminoles were making with the Eisenhower Administration."

Howard Kleinberg, "Do Seminoles, Miccosukee Come from the Same Tribe?," 15A.

Indian Activity. During the 1830s, settlers and Indians found themselves in conflict with one another over land around the Miami River. Events reached a climax in 1836, when the settlers sought refuge in the lighthouse on Key Biscayne, from which they hoped they could be taken to Key West. Indians attacked the lighthouse on 23 July, killing one person and wounding another. Settlers and their families fled to Indian Key or Key West, leaving South Florida under the control of the Indians. After the 7 August 1840 destruction of Indian Key by the Indians, Dade County was temporarily abandoned by the settlers.

The lighthouse was rebuilt and relit in 1846. In early December 1855, the Third Seminole War began. Many forts, including Fort Dallas and Fort Lauderdale, were reactivated. When the army returned to Fort Dallas in 1855, it completed the stone buildings. With the addition of many wooden buildings, the north bank now boasted more structures than the south bank. In 1857 the troops laid out the first road ever in the area to link Fort Dallas with Fort Lauderdale. Causeways were built over swampland and bridges over streams, except at Arch Creek, where there was a natural stone bridge. After the war ended in 1857, many soldiers stayed on in the area. Most of the Seminoles migrated out of the state; but a number, estimated at between one hundred and three hundred, disappeared into the Everglades. Demands for their removal were abandoned. An Indian agent reported in 1880 that there were sixty-three Seminoles living in the settlement in the Everglades above the headwaters of the Miami River.

Cities and Towns, 1896–1956

Archaeological excavations to date have revealed many Indian settlements and burial mounds. These include the former Tequesta village at the mouth of the Miami River, and sites at Arch Creek, El Portal, Flagami, Maddens Hammock, Surfside, Cape Florida, and Atlantis/Santa Maria.[24] Many of these places were later inhabited by the early pioneers and homesteaders. Some places in turn developed later into cities or towns, while others remained as districts. Yet others linger today only as place names. Incorporation of a city or a town eventually became an important feature.

Different paths of development were taken by the various communities. Miami, Coconut Grove, Arch Creek, Fulford, and Larkins began to emerge during the second half of the nineteenth century as settlements. Each would later incorporate. Some settlements of this period, however—Biscayne, Cutler, Lemon City, and Perrine—did not eventually develop into incorporated towns. At the beginning of the twentieth century, Homestead, Florida City, and Miami Beach were founded; all these later incorporated. The introduction of the railway after 1896 led to the development of many towns. Then in the first half of the 1920s, there followed another spate of settlement foundation and incorporation—Coral Gables, Hialeah, Miami Springs, Miami Shores, Buena Vista, and Opa-locka. Districts that were founded in the first two decades of the century and that did not subsequently incorporate included Redland, Silver Palm, Longview, Kendall, and many railway towns (Figure 3).

Metropolis, 1957–1977

In 1957, Dade County received a charter to become Florida's first home rule county under an amendment to the state constitution approved in 1956. Earlier attempts to consolidate the separate cities and towns into one large city had failed.

The 1950s and 1960s were watershed decades for Greater Miami. In the 1950s, the suburban municipalities showed a 114 percent population increase compared to a growth rate of 221 percent in the incorporated areas.[25] In the following decade, however, unincorporated areas continued to expand. Commercial and industrial establishments left the central city, and suburban sprawl eliminated any clear boundaries between municipalities. Suburban areas continued—and continue—to grow at a rapid rate. A new development, the first planned and built new community in Dade County since Coral Gables, was built by the Graham family: the first homes and a golf course that formed the nucleus of Miami Lakes were constructed in 1962. In the 1960s, college education was made available to almost everyone, and public schools began to be integrated. Jackie Gleason began his weekly television show from Miami Beach, and Miami had a new football team, the Dolphins. During the decade, the state system of colleges and universities expanded considerably. Miami-Dade Junior College, founded in 1960 as Dade County Junior College, became part of the state community college system in 1968. It was renamed Miami-Dade Community College in 1973. Florida International University opened in 1972. Other major schemes in Greater Miami included the transfer in 1967 of the port of Miami from its old site next to Bayfront Park to its new location on Dodge Island. The old site was converted to parkland and was renamed the New World Center-Bicentennial Park in 1977. Voters in 1970 passed a "Decade of Progress" bond issue for ambitious projects, such as a new rapid transit system, new cultural facilities, improvements to the sewerage system, and street lighting. Many projects were halted, however, by the recession of the early 1970s. The Metrorail rapid transit system and

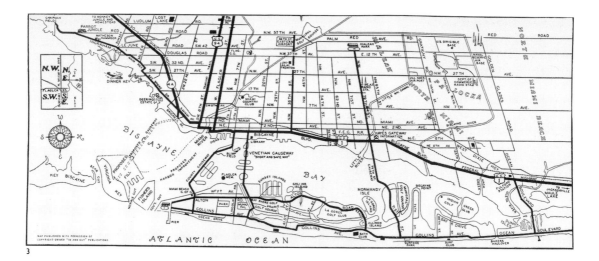

Metromover in downtown Miami, as well as the Government Cultural Center, were completed in the 1980s (Figure 4).

Cosmopolis, 1978–Present

The passage of federal and state banking acts in 1978 enabled foreign banks to open branches in Greater Miami. In addition, when the Free Trade Zone was established west of the Miami International Airport and multinational corporations located offices in the city during the 1970s, Greater Miami was transformed from a metropolis into a cosmopolis, a world city. A new era of international awareness and activity for Greater Miami as the city for international trade and commerce in the U.S. may be ushered in by the International Affairs, Economic Development and Trade Promo-

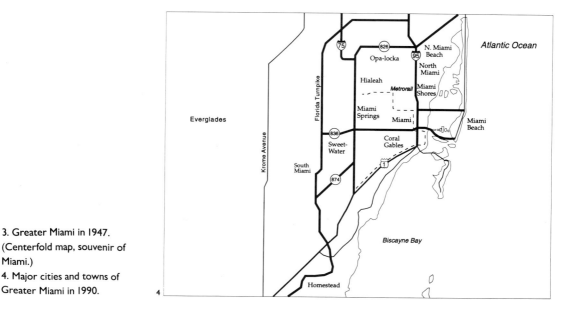

3. Greater Miami in 1947. (Centerfold map, souvenir of Miami.)

4. Major cities and towns of Greater Miami in 1990.

tion Act of 1990. Growth of international banking, which placed Miami second in the nation to New York, made the city of Greater Miami a bridge between the Americas. The International Insurance Exchange, similar to Lloyds of London, also established itself in Miami.[26] During the late 1980s, the Port of Miami became the largest passenger/cruise ship port on the globe. One-third of all cruise ships in the world operate out of the port; over one million tourists a year now go through the port. This figure is projected to reach four million by the end of the century. Miami International Airport, with over twenty million passengers a year, is one of the ten busiest in the world.

Greater Miami's growing international status as a global city was reflected in two events: the Chamber of Commerce Downtown Action Committee's choice of New World Center for the new city logo and the identification of the City of Coral Gables as one of three urban centers in the world that were spearheading the evolution of economic leadership for multinational companies.[27] By 1991 the global city of Coral Gables had become the regional headquarters for more than one hundred multinational enterprises,[28] though it may be losing its undisputed role as more companies begin to locate in the Waterford Office Park in Miami Lakes. To keep pace with the expansion in foreign trade, over fifty countries have established consular or other representation in Greater Miami.

The worldwide success of the television series Miami Vice during the late 1980s contributed to turning Greater Miami into an international status symbol. Furthermore, the series drew many tourists to the city and attracted several film studios of various sizes to the area, generating over $100 million in economic activity in Dade County.[29] Other significant developments during the 1980s were the completion of the James L. Knight International Conference and Convention Center, as well as the creation of Bayside Marketplace, and a tricounty rail system. Miami Arena became home to the Miami Heat basketball team and the Panthers hockey team. The Joe Robbie Stadium is shared by the Miami Dolphins football team and the Florida Marlins baseball team. Both the Panthers and Marlins opened their first seasons in 1993. Greater Miami in the early 1990s thus became one of the few metropolitan areas in the country to sponsor four teams in major-league sports. Also, major international events in Grand Prix auto racing, in golf, and in tennis take place regularly. Approval in July 1993 of a site near the Omni for a Performing Arts Center is expected to generate major dramatic change in downtown Miami. The $172-million center's complex of opera/ballet house, symphony hall, and community theater is scheduled to open in 1998.[30]

5a. Miami skyline at night, 1932.
5b. Miami skyline, 1992.

Imposing new office buildings resculptured the skyline of down-town Miami, which is now known all over the world as the "City of Lights" (Figures 5a, 5b). A neon sculpture on the Miami River Metrorail bridge is visible from I–95 in downtown Miami. The sculpture, by Rockne Krebs, is one of several in Dade County's vaunted twenty-year-old Art in Public Places program.[31] The build-ing most distinguished for its illumination is the CenTrust Tower. Significantly, the new owners who took over after the collapse of the CenTrust Bank renamed it International Place in 1991.[32]

chapter 2

Mosaic of Communities

FROM the beginning of its urban evolution, Greater Miami was always differentiated into a mosaic of identifiable communities. Each major community is described in this chapter and presented in chronological order based on the date of foundation of the settlement. The first major one to emerge was Miami. It incorporated at its birth as a city in 1896. Before this time there were only a handful of homesteads. In the first two decades of the twentieth century, several cities and towns were founded. Many of these still remain as municipalities. Other towns and districts that were created no longer exist as such or remain as names of places in Greater Miami.

Overview of the Foundation and Incorporation of Communities in Greater Miami

As there are so many communities to consider, it is convenient to arrange them into five groups defined by two criteria: the community's date of founding and its choice to incorporate as a municipality or not. Settlements in the first group were founded between 1856 and 1926, beginning with Miami and ending with Opa-locka. Almost half the communities in Greater Miami fall into this first group. After the incorporation of Miami as a city in 1896, the remaining communities in this group incorporated in two waves. Homestead, Florida City, Miami Beach and Coconut Grove incorporated in the first wave, between 1913 and 1919. Buena Vista, Arch Creek, Coral Gables, Hialeah, Fulford, Larkins, Country Club Estates, Miami Shores, and Opa-locka incorporated in the second wave, from 1924 to 1926. Various changes took place in the following years: Coconut Grove and Buena Vista were annexed by the City of Miami, while other communities altered their names.

> "... South Florida has one of the nation's most attenuated linear cities, a hundred miles long and averaging ten miles wide, squeezed in between the sea on the east and the still-uninhabitable Everglades wilderness to the west."
> Peter Muller, "The Urban Geography of South Florida," 64.

17

The second group consists of communities founded from the 1880s up to 1920 that never incorporated. These include Biscayne, Cutler, Lemon City, Perrine, Redland, Silver Palm, Longview, Kendall, Biscayne Park Estates, and many railway towns. The names of these communities remain today as designations of places.

This chapter describes the communities that fall into the first two groups. The third group consists of small communities that were founded and incorporated during the Great Depression of the 1930s. Although some of these communities were called towns, most had the word "village" in their name. The towns were those of Surfside and Golden Beach, incorporated earlier in 1928. Villages were Biscayne Park, El Portal, and Indian Creek.

Nine communities, all small, make up the fourth group. They were founded during World War II or in the postwar period of the 1940s. The last three in this group to incorporate—Hialeah Gardens (1948), Medley (1949), and Pennsuco (1949)—each had less than one hundred fifty people. Incorporation of these three towns led the Dade County legislative delegation to secure the passage of a special act in 1949 foreclosing further incorporation under the general laws of Florida.[1] The act stipulated that, in the future, municipalities in the county could be created only by special act of the legislature. Not only the small size of the "towns" was considered problematic, but also their siting in areas subject to severe flooding. The legislators had been spurred into action after developers attempted to establish still other municipalities.

Only two municipalities make up the fifth group, both of them created after the end of the 1940s. The first, Islandia, founded in 1961, is no doubt the strangest settlement in Greater Miami. Consisting of five islands in Biscayne Bay, Islandia is a "city" in name only. At the beginning of the century, it was a chain of thirty-three islands with its own school district and about one hundred permanent residents.[2] When the National Park Service took over Biscayne Bay, designated a national monument in 1968, it leveled all evidence of human structures. The Service then reduced the number of islands in Islandia, which had incorporated on the assumption that property owners could escape state and federal zoning laws. The dozen nonresident property owners are now under increasing pressure from environmentalists to sell their land; the remaining islands could then be added to the Biscayne Bay National Park. The second municipality in this group, the only one to be created in the last thirty years, is the Village of Key Biscayne.[3]

Incorporated Cities and Towns

Miami: founded with post office, 1856; incorporated, 1896. In the first locality established by the pioneers, on the south bank of the Miami River, Dr. Robert R. Fletcher opened a store in the late 1840s. Another store was built by George and Thomas Ferguson. They also erected a coontie starch mill and sawmill upstream near the rapids on the river (near N.W. South River Drive just west of N.W. 28th Avenue).[4] In 1855, William Wagner built a coontie mill one and one-half miles up the Miami River. From 1855 to 1858, he built his house on what became known as Wagner Creek. This house, now relocated, is one of the oldest known homes standing in Miami today.[5] In north Dade County, George Lewis and his Miami River neighbor Robert Fletcher built a coontie starch mill at the Arch Creek Natural Bridge. It was at the northern crossing point into Biscayne Bay country. The bridge was used first by the military trail, then became the first county road in 1892 and later the Dixie Highway. The Natural Bridge collapsed in 1973.

William F. English of Columbia, South Carolina, followed his uncle, Richard Fitzpatrick, to Biscayne Bay. He bought all his uncle's land for $16,000.[6] English then built a stone house and slave quarters, later Fort Dallas, on the north side of the river. His dream was to create a city on the south bank of the river. In 1842, he platted the "Town of Miami," but this plat has not been found. Very few lots were sold as tracts; up to one hundred sixty acres could be claimed by individuals under the Armed Occupation Act of 1842. The oldest deeds date from 8 August 1844 and 5 April 1845. A January 1846 deed describes conveyance of land by William F. English in the "Town of Miami/Village of Miami."[7] English worked the plantation for a while but abandoned it during the Third Seminole War. In 1851 or 1852, he went to California to raise capital for his venture. He died in the California Gold Rush from an accidental gunshot wound.

The area's first post office, named the Miami Post Office, was opened in December 1856. Mail delivery was from Key West by sailboat once a month. George Ferguson became postmaster in 1858. William H. Gleason and William Henry Hunt arrived in Biscayne Bay with their families in July 1866, and occupied the vacant Fort Dallas buildings. Over the next decade, Gleason managed to obtain absolute power over Dade County until the election of November 1876. Despite his shortcomings, he did attract new settlers to the area. In 1869, however, when Dr. Jeptha V. Harris purchased the Fort Dallas property from William English's heirs, Gleason and Hunt were forced to move out. They moved to Hunt's homestead to the north, now Miami Shores, taking the post office with them.

In December 1870, they renamed it the Biscayne Post Office, so that until 1874 there was no Miami.

The Gleason and the Harris claims of the James Hagan grant were purchased by George M. Thew for the Biscayne Bay Company for $6,100 and a thousand shares of stock. In 1874, J. William Ewan arrived with Jonathan C. Lovelace to manage the Biscayne Bay Company property. They reopened the post office and named it "Ma-ama," which Ewan believed was the Indian way. The name was changed back to Miami in September 1877.[8] Ewan also opened a store and trading post that he ran with the help of Charles and Isabella Peacock, who had arrived in Miami in 1875. The Fort Dallas buildings were occupied by the Lovelace family and then by Ewan, the "Duke of Dade," and his mother.

William B. Brickell and Ephraim T. Sturtevant, both from Cleveland, arrived in Biscayne Bay on a scouting trip in 1870. They came in search of a freer life in Florida. Brickell acquired three tracts of land, opened a trading post, and established a home south of the mouth of the river. The spot became known as Brickell Point. Sturtevant built a house to the south of the Brickells. A year later he moved into a vacant bayfront house nine miles to the north (today's N.E. 103rd Street).

Julia Tuttle, daughter of Ephraim T. Sturtevant, first visited the area in 1875. On his death, she inherited his homestead in today's Miami Shores. She then purchased the rest of the substantial Hagan tract from the Biscayne Bay Company. On 13 November 1891, she moved permanently to the bay, occupying the Fort Dallas officers' quarters. The "Duke of Dade" moved out and went to live in the Peacock Inn. Her dream, like English's before her, was to build a city. Tuttle's business acumen told her, though, that the railroad needed to be extended to Biscayne Bay. She approached Henry Flagler to bring his railroad beyond West Palm Beach to Miami. He wrote Tuttle in April 1893 that the completion of the inland waterway might serve the same purpose. The big freeze in northern and central Florida in 1894–1895 apparently provided her the opportunity to persuade Flagler to change his mind. It is widely held, but not substantiated, that she sent him a box of fruit with fragrant orange blossoms to prove that South Florida was frost-free. Flagler came to Miami in June 1895.

On 24 October 1895, Henry Flagler and Julia Tuttle signed an agreement for Flagler to bring the railroad to Miami. He agreed to extend his railroad in exchange for each alternate lot in Tuttle's property. This property consisted of 520 acres on the north bank of the river and 100 acres along the bay and river for a hotel. He was also to get alternate lots in William Brickell's 400 acres south of the river. Flagler committed himself to several projects: he was to build a hotel—the Royal Palm, to establish streets, and to finance improvements, including a water works and an electric light plant.[9] Planning and construction were the responsibility of John Sewell, who arrived to turn ". . . a scraggly excuse for a village . . . ." into a town.[10] He liked to call himself the "Daddy of Miami."[11]

Miami began to grow with the laying of the railroad tracks in September 1895. The first train arrived with a load of building material on 15 April 1896. Supplies were earmarked mainly for the building of Flagler's Royal Palm Hotel (now demolished) on the south side of today's Dupont Plaza. The first passenger train reached Miami at nine o'clock on the night of 22 April 1896, and thus a city was born. Miami was incorporated on 28 July 1896, with three hundred forty-four voters, enough to enable it to incorporate as a city instead of a town from the beginning. In 1897, Tuttle platted her almost nine hundred acres into ten- and twenty-acre plots.[12] She built a barnlike structure to house workers across and to the south from where the *Miami Herald* building now stands. The structure soon was called the "Miami Hotel" although it really was no such thing. Behind it Tuttle built basic two-story buildings and rented space to businesses, the first to J. E. Lummus of Bronson for a general store. She also built an office for Dr. James Mary Jackson, the son of a Bronson grove owner and doctor. Julia Tuttle died suddenly on 14 September 1898, at the age of forty-nine.

Miami's first downtown school was opened in 1897 in a store building. In 1889, the state legislature made statutory provisions for the return of county and local control of school management. The state superintendent of public instruction aimed to have at least one high school in each county.[13]

In its first issue on 15 May 1896, the *Miami Metropolis* stated, "This is the first paper ever published on beautiful Bay Biscayne, the most southern newspaper on the mainland of the United States, published at the most southern telegraph terminal and express office on the mainland at Marvelous Miami, the town with one thousand souls and the survey of the place yet to be completed. The coming metropolis of South Florida." The newspaper campaigned for a city charter, street paving, a bridge across the river, and relocation of the post office from Brickell's trading post, then located inconveniently across the river. The newspaper also urged that a sewer be installed, which was eventually laid but ran into the sweet water of the Miami River. The city grew so rapidly that it came to be called "The Magic City," a name coined by E. V. Blackman and later adopted in the 1904 official city directory. Explosive growth continued for two decades.

When Josiah F. Chaille was selected in October 1920 to fill an unexpired term as a member of the Miami City Council, he accepted the United States government's ultimatum to correct the haphazard naming of streets—there were many streets with the same name, and sometimes the name of a street would change every few blocks—or face withdrawal of mail deliveries. Chaille, modeling his approach on Washington, D.C., divided Miami into four quadrants. He took Twelfth Street and Avenue D as the starting points, named the former Flagler Street and the latter Miami Avenue, and replaced the names of all other streets by numbers. His system was approved by the City Council, after some pressure, and by the federal government. At the next election, however, when Miami adopted a City Commission form of government, one of its first acts was to change the name of S.E. 2nd Street back to Brickell Avenue.

In 1923, the City of Miami was at its height as a developer's dream. It had an increasing population, a record rate of building, and a city-sponsored facelift of the bayfront. In addition, various groups sought to establish a university, a music conservatory, and a civic theater. Nevertheless, certain problems could not be glossed over, including dense traffic in narrow downtown streets that made Miami one of the most congested cities in the nation in the 1920s.[14] In a referendum on 2 September 1925, the voters of Miami decided to annex Allapattah, Buena Vista, Lemon City, Little River, Silver Bluff, and Coconut Grove into a larger Miami. About the same time, Coral Gables and Hialeah incorporated as cities. The wave of development was reflected in increased bank deposits, voter approval of bond issues for much-needed public services, and a charter for the new University of Miami. Another testimonial to the city's economic vigor was the hundreds of advertisements published in an enormous issue of the *Miami Daily News* on the city's twenty-ninth birthday.

During the Depression years of 1931 and 1932, Miami withdrew from much of the land it had annexed six years earlier, primarily because it was unable to provide services and secondarily because property owners of the new areas failed to pay their fair share of taxes.[15] In these areas, market values of land had fallen to a level less than one percent of comparable properties in the areas closer to the city center. There was relatively little interest in annexation after the deannexation of 1931, with the exception of the Liberty City area, annexed in 1937 for a public housing project. Residents in outlying areas also felt dwindling interest in annexation as there was a diminishing need for city services owing to the county's extension of less expensive services.

Brickell Avenue. A bridge was built across the river at Miami Avenue in 1904. The city began to expand southward as the Brickells opened Brickell Avenue. Soon the avenue became known as "Millionaire's Row," home to art-glass pioneer Louis Comfort Tiffany, developer Carl Fisher, and politician-turned-pitchman William Jennings Bryan.[16] In 1905, the Brickell subdivision was added to Miami with large estate-sized lots along the bayfront. James Deering bought 130 acres of land from Mary Brickell. He added another 50 acres to create an estate on the bayshore two miles south of Miami. He began to build a Venetian palazzo, Vizcaya, on his estate in 1914. When it opened on Christmas Eve of 1916, the palazzo had cost an estimated $22 million.[17] By the beginning of the 1980s, the last mansion on Brickell Avenue north of Vizcaya was swept away by a wave of high-rise condominiums that changed Miami's skyline. At the end of the decade, the southern section of the Avenue was lined by almost twenty condominium buildings. The northern section from S.E. 15th Road to the Miami River, meanwhile, became the location of over thirty major office and bank tower buildings.

Biscayne Bay Islands. Fisher's Island was created from the southern tip of mainland Miami Beach when Government Cut was opened in 1906. The wealthy Vanderbilt family built a twelve-structure housing estate, which was completed substantially by 1936. After changing hands a few times, the estate has been developed presently into an exclusive private resort, Fisher Island. In 1918, Carl Fisher created Star Island, just west of the southern tip of Miami Beach, from bay bottom spoil. He was followed by a rush of developers who soon developed Palm Island, Hibiscus Island, Fair Island, La Gorce, Sunset islands and Venetian Isles in Biscayne Bay. Dredged material from the bay was also used to create Bayfront Park in 1926. A bandstand was added in 1934. Before the establishment of the Park, the edge of the natural coastline had been defined by Biscayne Boulevard.

Biscayne Boulevard. In 1926, the Shoreland Company of Hugh Anderson and Roy Wright, using private capital, became involved in creating Biscayne Boulevard as an imposing approach to Miami from the north. The purpose of the Company's participation was to enhance its Miami Shores development. Before the Boulevard was constructed, the approach from the north was West Dixie along N.E. 2nd Avenue. This thoroughfare angled across the railroad at N.E. 36th Street and then proceeded southward through a nondescript area. The road followed this path as Charles Deering did not want the highway to follow the railroad through his estate. Two hundred twelve acres in extent, his holdings stretched north of Buena Vista to the bay. To build Biscayne Boulevard, the private Shoreland Company bought the Deering estate, a step toward fulfilling the dreams of Hugh Anderson and Roy Wright to create an imposing four-lane thoroughfare approach to Miami. Biscayne Boulevard already extended along the bayfront hotels up to about N.E. 13th Street. Anderson and Wright bought all the property between N.E. 15th Street and the northern boundary of the Deering Estate (along a line corresponding to N.E. 3rd Avenue). They were helped by the condemnation rights exercised by the City of Miami: to make way for the highway, twelve buildings were moved; about eighty-five houses, twelve apartment houses, two hotels, and a synagogue were demolished; and most other houses had a wing or a porch removed. The boulevard then merged with the new federal highway at N.E. 55th Street to become U.S. 1. It is estimated that the last eight miles cost one million dollars a mile. Seven million dollars was lent by the J. S. Phipps estate; when the boom ended, it took over Biscayne Boulevard to protect the family investment. Biscayne Boulevard was dedicated on 11 November 1926 and was opened to traffic on 12 February the following year.[18] In the early 1930s, a group of buildings sprang up between N.E. 13th and 16th Streets in an attempt to create "the Fifth Avenue of the South."

Coconut Grove: founded with post office, 1873; incorporated, 1919; annexed by Miami, 1925. In the area one mile south of the Miami River, Temple Pent and his family from the Bahamas were apparently the first to settle there. In 1821, he attempted to confirm a Spanish donation of 640 acres at "Key Buskin Bay" but was unsuccessful in his claim. The land was opened to homesteaders after the 1846 survey of the area, which included present-day Coconut Grove and extended to the Cocoplum tract. Simeon Frow, keeper of the Cape Florida Lighthouse from 1859, and his ten children frequented the area. They called it the "land across from the light."[19] There were, however, no homestead applications until one was made by Edmund D. Besly (his name has been spelled several different ways) on 14 November 1868. He probably settled in the area much earlier as he may have been the Edward Beasley recorded as a resident of the Cape Florida area in the 1830 census. Other residents were Temple Pent and Richard Fitzpatrick. On a coastal map of 1850, "Beasley's Point" (Coconut Grove) was featured as a point of triangulation. The other two points were the Cape Florida Lighthouse and "Lewis Point" just south of the Miami River.

In 1866, Dr. Horace Philo Porter decided to move to South Florida, where he intended to plant coconuts, mangoes, limes, and avocados. Before his move, he had practiced medicine, briefly in

Ohio and then in Michigan after his discharge from the United States Army on 4 November 1864. His agricultural pursuits were cut short when his young plants were wiped out by a hurricane. On 26 November 1872, he applied for an 80-acre homestead on then unoccupied land (later the Pent homestead) in present-day Coconut Grove. He amended his claim in July 1873 and added another 80 adjoining acres to his original claim. The claim was contested and patented to Anna Besly on 20 May 1875, five years after her husband Edmund Besly had died. Porter, discouraged, left and never returned. Ironically, in 1877, Anna Besly sold her entire homestead to John W. Frow for $100. Francis "Jack" Infinger, an early settler, arrived after the Civil War and established a home near the present Cocoplum area. In the late 1880s, the 186-acre Infinger tract was bought by Adam Richards. The property extended from the bay to what is now Old Cutler, and from the Coral Gables waterway to Matheson Hammock.

Edmund Besly's homestead was the first recorded one in Coconut Grove. It was 160 acres in area and extended from present day S.W. 27th Avenue to south of the Moorings. The second homestead was made to J. William Ewan in 1882.[20] In 1884, John W. Frow became the first subdivider in Coconut Grove when he sold part of his land. John Thomas Peacock came from England in 1870, and was one of many squatters in the area. His solitary presence at the south end of the Grove led it to be named "Jack's Bight." He later established a homestead in the Silver Bluffs area. His brother Charles, who arrived with his family in 1875, later bought 31 acres of the original Besly homestead from John Frow. There he established Bay View House, which became the first hotel in the Miami area. Its site is on the ridge that is Peacock Park today. The hotel catered to the area's first winter tourists, who came by sailboat from Key West. In 1887, as soon as the ten children necessary to open a school were registered, the first public school opened in Coconut Grove. Dinner Key, then an island, was used by boaters from Homestead to Miami as a convenient stopping place for mid-day meals.

Ralph Middleton Munroe, a young Staten Islander, paid many visits to the Coconut Grove area. The first was in September 1877, on a sailing vacation. Other visits were in 1881 and in 1884. He settled permanently in Coconut Grove in 1885 and in 1891 he designed and built his home, the "Barnacle." In 1887, the Biscayne Bay Yacht Club was formed, with Ralph Munroe as Commodore. In the following year, the Club leased the then-dark Cape Florida Lighthouse and surrounding property and later constructed a clubhouse. The women of Coconut Grove formed a Housekeeper's Club on 19 February 1891. The Exchange Library opened in January 1895, and a building was constructed in 1901. In one of his early visits to the area south of the Miami River, Ralph Munroe made an interesting discovery in an old postal guide. There had been a post office "Cocoanut Grove" in the area. He also found that Horace Porter had been appointed postmaster in Coconut Grove on 6 January 1873. Porter, who had been unsuccessful in his attempt to claim the Pent homestead, now achieved fame after his death. For Porter and others, a post office in the Grove had become necessary when the Miami post office, formerly at the mouth of the Miami River, was moved in June 1870. It was established on a site between Buena Vista and Little River and named Biscayne. The seven or so miles between the mouth of the river and Biscayne became a hardship for those living near the river. The life of the Coconut Grove post office was short; it was discontinued on 8 February 1874, when Porter left to follow his wife to Boston. According to a local historian, "All efforts to discover why the area was called Coconut Grove (Cocoanut Grove at the time) have met with failure."[21] Ralph Munroe arranged to have the post office reopened on 25 August 1884, with Charles Peacock as postmaster.

The first black settlers arrived in the latter half of the 1890s to work at the Peacock Inn. Soon a community, almost exclusively from the Bahamas, grew up across the "back road" (Main Highway) and became the first black settlement in the Miami area. Black pioneers, in particular E. W. F. Stirrup, purchased land, mostly from Joseph Frow. Later the irregular footpath that was called Evangelist was paved and the street renamed Charles Avenue after Charles Frow, Joseph's son.

Coconut Grove was the largest and most influential settlement in the Biscayne Bay area between 1884 and 1896, before Miami became an instant city. The Grove had the only hotel, the Peacock Inn, south of Lake Worth. There was also a school, a church, a library, and a women's club. The arrival of the railroad changed Coconut Grove. Nearly all of the present area and much of Coral Gables was turned into grapefruit groves. Packing houses and a railway siding were established at Douglas Road and Dixie Highway. Coconut Grove received national attention as the birthplace of two tropical fruits—the Hayden mango and the Trapp avocado. In 1896, a road was built to link Coconut Grove and Miami. It was called the Country Road, now Brickell Avenue, and followed the shoreline. The road was rerouted around Vizcaya when James Deering built his mansion in 1916. Part of the road was renamed South Bayshore Drive.

The land boom began in the Grove when the Coconut Grove

Park Subdivision was platted in 1919. This subdivision offered a unique idea later adopted by other developers—four different types of plans. Each plan varied by site location, and each had a grapefruit tract. This development added a new dimension to the Grove's attraction. Wealthy or famous persons such as William J. Matheson, William Deering, John Bindley, Arthur Curtis James, the Calverts, David Fairchild, and the widow of the sculptor Augustus Saint-Gaudens, all built homes in the area. Coconut Grove also attracted members of the northern professional and academic community after 1903 when Camp Biscayne (across from the present day Grove Playhouse) was established. A visitor to the area, Paul Ransom, established the private boys' Florida–Adirondacks School. The boys spent the summers in the Adirondacks and the winters on Biscayne Bay.

The two communities of Coconut Grove and Miami came into conflict when the government, at the urging of the Miami Chamber of Commerce, leased land at Dinner Key to build one of the nation's first naval air stations. Residents of the Grove complained of noise, hazards to yachtsmen and fishermen from the seaplanes, and the pollution of the crystal-clear bay waters. At a meeting held at the Coconut Grove School on 18 March 1919, the residents voted to incorporate. They also voted to drop the "a" from "Cocoanut Grove," a pet complaint of author Kirk Munroe and botanist David Fairchild. Improvements to streets, sidewalks, parks, sewage disposal, water, street lights, and fire and police protection were considered. In July 1920, the Town Council hired a Philadelphia architect, John Irwin Bright, to prepare a town plan. It is unclear why the plan was never carried out. A large portion of the Council's time was spent on the approval of subdivision plats. By 1923, the town had three hundred registered voters, enough legally to be called a city. Since 1918, the *Miami Herald* had advocated that the City of Miami annex Coconut Grove. In 1923, it pressed also for the annexation of Silver Bluff, Little River, Buena Vista, Allapattah, and Lemon City to form a Greater Miami. In an election on 2 September 1925, most of the voters approved annexation and the Grove became part of a larger Miami.

Coconut Grove retains its identity today, whereas those of the other areas annexed have almost been forgotten. In another election sixty-six years later, the voters in Coconut Grove voted overwhelmingly to establish a Village Council. Voters were unhappy with the City of Miami's lack of attention to local issues,[22] an apparent instance of history repeating itself. The desire to secede from the City and to form an independent town remains strong.

Arch Creek: settled, 1880s; post office, 1903; incorporated as Town of Miami Shores, 1925; name changed to North Miami in 1927 and later to City of North Miami. When Adam C. Richards arrived in Biscayne Bay in 1875, there were only two families that lived near the Miami River, the Brickells and the Wagners. On the north side J. W. Ewan, the "Duke of Dade," lived in the old officers' quarters at Fort Dallas. Richards joined Lewis and Fletcher at Arch Creek, where he also built a coontie starch mill. In 1888, he sold part to Kirk Monroe and the rest to a northern corporation.

In 1903, the Florida East Coast Railway built a new depot at Arch Creek to serve the farms in the area. The depot was located on high land half a mile south of the Natural Bridge. This is where the county road turned east to the coastal ridge. Soon the Elmiran family was joined by others to form an agricultural community. The post office was established in 1903, and the school in 1905.[23] By 1912, Arch Creek had eighteen homes, a population of over one hundred, a post office, school, church, small business district, and a railroad station. Arch Creek extended between N.E. 115th Street and 127th Street and had East Dixie on the west and the bay on the east. On 5 February 1926, the community was incorporated as the Town of Miami Shores, not to be confused with the large subdivision of Miami Shores just to the south. In the same year, Sunny Isles, Golden Beach, and all of the ocean front up to Broward County were annexed. The plan was to have a causeway to Miami Beach, a mile and a half away. A large island across the bay from Miami Shores was filled, bulkheaded, and laid out with lots. The area is today Indian Creek and Bay Harbor Islands. By an act of the Legislature the name of the town was changed to North Miami on 6 June 1927.[24] With the growth after World War II the town was large enough to change its status to the City of North Miami.

Fulford: founded, 1891; incorporated as a town in 1926 and designated a city in 1927; became part of North Miami Beach, which incorporated in 1931. On the north end of Biscayne Bay was the two-thousand-acre Graves Tract. It contained the meandering Snake Creek delta of mangroves. The creek flowed into a shallow, brackish lagoon but was later opened to the ocean by the Baker's Haul-over Cut. Part of the tract is now occupied by the Bay Vista campus of Florida International University.

In October 1891, Captain William Hawkins Fulford filed an application for a homestead, a hundred acres in extent, near Snakes Creek, known today as Oleta River. The town of Fulford, now part of North Miami Beach, eventually developed in this location. Captain Fulford was keeper of the Biscayne House of Refuge at Lemon

City. The Houses of Refuge were established by the United States Life Saving Service. Houses had keepers who were to help stranded people, note passing ships, collect weather information, and assist in the repair of ships and boats. In 1874, the government planned five houses of refuge along the east coast of Florida. One of the five was built at present-day 71st Street on the ocean. William J. Smith occupied the Biscayne House of Refuge as the first keeper on 7 October 1876.[25]

In 1900, Fulford was already a thriving farm center with a railway depot and siding, while Arch Creek was just beginning. Little Snake Creek became known as the "Gateway to the Glades." Between 1900 and 1920, dredges worked continuously to dig ditches and drain the land in and beyond the Snake Valley. A main canal that ran northwestwards of Fulford virtually eliminated the Little Snake Creek. The settlement developed into a community with a Methodist Church in 1906, a Community Club, and the Hotel Alabama in 1912. In 1920, Fulford had a population of 182, less than the 307 residents at Arch Creek and the 538 at Ojus, where rock quarrying and thriving farming industries were located.

Ojus (Seminole for "plenty") was founded in 1897 by Albert Fitch and soon became a rich farming area where all types of crops grew. The rock in the area was found ideal for road building, and at one time fifty to sixty carloads of rock were shipped out daily.[26] In 1913, the Miami Gardens tract of 6,000 acres was subdivided and sold in 5- to 20-acre plots. By 1922, the prairies were drying up; as tomato crops declined, farmers planted groves, raised poultry or dairy herds, or moved to South Dade.

Larkins: founded, 1899; incorporated and renamed Town of South Miami in 1926 and City of South Miami in 1927. On 6 July 1899, Wilson A. Larkins' application to establish a post office in his store was approved. The post office, together with the surrounding settlement, was named Larkins despite Wilson Larkins' own preference for the name Manila. When the railroad came through later, the rough sandy track between the Cutler trail and the railroad crossing was found unsuitable for regular travel. The track was improved and was known for years as Larkins Road before it was renamed Sunset Drive. By 1917, Larkins had a population of about three hundred, with fifty-nine subdivisions.[27] In 1926, the town of Larkins was incorporated as the town of South Miami to prevent annexation by neighboring Coral Gables.

Homestead: founded, 1904; incorporated, 1913. After the survey for the Miami-Homestead railroad extension was completed in late

1903, William Alfred King constructed the first permanent buildings on what was to be the site of the City of Homestead. He was the Florida East Coast Railway section supervisor. A depot, offices, and homes for the station agent and section supervisor, as well as a tool shed, were constructed. The area did not have a name; it was described simply as "Homestead" on engineers' maps, from the label "Homestead Country" chalked on cars carrying supplies and building materials to the end of the line. In September 1904, William D. Horne opened a store and boarding house.

John S. Fredericks laid out the town in June 1904 for Henry Flagler. The tracks reached Homestead in August; and the first passenger train arrived on 15 December 1904. By 1907, there were enough children to open one school; and by 1913, enough for a second, owing to a large influx of settlers from the Southern states after the destruction of the cotton crop by the boll weevil in 1912.[28] On 27 January 1913, all twenty-seven registered voters met and decided to incorporate Homestead. The city limits were set at one and one-quarter mile square. The first bond issue was used to pave the two main streets, build a City Hall, and buy a fire engine. With the boom of the 1920s, the population reached over one thousand three hundred. Krome Avenue became a busy business section. New water and sewer systems were put in place in 1925, and the road to Key Largo opened on 1 September.

In 1903, David Webster Sullivan was the first person to establish himself west of the area that was later to become the City of Homestead. This area, located north and west of Homestead and south of the Silver Palm and Redland Districts, was opened to homesteading. It was never given a name as a community. After completion of the railroad survey, William J. Krome decided to settle in the area. He filed a claim in October 1903, for land on both sides of what is now Krome Avenue and the north side of Avocado Drive. Several other members of the survey team also filed claims in the area. The completely agricultural character of the area changed in the 1950s when Homestead Air Force Base was opened and military personnel with their families established homes in the city, Homestead retains the essentially agricultural base of its economy.

Florida City: founded, 1908; incorporated, 1914. The Tatum brothers purchased twenty-two thousand acres in the east glades south of Homestead. In 1908 they set up the Miami Land and Development Company. Edward Stiling was hired to organize a town and sell the land. The first families arrived by railroad on 28 October 1910. He named the city Detroit, after his home city in Michigan. Stiling's plat for the town included a 100-foot-wide main street and 70-foot wide secondary streets. A school was opened in 1911. Soon stores lined both sides of Palm Avenue and formed a larger business area than Homestead. By 1914 so many newcomers had arrived that it was decided to incorporate and to change the name of the town to Florida City.

Miami Beach: founded, 1912; incorporated, 1915. Miami Beach originally consisted of three development companies: the Miami Beach, Ocean Beach, and Alton Beach Improvement Companies. In the early 1880s, Elnathan T. Field and Ezra Osborn purchased sixty-five miles of oceanfront land from the federal government for 75 cents to $1.25 an acre. Their property stretched from Jupiter to Cape Florida. In 1883, they planted 38,000 coconut nuts from Trinidad on Miami Beach and another 62,000 on Cape Florida.[29] In 1886, Charles H. Lum built a two-story house with a porch on the peninsula that would be Miami Beach. It was the only building except for the House of Refuge and a few fishermen's shacks. The Field and Osborn project was not successful for many reasons, one being that the trees largely failed to bear fruit; another, that the partners had underestimated the costs of the project, and still another, that they lacked a transportation and marketing program. John S. Collins, a man knowledgeable about plant life, bought out the enterprise in 1909, becoming the sole owner of 1,670 acres, nearly five miles of oceanfront on the Atlantic, and one mile along Biscayne Bay. Collins organized his Miami Beach Improvement Company on 3 June 1912 to sell land for residences. The first plat was filed on 11 December 1912. Despite the protests of the owners of boats that ferried people across Biscayne Bay, he obtained a grant to build a wooden bridge across the bay to connect the beach land with Miami. Collins then constructed the longest wooden bridge in the world—two and one-half miles long—to connect Miami Beach at Dade Boulevard to Miami at N.E. 15th Street. On 23 May 1913, Thomas Pancoast and his family were the first persons to drive across Biscayne Bay from Miami on the newly constructed Collins toll bridge, opened formally only on June 12, a few weeks later. In 1925, this bridge was replaced by the Venetian Causeway.

J. E. and J. N. Lummus, two brothers each of whom was the president of a bank, lent money to Collins to build his bridge. They decided to buy up the south end of the island, 605 acres of swampland from Lincoln Road south. They began their Ocean Beach development program in May 1912. A plat was filed on 9 July 1912, and they began to auction real estate at Ocean Beach early in 1913, even though the bridge had not yet been completed. The arrival of Carl Graham Fisher, a self-made millionaire and builder of the Indianapolis Speedway, on the peninsula in 1910 changed that area forever. Fisher advanced Collins $50,000 for the completion of the wooden bridge. In return, as a gift, Collins gave Fisher 200 acres of land with access to the ocean. Fisher also lent the Lummus brothers money for their development. In return, he was given 105 acres of swamp from Lincoln Road south to 15th Street. He bought an additional 260 acres of land and formed the Alton Beach Realty Company to create his vision of an American Riviera. The first plat was filed on 15 January 1914. He, as well as the Lummus brothers, spent a fortune dredging sand from Biscayne Bay to spread over the swampland to create land suitable for development (Figure 6). Fisher also spent large sums of money on planting to prevent the sand from blowing away. He had a difficult time with his dream city. There were no takers, even though he offered free lots to anyone who would build a home and settle his land.

Thus begins the history of Miami Beach. It grew rapidly in the next few years and was incorporated as the City of Ocean Beach on 26 March 1915 with 300 residents, but only thirty-three voters.[30] The name of the city was changed to Miami Beach the following year. After World War I, Fisher merged with Collins and Pancoast, he supplying the funds and they the land, for a large tourist development. Land began to be sold in considerable quantity in 1920. By 1921 there were five hotels in operation,[31] including Fisher's domed Flamingo Hotel. He named the broad highway, Lincoln Road, after his idol, Abraham Lincoln. In the early 1950s it was called (by its

6. The Surf Club, Miami Beach.

TABLE I Miami Beach: Buildings Completed

Year	Hotels No.	Hotels % Increase	Apartments No.	Apartments % Increase	Houses No.	Houses % Increase
1930	77		233		1,153	
1935	112	45%	397	70%	1,915	66%
1940	279	149%	890	124%	3,338	74%

Source: Adapted from Keith Root, *Miami Beach Art Deco Guide*, 9.

merchants) the "Most Beautiful Shopping Street in the World," or the "Fifth Avenue of the South."

During the decades of the 1930s and 1940s, Miami Beach became the winter haven and retirement home for the wealthy class. It was also regarded as one of the world's most glamorous winter playgrounds. The original city plan allowed only three types of residential uses: homes, apartments, and hotels. There was no provision to house the thousands of workers employed in the predominant tourist industry; they were forced to live across the bay in the City of Miami. After World War II, the older residential sections at the south end of Miami Beach began to decline, and the process spread slowly northward. Wealthier residents moved to new areas north of the city, where modern hotels also sprang up.

The population of Miami Beach swelled each season with the arrival of tourists. In 1930, the resident population of 6,494 increased to 35,000 during the winter months. Ten years later, in 1940, the resident population of 28,012 expanded to about 80,000 in the winter season.[32] Hotel and apartment construction went on apace (see Table 1).

In 1979, a one square-mile district of South Beach[33] was added to the National Register of Historic Places.[34] In the district are concentrated well over eight hundred notable buildings. Commonly known as the Art Deco District, it became the first twentieth-century "historic" district on the Register. The boundary of the district is approximately the area bounded by Ocean Drive to Lenox Avenue between 6th Street and 17th Street, with a northeastern "peninsula" from Collins Avenue to Washington Avenue up to 22nd Street.

While national designation of the Art Deco District lends prestige, among other benefits, the buildings themselves are protected by the Miami Beach Historic Preservation Ordinance. Since 1986, the City Commission has approved four local historic districts for this purpose. The Miami Beach Local Historic Preservation Districts are Ocean Drive/Collins Avenue, Flamingo, Espanola Way, and Museum. On account of the objections of some property owners, a pocket east of Collins Avenue, between 15th Street and Lincoln Road, and another between 20th Street and 21st Street, were excluded from the local districts. In general, the city planning board supported the extension of local historic districts to coincide with the National Register of Historic Places boundaries. Controversy continued when the Miami Beach City Commission passed a historic districts zoning ordinance in October 1989. Preservationists severely criticized the ordinance for emasculating the districts.[35] In addition, many other proposals threatened to reshape the historic district and the whole of South Beach.[36] The razing of the splendid New Yorker hotel in 1981 and the demolition of the Senator Hotel, "jewel of the Art Deco District," in 1988,[37] were ominous warnings of erosion to America's only twentieth-century Historic District.

Although the area north of 6th Street was historically designated and its buildings thus were protected, the area south of 5th Street to the island's tip at Government Cut was subject to a moratorium on restoration and rebuilding that lasted from 1973 to 1982. The whole area of about two hundred fifty acres was to be flattened and rebuilt with high-rise buildings and canals, a "tropical Venice." The City Commission eventually abandoned this anachronistic scheme to raze the area, but the moratorium had created a rundown area and led to the loss of landmarks such as the greyhound racetrack and the Coast Guard house. Somehow the famous Joe's Stone Crab Restaurant, opened in 1913, survived and is now a prominent feature in a new plan. The current intention is to rehabilitate many old hotel and apartment buildings in the interior of the area and to redevelop the western and southern strips along the Intracoastal Waterway and Government Cut. With a refound confidence in the area, renamed South Pointe in 1983, the City of Miami Beach invested funds in the area's roads and sewers. For its part, the private sector built the first new building in the area in 1987, a multistory condominium tower in "Modern Deco" style at the southern end of the area facing Government Cut.

Coral Gables: founded, 1921; incorporated, 1925. George Edgar Merrick inherited a 160-acre grapefruit grove from his father. He expanded it to 3,000 to build his dream city. Merrick's vision met with difficulty as bankers would not lend him money when apparently the growth trend was in the direction of Miami Beach. He persisted in his goal to establish his "Master Suburb," selling a few lots and all the time buying up more land. His dream city was to be called Coral Gables, after the family home. The first lot was sold on 28 November 1921. In the following year the first street and first store were opened. Coral Gables was incorporated as a municipality on 27 April 1925. This was followed by the opening of the lavish Miami-Biltmore Hotel on 15 January 1926. This building was one of many remarkable architectural features along with gateways, fountains, boulevards, and distinguished mansions and smaller hotels, which Merrick introduced. At first sight, it would appear that the street names in Coral Gables are of Spanish origin. In reality, some names are Italian or common English: "There is no rhyme or reason to the names. Some were chosen because they sound good or sound Spanish or sound Italian."[38]

During the land boom in 1925, Merrick persuaded the sponsors of a college in Miami to locate the institution in his city instead. He donated one hundred sixty acres for the site and pledged $5 million. So the University of Miami in Coral Gables was founded. The severe hurricane of 1926 halted construction. During its first decade the school struggled for survival as the Depression persisted. The university opened in the fall of 1926, and was known as the "Cardboard College" from the cardboard partitions used to divide some rooms into classrooms in its temporary accommodation, the unfinished Anastasia Building in Coral Gables. The San Sebastian Hotel nearby was purchased in 1939 and converted into administrative offices and a women's dormitory. Construction began on the Merrick Building in 1945 on the original site donated by George Merrick. In 1947, the University moved to its vacant campus in Coral Gables. The Memorial Classroom Building and some temporary buildings were added, and the skeleton structure of the original administration building was completed and renamed the Merrick Building. "City Beautiful," as Merrick renamed his creation, was a victim to the collapse of the land boom and the Depression of the 1930s. He died on 26 March 1942, as Miami's postmaster.

Hialeah and Country Club Estates: Hialeah, founded 1921, incorporated 1925; Country Club Estates, founded 1922, incorporated as Country Club Estates in 1926 and renamed Miami Springs in 1930.
James H. Bright arrived in Miami in 1909. He purchased from the Tatum Brothers 14,000 acres of Everglades land that he turned into a cattle ranch. In 1917, Glenn H. Curtiss moved his flying school onto the property. Curtiss and Bright then platted the subdivision of Hialeah (Seminole for pretty or high prairie)[39] in 1921. Four years later they turned Hialeah into Dade County's sports and amusement center with a dog track. Later they added horse racing and a jai alai fronton. The partners also built the Miami Studios hoping to turn the area into another Hollywood. Later,

Hialeah began to attract industries due to the large concentration of suitable labor in the city. Other inducements were added by the city commission, and in response, many new industries flocked to the area. After the war the city became, and continues to be, the manufacturing center of Greater Miami.

The artesian well discovered on land owned by Bright and Curtiss led to the development of Country Club Estates, followed by the settlement of Opa-locka with its Moorish mosques and domes. Curtiss was involved independently in these two developments on the 1200-acre Curtiss-Bright ranch. The dismay he felt at the rapid and uncontrolled growth of Hialeah led him to develop what is now Miami Springs with strict regulations in place.[40] The development of Country Club Estates was incorporated as a town in 1926, and renamed Miami Springs in 1930.

Miami Shores: founded, 1922; annexed by Miami, 1925; withdrew and was incorporated as the Village of Miami Shores, 1932. In 1922, L. T. Cooper, in partnership with G. E. Willis, put together a land package of 1,100 acres, starting at N.E. 87th Street, continuing one mile along West Dixie, and widening to the bay. They developed El Portal with wide streets and sidewalks, large lots, and a stone Alhambra Gateway. This development was 300 acres in extent, located north of N.E. 87th Street. They also established a larger tract with four thousand lots, which they called Bay View Estates.

Their major project was Miami Shores, the single largest land development in Dade County at the time. Miami Shores included several developments. Both East Dixie and West Dixie highways were included and the designated route for a new federal highway. The railroad also passed through the area. On the site of Miami Shores there were many old homesteads, as well as an extensive bayfront. Before the project could be marketed, however, it was purchased by the Shoreland Company and developed as the Miami Shores subdivision. In 1932, the community of Miami Shores withdrew from Miami, which had annexed the subdivision in 1925, and incorporated as the Village of Miami Shores.

Buena Vista: incorporated, 1924; annexed by Miami, 1925. Buena Vista, so-called for its beautiful view of Biscayne Bay, began as a farming area and the pineapple plantation of T. V. Moore, the "Pineapple King of South Florida."[41] By 1924, the community had grown large enough that it incorporated. The Town Hall building on N.W. 40th Street and 2nd Avenue still survives. Miami annexed the short-lived city the following year.

Opa-locka: founded, 1926; incorporated as a town in 1926 and designated a city in 1927. The disappointment Glenn Curtiss had with the development of Hialeah was repeated in his second development, Country Club Estates. It did not become the garden city that he envisioned. Curtiss began to plan another dream city to the north. The introduction of a new railway line by the Seaboard Air Line Railway through the area provided the stimulus for the development of Opa-locka. Curtiss insisted that his new city have arabesque architecture. In January 1927, the first train arrived at the railroad station in Opa-locka, shortened from the Seminole name Opatishawockalocka (hammock in the big swamp). After World War II, industrial enterprises located in the city and open spaces and warehouses were replaced by low-income apartment buildings.

Nonincorporated Towns and Districts

Biscayne District: settled, 1870s; post office, 1870. Biscayne Prairie, as northeast Dade County was known during the 1870s, consisted of four bayfront tracts. These were occupied, from north to south, by the Sturtevant, Hunt and Gleason, and Barnott families, and the Potter brothers. William Gleason had attempted to acquire the Sears tract, three miles north of the Miami River, as a federal homestead. With his partner William Hunt, they named the area north of the tract Biscayne. The mangroves in the area made the bayside almost impenetrable except for five places in the upper bay. When the railroad came, the depot was named Biscayne. Later developments were Biscayne Heights, Biscayne Park, Biscayne Gardens, and Biscayne Canal. By 1895, the area of East and West Biscayne was designated the Biscayne District so that the area could justify having its own school.

Cutler: settled with post office, 1884. A full township of thirty-six sections on Biscayne Bay below the 26th parallel was granted by Congress in July 1838 to Dr. Henry Perrine, at the time the American Consul in Campeche, Yucatan, Mexico. One provision of the grant was that each section was to have a settler engaged in the cultivation of tropical and semitropical plants of commercial value. Plants were to be nonindigenous to the United States. The government's intention was to introduce large-scale tropical planting to Florida. The Perrines arrived at Indian Key on 25 December 1838. On 7 August 1840, rampaging Indians killed Dr. Henry Perrine. As ownership of the huge Perrine grant was unclear, pioneers were forced to "squat." This situation was hardly conducive to the

Dr. Henry Perrine described his selected land as "the sheltered sea shore of an ever-verdant prairie in a region of ever-blooming flowers, in an ever-frostless tropical Florida."
Jean Taylor, *The Villages of South Dade*, 2.

emergence of settlements. Only William Fuzzard was successful in establishing Cutler. Northern Dade County had no such problem.

The first recorded settler along the Ridge, the area along Biscayne Bay between Coconut Grove and Cutler, was Isaiah Hall. He established his home at Hall's Creek, just south of the present wading beach at Matheson Hammock. John Addison arrived in April 1864. He had fought in the Third Seminole War at the Manatee River Settlements and was there when the Civil War began in 1861. Addison chose the "Hunting Grounds," the last place where the rock ridge touches the water on Dade County's southern coastline. He became a squatter on the Perrine Grant and built an impressive home regarded as one of the finest on the bay.

In 1876, Henry E. Perrine, son of Dr. Perrine, arrived with the aim of building a new town to be called Perrine. Land for the town was a place the locals called "[Big] Hunting Grounds" or "Addison's Landing." The venture was a failure, and Henry Perrine left South Florida and returned to New York. In 1883, Dr. William Cutler, from Chelsea, Massachusetts, bought a tract of six hundred acres with two miles of waterfront north of the Perrine Grant. He intended to establish a fruit and vegetable plantation and erected a small shack where Ingraham Highway crossed Snapper Creek.

William Fuzzard settled on land in the Perrine Grant in 1884. His property was south of where the Cutler Light Plant now stands and north of Addison's Hammock. He began with starch making but gave this up for growing pineapples. By 1892, Fuzzard had 25,000 pineapple plants and several mangoes and guavas. To bring in supplies, he blazed a trail from his home to Coconut Grove. This trail was the beginning of Old Cutler Road that ran north from his home along Ingraham Highway to Coconut Grove. In 1884, his application to establish a post office was approved as there were enough residents in the area to justify one. He named the post office "Cutler" in honor of his friend and mentor Dr. Cutler. The great freezes of 1894 and 1895 persuaded many pioneers in central Florida to move south. As most of the land available for homesteading in Miami and Coconut Grove was not available, the new settlers were attracted to Cutler because of its rich farmland. By the end of 1895, over twenty families had homes, cultivated fields, and groves in the area. A school was opened in 1896 and remained in operation until 1908. The town of Cutler declined, however, when the railroad extension was built to the west and the post office was moved to the south. By 1906, there were only about ten or twelve families living in Cutler.[42] Three years later the school was closed as there was a school in the new town of Perrine, which opened to the west along the railroad.

Originally the railway extension southward from Miami was to run along the bay ridge through Coconut Grove and Cutler. Opposition from Commodore Munroe and his friends blocked the proposed extension, however. These landowners wished to preserve the character of their estates from the intrusion of commercialism. The railroad was laid to the west, thus bypassing both Coconut Grove and, farther south, Cutler. Between 1913 and 1926, Charles Deering consolidated land for his estate.

Lemon City: founded, 1889; post office, probably 1889. John Saunders arrived at Mettair's Bight, five miles north of the Miami River, in 1876. In 1889, he produced final proof to claim a homestead on Biscayne Bay at N.E. 61st Street. He sold one tract to Eugene C. Harrington, who called his subsequent subdivision Lemon City. It was named after the unusually sweet lemon trees that grew in the area. The "city" in name only had no fixed boundaries.[43] Soon there were a post office, a store, and the Lemon City Hotel. After the introduction of the steamboat service to the Indian River area, the many settlers there exhausted the lands. Homesteaders then made their way from Indian River to settle at Lemon City. By 1891, the settlement had become a sizable community of about eighty houses with a school, a church, a post office, several boarding houses, and a sawmill. A railroad station was added later. The original subdivisions were subsequently replatted and the old places demolished. In the 1920s many pioneer black families relocated to Overtown and other areas. Today Lemon City is only a name but its place remains in the history of Greater Miami as one of the first organized communities. Since 1980, the area has become "Little Haiti" as many Haitian merchants arrived and opened stores along N.E. 54th Street between Miami Avenue and N.E. 2nd Avenue.

Perrine: founded, 1897. On 28 January 1897, the Secretary of the Interior issued the patent to the Perrine heirs when the terms of the grant of 1838 finally had been fulfilled. During the preceding period, land in the huge Perrine tract could not be bought or homesteaded. As a result, the families who had settled on the land formed a "Squatter's Union" to press for their rights. They were helped in their efforts by J. E. Ingraham, vice president of the F.E.C. Railway. He also attempted to find settlers for the remaining sixteen unoccupied sections. The patent allocated 40 acres of land to every settler on the grant, 10,000 acres of the total of 22,000 acres to the Perrine heirs, and 5,000 acres each to the Florida East Coast Railway and the Florida Central and Peninsular Railroad. Dr. S. H. Richmond, an engineer for the F.E.C. Railway, began to make preliminary surveys for the platting of a town and laying out of roads.

Redland: founded, 1900; post office, 1907. The first homesteaders in the Redland area were Daniel Roberts and Claude Jenkins. In April 1900, Roberts filed a claim for a homestead in the Redland District, the second area to be opened for homesteading in South Dade. Although all the area south of Perrine is now called the Redland, it used to have definite boundaries. These were what is today Eureka Drive to Biscayne Drive between Krome Avenue and the Everglades. The name was derived from the rich and tillable red soil in the area. In 1905, John Bauer built the first store at the corner of Redland Road and Bauer Drive; it was to become the nucleus of the town of Redland. A year later there were enough families with children to open a school. In 1907, Bauer became the first postmaster. Redland did not develop into a thriving town even with the coming of the Seaboard Railway through the area in the early 1930s. The post office was discontinued in 1934 during the Depression. Each year the Redland District shared with other South Dade grove owners and vegetable owners bigger and bigger displays in the annual Dade County Fair. There they garnered many prizes and trophies. The Redland District Chamber of Commerce (based in nearby Homestead) sent its own band and float to the fair in 1915. In 1924 Redland held its first fruit festival in Homestead, a week before the county fair.

Silver Palm: founded, 1900. In 1900, the Silver Palm District became another area south of Cutler to be settled. Charles Gossman was the first to take up residence in the district. Its name comes from the little palm with silver-backed fronds that grew in the thick pine woods of the area. By 1902, there were enough families with children in the Silver Palm District to start a school, the first south of Cutler. The school was merged with Redland's school in 1916.

Longview: founded, 1902. William J. Krome, surveyor of the railway route from Homestead to Key West, established a camp at the edge of the Everglades in 1902. He chose high land west of present-day Florida City. It was shown on 1903 survey maps as an area at the end of the Longview Trail. Krome named the camp Longview after the "long view" of the prairie that a two-story tower afforded hunters searching for game. In 1910 the area was settled when Ruben N. Moser persuaded eight families from Topeka, Kansas, to join him in homesteading the Longview locality. New settlers built a school that operated from 1910 to 1913, when the big new school was opened in Homestead. During its short life of three years, the little school of Longview was voted by a state evaluation group the best small rural school in Florida.

Kendall: settled, 1900s. Early in the 1900s, Henry John Boughton Kendall arrived from England as one of the trustees of the Florida Land and Mortgage Company. He came to manage the company's groves and landholdings. These stretched west of Red Road from S.W. 88th Street to S.W. 104th Street. In the early 1920s, Dan Killian, the county commissioner, renamed these streets North Kendall Drive and South Kendall Drive respectively. Henry Flagler decided to sponsor a model grove in the area, now known as Kendall. He wanted to prove the worth of the land he had opened after the extension of the railroad from Miami to Homestead. Because of Flagler's tract and the presence of Seminole Indian villages, the Kendall area was slow to develop; little land was available for homesteading. One Indian village was west of what is now Baptist Hospital. A second village was on what is today S.W. 107th Avenue between North Kendall Drive and Sunset Drive. There was also an Indian camp between Snapper Creek Road and Davis Road just west of Galloway Road. A school for the Kendall area was opened in September 1929, at 9300 S.W. 7th Avenue. Today only vestiges of Kendall's first homesteads survive. About eighty years ago, though, when the rains came, residents had to contend with alligators, rattlesnakes, mosquitoes, and five feet of water outside their kitchen doors.[44]

Railway Towns: founded, 1903. As the F.E.C.R. extended its rail lines south, sidings were built, usually on section lines. Sidings were used for the loading and unloading of goods. The first siding after Kendall was at what is now S.W. 136th Street. An F.E.C.R. depot was built east of the tracks at the northeast corner of 136th Street and U.S. 1. Benson's Siding, called after the person who operated the siding, was later known as the town of *Benson*. It was renamed Howard around 1923, and the east-west road named Howard Drive.[45] One mile south of Benson was the town of *Key*. It had twelve to fourteen houses for whites on the east side of the tracks, and many more houses for blacks on the west side. A Captain Key managed the town. South of the town was the settlement of *Rockdale* at what is now Coral Reef Drive and U.S. 1. The Rockdale road ran from the northeast corner of Coral Reef Drive and U.S. 1 west for three blocks where the Richmond Inn was located. Cutler School was located on Rockdale Road about two or three blocks north of Richmond. In the early 1900s, the F.E.C.R. company built a siding and a large rock-crushing plant at the settlement of Rockdale. This plant provided material to create a solid bed for the railway tracks. At the next stop south, at what is now Richmond Drive, the F.E.C.R. established in 1903 a complex for the southern end of the line. A general camp and supply depot made up the complex. The town of *Perrine* developed and soon grew to include three hundred people. At Quail Roost Drive and the railroad the town of *Peters* was established. Tom Peters owned the packing houses, a commissary, and a hotel in the settlement. Also in 1903, the town of *Goulds* came into being when a siding, operated by a Mr. Gould, was established. It was situated at what is today S.W. 216th Street. Land in the area had already been homesteaded by William Johnson and William Randolph. In 1904, Gaston Drake bought land on both sides of the railroad north of Coconut Palm Drive. He brought in a sawmill and built over a hundred homes for his workers. He named his town *Princeton*. He painted all the buildings orange and black, after his alma mater. His operations covered about forty square miles of pine land. From here he supplied lumber for much of the building in Miami, Vizcaya, for the causeway bridge to Miami Beach, and for Flagler's railroad extension to the Keys. The mill was closed down in 1923, when the timber supply was depleted. In 1906, S.A. Murden filed a claim for a quarter section west of the railroad, which had come through in 1904, in the area of Modello. He platted his land, applied for a post office, and, being a sales agent for the Model Land Company, named the town *Modello*. Other homesteaders included Hannah I. Bauer, whose land is now occupied by the Orchid Jungle. Modello never grew much beyond its railway siding status. Nothing is left of the town now except the name and a park around an F.E.C.R. excavation lake. On 6 May 1907, Wilbur Albury received a grant for land bisected by the Miami-Homestead railway. On 4 February 1908, he sold his grant to George Washington Moody. He subdivided the tract and named the town *Naranja* (Spanish for orange) after the many orange trees in the area.

Biscayne Park Estates: founded, 1920. Arthur Mertlow Griffing moved to northern Dade County in 1903 to manage the family's nursery at Little River. He built a large home on land along East Dixie Highway that was once part of the Potter homestead. After about a decade, in January 1914, he branched out into land development. Biscayne Heights was his first venture. In 1920, he began one of the earliest large developments, the 700-acre Biscayne Park Estates, in the Biscayne area. This was among the first signs of the upcoming land boom. The construction of the Biscayne Canal in

1923 helped drain Griffing's "Gateway to Miami" and other areas along its ten mile length from the Miami Canal near the Pennsylvania Sugar Mill to the bay. About half of Griffing's development became part of North Miami. Another part was incorporated as the Village of Biscayne Park. The Charles Deering Estate, which extended from the bay to N.E. 2nd Avenue, was purchased in 1925 by Hugh Anderson, President of the Shoreland Company, and Roy Wright. They wished to develop it as a high-class residential area, Miami Plaza (today's Bay Point). Charles Deering moved to Cutler, where he established a new estate.

Special Developments: Parks

In 1847, the Royal Palm Hammock was discovered by Jack Jackson and visited by Flagler's civil engineer, J. S. Fredericks, in 1883. They and others reported on the extraordinary beauty of the hammock and hoped it would be preserved. The Royal Palm State Park was dedicated on 23 November 1916 and later became Florida's first national park. The Royal Palm Hammock is located about ten miles southwest of the Florida City juncture of the Ingraham and South Dixie highways. About half of the land was a donation from Mrs. Henry Flagler to the Florida Federation of Women's Clubs. The buildings at the Park were completed by January 1918.

Ernest R. Coe campaigned tirelessly through the 1920s to turn the Everglades into a national park as a sanctuary for animals, birds and plants. The land area amounted to half a million acres that had been transferred to the state of Florida by the Great Swamp Lands Act of 1850. In the early thirties, U.S. Representative Owen sponsored a bill in Congress to create the Everglades National Park. In 1939, a government geologist, Garald G. Parker, was sent to Miami to find out why the water wells were going salty during the drought. Over the next five years Parker and his team of scientists were the first to chart the movement of the water in the Everglades. He discovered the limestone wedge of the Biscayne Aquifer, an underground network of cavities, interconnected "much like the holes in a sponge."[46] His explanation of the route surface water took south from Lake Okeechobee, and how the water above the ground was an integral part of the water beneath it, led Marjory Stoneman Douglas to name her famous book about the Everglades *River of Grass* (Figure 7). On 6 December 1947, the Everglades National Park was officially dedicated by President Harry Truman as the nation's third largest and only tropical park. Forty-two years later President Bush signed a bill authorizing an expansion of Everglades National Park.[47]

Other major parks were also established in the twentieth cen-

"Until . . . 1947, most Floridians thought the Everglades as a wasteland to be conquered and put to a 'good use' such as farming. State policies actively encouraged drainage and development. Marjory Stoneman Douglas' book *The Everglades: River of Grass* changed all that, now . . . Floridians understand the importance of the Everglades to South Florida's water supply and to the ecological well-being of Everglades National Park, Florida Bay, and the Keys."

Robert Sanchez, "It's Time to Appreciate One of Florida's Resources," 26A.

tury. Major examples are Tropical Park, Greynolds Park, Matheson Hammock Park, David Fairchild Tropical Garden, Redland Fruit and Spice Park, and Crandon Park. In December 1931 the 245-acre Tropical Park in western Dade County opened as a race track. The track was closed in 1972 and in May 1974 the Metro-Dade Commission bought the land. An adjacent 30 acres were added to create one of the county's largest parks. Dade County decided in 1933 to build Greynolds Park on the Oleta River in the northern part of the county. It was named after A. O. Greynolds, the owner of the rock pit on the land. The park was dedicated in 1936 and in 1983 was declared an historic site.[48] In 1938, Robert H. Montgomery's botanical garden was dedicated as the David Fairchild Tropical Garden, after the world-famous plant explorer. The 80-acre garden is south of Matheson Hammock in southeast Dade County. In 1944, Dade County purchased 20 acres for a subtropical park from the 40-acre nursery operated by Mary Heinlein and her husband Herman. Mary was appointed the first superintendent and chief planner of the new Redland Fruit and Spice Park, a position she held until her retirement in 1959. It was renamed the Preston Bird and Mary Heinlein Spice Park. Crandon Park on Key Biscayne was opened when access became available from the Rickenbacker Causeway, dedicated in 1947.[49] Many of Dade County's parks, such as Matheson Hammock, Crandon, Baker's Haulover, and Greynolds, were designed by the landscape architect William Lyman Phillips.[50]

Factors of Growth

THREE major factors enabled Greater Miami to grow from a small settlement into a vast urban area: the area's location and natural advantages, improvements in transportation along with drainage of swampland, and the influx of Cuban and other refugees. This chapter recounts these factors. Biscayne Bay had natural advantages that fostered growth. Foremost were the availability of fresh water and the favorable climate, which still attracts many tourists today. Human interventions—mosquito control and the use of air-conditioning in buildings—were necessary, however, to make living in the area more comfortable. Significant transportation improvements in the last decade of the nineteenth century and in the first third of the twentieth century were the railroad, major road and bridge construction, and air service, primarily to Latin America. The drainage of swampy ground became essential to provide sites for hotels to accommodate tourists and land for the houses, apartments, and other facilities to serve the ever-increasing number of residents.

Natural Advantages of Location

Fresh Water and Climate. The key to the early development of the Biscayne Bay area was fresh water. For centuries Indians and seamen of all kinds sailed up the Miami River for fresh water. The best-known spring, shaped like a large bowl (the Devil's Punch Bowl), was located on the river's south bank below Brickel Point.[1]

In the last three decades of the nineteenth century, South Florida's subtropical climate was becoming well known as beneficial to those with respiratory disorders, which were quite common then. Despite the favorable climate that prevails most of the time, Florida

In R. L. Gardiner's *A Guide to Florida, the Land of Flowers* (1872, 82), Lieutenant-Governor Gleason was quoted as follows: "... the pure water and other mineral springs, the magnificent beauty of its scenery, the salubrity and equability of its climate, must make Biscayne Bay at no distant day, the resort of the tourist and the lover of adventure." F. Trench Townshend tendered a more critical description of Miami in his book *Wild Life in Florida* (1875, 236): "... in reality a very small settlement on a ridge of limestone, ... the climate is equable but very hot, the scenery is pretty but never approaches magnificence, while the multitude of insects makes life hardly durable."

did, and still does, experience some poor weather. At the end of December 1894, for example, northern and central Florida experienced the worst freeze within living memory. The thermometer fell to fourteen degrees in Jacksonville and to twenty-four as far south as Jupiter (northern Palm Beach City). A second freeze the following February meant financial ruin for fruit and vegetable growers.

Tourism. Besides those seeking a healthy climate, South Florida's weather also began to attract tourists. E. G. ("Ev") Sewell, the area's first superpromoter, organized Miami's fifteenth celebration in July 1911 as the city's largest ever. He also devised a plan to advertise the city all over the country. In addition, Sewell persuaded Glenn Curtiss to open a flying school in Miami after he was turned down by the Wright Brothers. By 1915, several famous people began to winter in Miami and the "Magic Knights of Dade" held a Mid-Winter Festival to entertain tourists. Miami Beach became the "Playground for the People" with casinos and second homes. After World War I, Carl Fisher raised the level of the tourism campaign to new heights with the introduction of the publicity stunt. He brought national attention to Miami Beach in the 1920s with a constant stream of politicians, movie stars, and socialites. Meanwhile, public officials turned a blind eye to gambling and bootlegging to attract tourist dollars. During the 1930s, slogans such as "Stay Through May" were used to attract tourists, for whom special events were staged. In April 1931, the first Pan American Day was held to entice Latin American tourists. The Palm Festival of 1932 and 1933 blossomed into the world-renowned Orange Bowl Festival that is still a feature of Greater Miami life today. South Florida became a major resort area when motoring became widespread

8. Summer tourist group at the Pancoast Hotel. (Photo dated 1933.)

before World War II, with three-quarters of all tourists entering Florida arriving by automobile (Figure 8).[2]

Visitors continue to be attracted to the area. In 1980, there were 12.6 million tourists, including many foreign vacationers, who came to Greater Miami.[3] This was up considerably from the 6.0 million in 1970 and the 5.5 million in 1960, and vastly more than the 2.0 million in 1940. Despite the crime image that Greater Miami suffered during the 1980s, the tourism rate has climbed steadily since about 1984, reaching a high of nearly 8.5 million overnight visitors in 1991.[4] In 1980, tourists spent $9.1 billion in local hotels, restaurants, and retail stores. With more than 1.6 million passengers, Miami was the leading cruise ship port in the nation. When tourism lagged in the early 1970s, an attempt was made to legalize casino gambling on the Gold Coast, primarily Miami Beach, through a constitutional amendment, but this measure was resoundingly defeated in the November 1978 elections.

Certain human interventions in the natural environment were necessary to overcome two major and perennial discomforts: mosquitoes and heat with high humidity (Appendix A). The area is favorable not only to humans but also to insects, particularly mosquitoes, which have plagued the area since the beginning. Indians and early settlers used smoke in an attempt to keep the insects away, nowadays the primary countermeasure is spraying selected areas of Dade County.[5] The uncomfortable effects of the heat and humidity that prevail for almost six months a year are overcome by air-conditioning homes and buildings used for work, recreation, and education, as well as transport vehicles.[6] In Greater Miami, air conditioners began to appear on a large scale in commercial buildings in the late 1950s. They were introduced into residential structures in the mid-1960s, when developers introduced "cracker-box" houses. Until that time homes were designed for natural cooling, relying extensively on attic fans and prevailing breezes for relief from the hot climate.[7]

Transportation

Sea. The main means of communication for pioneers in the nineteenth century was by small sailing craft on Biscayne Bay. Mail had to be brought in by sailboat from Key West because South Florida was then separated from the rest of the state by swamps and rivers. The mail schooner from Key West came bimonthly, eventually weekly, after Ralph Middleton Munroe reactivated the Coconut Grove post office. Fowey Rock Lighthouse was completed by the government in 1878 after continual complaints that the Cape Florida Lighthouse was ineffective.

In 1898, Henry Flagler invited his rival Henry Plant
to Miami. Plant sent back
a query: "Where on earth
is Miami, and how do I get
there?" Flagler replied,
"Go to the terminal in
Jacksonville and follow the
crowd."

Arva Moore Parks, *Miami: "The Magic
City,"* 76.

Government Cut was opened in 1905 to provide a navigable
channel between the Atlantic Ocean and Biscayne Bay. With an ap-
propriation from the Rivers and Harbors Committee of the United
States Congress, large dredges cut through the peninsula at Miami
Beach. At the lower end of the long peninsula that was to become
Miami Beach, the 500-foot-wide cut improved access to the port
of Miami. Fisher's Island was created at the same time.

Rail. Henry M. Flagler first came to Florida in the winter of 1883.
He began the Florida East Coast Railway (F.E.C.R.) and in 1892
started building a railroad south from Saint Augustine to West
Palm Beach. In 1893, he secured a charter to build toward Miami
from Daytona with a land grant of 8,000 acres per mile for construction. By November 1894, the railroad reached West Palm
Beach. With his railroad, Flagler built hotels—the Royal Poinciana
Hotel on Lake Worth, the Breakers in Palm Beach, and the Ponce
de León and the Alcazar in Saint Augustine. The construction of
these hotels illustrates the importance of the railroad in the development of towns along the east coast of Florida. Flagler's F.E.C.R.
company extended the railroad from West Palm Beach to Miami;
and the first locomotive carrying supplies reached what is now
downtown Miami on 15 April 1896.

Construction of the railway led to the foundation of several
settlements at railway sidings and depot buildings.[8] In North Dade
these were—from north to south—Ojus, Fulford, Arch Creek, Biscayne, Little River, Lemon City, and Buena Vista.[9] The Biscayne
depot was designed for whistlestops, consisting only of one room
for storing freight and an open-sided roofed loading platform. The
depot was probably at N.E. 99th Street, near the present Miami
Shores Golf Course. The depot building was destroyed in the 1926
hurricane, but it had already outlived its usefulness. It was necessary to use fill or trestle for the railroad to cross the Biscayne
prairie, thus creating a boundary that separated East and West
Biscayne.

In December 1902, William J. Krome led a group to survey the
area south of Miami for the Florida East Coast Railway. A route
was needed for the railroad extension from Miami to Key West.
Flagler wanted to extend the railway southward to Homestead so
as to open the agriculturally rich Redland area and to complete
the link with Key West. Construction on the railroad from Miami
to Homestead began in 1903 and continued to Key West, where
the first train arrived on 22 January 1912. The railway sidings in
South Dade, some with station houses, were Kendall, Benson, Key,
Rockdale, Perrine, Peters, Goulds, Princeton, Naranja, Modello,

9. The Miami depot, typical of the Florida East Coast Railway buildings.

and Homestead.[10] These were the focal points of small communities. Some remain as place names today, while others have disappeared as settlements. Perrine was a significant stop with full station facilities.

Railroad construction in all of Florida was at a virtual standstill between 1900 and 1920 but reached new heights in the 1920s. Under the leadership of Davies Warfield, the Seaboard Air Line extended its lines and services, including a track down the coast to Miami in 1927. Meanwhile, the Florida East Coast Railway double-tracked its line from Jacksonville to Miami.

Road. Lantana at the lower end of Lake Worth was linked with Biscayne Bay by the first county road that was opened in 1892. The road followed the old military trail on the coastal ridge. There were wooden bridges across the Little Arch Creek and over Little River. This section of the trail had been built by Captain N. Brannen in December 1856 during the Third Seminole War. Today N.E. 12th Avenue in Miami Shores almost coincides with the military trail and earliest county road. The first hack, a springless wagon drawn by mules, began running from Lantana to Miami in January 1893. Connections three times a week between the two settlements by the stagecoach line put the "barefoot" mail carrier out of business.[11] For the first time Biscayne Bay was accessible by land, and thus began the first land boom along the bay. The original settlers, though, saw this as a threat to the seaman's way of life—to their tropical paradise.

In 1917, after the Collins Bridge was built, the County Causeway (later renamed the MacArthur Causeway) was begun. By 1919, its damming effect prevented the tidal flushing of the upper bay, which thus became foul-smelling with dying fish and a breeding area for millions of mosquitoes. In the early 1920s, a cut was made, spanned by a steel bridge, at Baker's Haulover. The first automobiles crossed over the new causeway to Miami Beach on New Year's Day, 1920. Miami–Key West Overseas Highway was completed on 29 March 1938, and the new Seven Mile Bridge was opened on 23 May 1982.[12] Rickenbacker Causeway, dedicated in 1947, provided access to the new Crandon Park on Key Biscayne.

On 25 April 1928, the Tamiami (a combination of *Tampa* and *Miami*) Trail, 274 miles across South Florida, was opened officially (Figure 10). Construction had begun in 1915 and 1916. Grading of the road in Dade County was completed in 1918. But the creation of Collier County in 1923 was required before construction in Lee County could be completed by the State Road Department. Barron G. Collier owned some three-quarters of the land in the new county. He promised the legislature to initiate construction of Tamiami Trail if a new county was created. Completion was also delayed by difficulties in construction through expanses of trackless swamp, areas least able to pay, and stretches with expensive engineering problems. In 1924, when John W. Martin was elected governor, there was a dramatic increase in road improvements under the State Road Department.

10. Everglades drainage canal at Tamiami Trail, looking east at the mile-20 point. (Photo dated 1927.)

11. Pan Am Seaplane Terminal, Dinner Key.

Air. During World War I, Miami became an air-training center for Marines at Glenn Curtiss's facility, near what is now Hialeah. Naval aviators trained at Dinner Key in Coconut Grove. When Arthur Burns ("Pappy") Chalk set up an amphibious aircraft service from Miami to the Bahamas in 1919, he did not know that seaplanes would become a Miami institution.

After the passage of the Kelly Air Mail Act of 1925, Juan Terry Trippe's Pan American Airways received the first foreign mail contract. Service began between Key West and Havana on 28 October 1927. Soon afterwards Pan Am moved its headquarters to Miami. Trippe purchased 116 acres and built the Pan Am Field (later to become the Miami International Airport) at N.W. 36th Street and Le Jeune Road. Many other Latin American cities were added between 1928 and 1930 when Miami became the "Gateway to the Americas." Pan Am then moved its operations to Dinner Key, where it established a seaplane base in 1931 (Figure 11).[13] In 1930, Eastern Airlines, formerly Pitcairn Airways, which had been formed two years previously, began service to points north of Miami and took over Pan Am's 36th Street field. Later a municipal airport was created on Glenn Curtiss's 160-acre field at N.W. 112th Street and 42nd Avenue. National Airlines was founded in 1934 and initially served Florida cities. Delta Airlines began as a Florida crop-dusting operation in 1934 but became more actively involved in air transportation after World War II.

Greater Miami's year-round ideal flying weather encouraged the federal government to construct training airfields in the area during the war years of the early 1940s. The local economy was transformed from a seasonal tourist one to a year-round hotel industry to accommodate military personnel, who stimulated the retail and service trades. In addition, thousands of civilian workers came to the area to provide services and maintain military installations. The economy of the area was further enhanced when additional tourists were attracted to Miami by airline companies. Pan Am introduced a new class of service (economy class) in 1948, and National offered its "A Millionaire's Vacation on a Piggy Bank Account" in the 1950s. After the failure of Eastern Airlines at the end of the 1980s, Pan American World Airways also reached "a bitter end" in December 1991.[14] Pan Am, which had grown from its South Florida roots into a worldwide symbol of United States aviation, had many firsts: it was the first airline in the United States to adopt "flying boats," the first to offer trans-Pacific service, the first to extend transatlantic service, and the first to fly a commercial jetliner.

Land Settlement and Drainage

Passage of the Armed Occupation Act of 1842 and the survey of Biscayne Bay by George McKay in May 1846 made it possible for land to be readily acquired. The Act provided for the head of a family to obtain 160 acres of surveyed land if he lived there for five years. He was also required to clear five acres and build a home there. The purpose of the Act was to settle the frontier territories with homesteaders. In 1850, the federal government passed the Swamp Act. Each state now had the right to select certain areas as swampland and petition to have the title transferred to the state. Then the state could sell land to individuals, donate land to encourage the building of railroads and canals, or reserve land for state use. In addition, the federal government passed the Homestead Act in 1862 to make further land available to settlers. Any citizen could receive a maximum of 160 acres of public land provided that he lived continuously on it for at least five years and improved it.

The desirability and feasibility of the drainage of the Everglades was made in the Buckingham Smith report in 1848. Governor Napoleon Bonaparte Broward, in his inaugural address on 4 April 1905, presented a comprehensive list of proposals, including the drainage of the Everglades. In the same year the Florida legislature passed the first comprehensive drainage law. A Board of Drainage Commissioners was empowered to construct a system of canals to drain and reclaim swamp and overflowed lands. The thinking at the time was that the complex system of water control in Florida, and the Everglades in particular, was needed for two reasons: One was to remove overflow water and the other was to conserve water to avoid water scarcity, paradoxical as this may sound. The workings of the system were illustrated dramatically in 1922, when rains flooded the Everglades but were followed by glades fires over the drained areas during the dry years of 1924 and 1925.

In 1906, the commissioners created the Everglades Drainage District of over four million acres. Before large-scale drainage began, the Everglades boundary was at the location of present N.W. 17th Avenue in North Dade, at 31st Avenue on the Miami River. In South Dade it was a few miles farther west where the high, dry ridge that ran down the East Coast was at its widest point. The Everglades Land Sales Company opened a Miami office in 1909 and started extensive draining of the Everglades. Sales of real estate and dredging of the Miami Canal began. As part of the drainage canal program, the rapids of the Miami River were breached to extend the river into the Miami Canal and allow boats to make a smooth passage upstream. As a result, the rock ledges could no longer hold back the intrusion of salt water from the sea and many springs dried up.[15] The Miami River's "sweet water" became a thing of the past. After the completion of the Miami Canal, Everglades water poured into Biscayne Bay for weeks. The water table dropped, and muck from the Everglades slid into the Miami River and into the bay. The waters of Biscayne Bay turned from a crystal blue to a murky brown as millions of tons of sediment-rich fresh water from the drained Everglades poured into the bay. By 1916, when the massive drainage project was completed, huge areas of the Everglades had been drained dry and opened to development. The dredge changed the face of south Florida forever as two million acres were dried out for real estate development (Figure 12).

Continued drainage of the Everglades to open new land, primarily as the winter garden of the United States, disrupted the delicate balance between fresh and salt water. Problems of overflow and scarcity remained, and efforts to reclaim wetlands were ineffective. Higher than average rainfall and two hurricanes in September and October of 1947 created vast sheets of water, twenty and forty miles wide and up to ten feet deep. As much as five million acres of the Everglades and low-lying coastal communities were covered with water. In 1949, the state legislature created the Central and Southern Florida Flood Control District that took over the responsibilites of the Everglades Drainage District in 1955. A flood control plan prepared by the Army Corps of Engineers involved additional canals, locks, and levees. These drained more of

12. The ubiquitous dredge: the dredge *Magic City* deepening Miami harbor. (Photo dated 1926.)

the Everglades, which up to that time reached to a line west of Red Road and north of N.E. 125th Street. Drainage activities made vast amounts of new land available for development. In 1946, Miami citizens voted to extend sewers to areas served by septic tanks. Six years later, in 1952, they voted for general obligation bonds to establish a treatment plant on Virginia Key to clear the sewage that was pouring into the Miami River and Biscayne Bay.

From earliest times, then, there has been concern with the control of floods and the reclamation of land. The problem, a surplus of water, and the solution, getting rid of the excess, at first seemed simple. First efforts proved, however, that the solution was more complicated and costly than anticipated and that a new problem was created, paradoxically, that of water scarcity. Even now, after a long arid spell, when the endless prairie of grass burns and the winds blow toward the city, people in the western parts of Greater Miami choke on the smoke. Some flood control of the Everglades is needed, however. It is required, first, to prevent an inundation of the coastal strip where over two million urban dwellers now reside, and second, to keep the water table high enough to ensure that residents have an adequate supply of fresh water.

The Land Boom of 1921–1926. The land development boom that began in 1921 was soon a frenzy of men attempting to turn Florida sand and swampland into gold. In the early 1920s, the "Boom, Bust, and Blow" brought an extension of the Miami city limits, a change in its skyline, continued drainage of the Everglades, and the foundation of new cities. In the fall of 1925 the boom began to weaken following a series of setbacks.[16] During the boom in Greater

Miami, some hundreds of residential subdivisions sprang up that made the real estate and construction activities major factors in the local economy.[17] Many places changed or adopted names to cash in on the magic name "Miami." Ocean Beach became Miami Beach, and other settlements renamed themselves North Miami Beach, North Miami, South Miami, West Miami, Miami Shores, and Miami Springs.[18]

There is no general agreement as to the causes of the land boom in Florida. Contributory factors were no doubt the increased use of the automobile and the roadbuilding program. Migration of people from the northeast was an additional factor. People were seeking escape from the strains of urbanization and industrialization that had intensified during World War I. Also, the material prosperity of the country provided means for travel and speculative enterprise in the new and less developed areas. Furthermore, there is no adequate explanation of why the land boom occurred in Florida and the greatest activity in Greater Miami. An attractive climate, good accessibility to the populous northeast seaboard, and the lack of state income and inheritance taxes could account for the interest. Early successes and reports, such as the transformation of Miami Beach from a mangrove swamp to a modern city almost overnight, provided the evidence for potential investors.

The year 1923 showed significant increases over the previous year in the building permits granted, in taxable real estate, in retail sales, hotel room occupation, steamship freight tonnage, and telephone facilities.[19] At the height of the land boom in 1925, the *Miami News* opened the News Tower (to be called the Freedom Tower in the 1960s). It printed the largest single issue of a newspaper—five hundred four pages of mainly advertising lines—in the country. A measure of the extent of the land boom can be gathered from the increased development in the City of Miami in the five-year period between 1921–22 and 1925–26.[20]

There were signs of an impending bust in the land boom during the peak year 1925. After the 1924 winter season, instead of there being a slowing down of business, more and more people arrived. By the late summer of 1925, speculative projects reached such a pitch that sound ones were ruined by being pushed too far in the pursuit of customers. There was a shortage of housing for the rapidly growing population; some developers even attempted to accommodate customers in tents. Perhaps the most significant sign was the breakdown in transportation. On 17 August 1925, the Florida East Coast Railway announced an embargo—a permit system—on shipments to Miami and later extended it statewide. The drastic measures were taken because consignees were using freight cars as storage facilities for lack of sufficient warehousing in the city. In Miami, at the time, there were 851 carloads of freight on sidetracks, 150 at waiting areas, and 700 cars en route. Although most of the restrictions were removed on 15 May 1926, by then the building boom had lost momentum.

Steamship service was also under strain from the feverish activities. In late December 1925, there were thirty-one ships anchored off Miami Beach waiting to come in and unload (Figure 13). The situation worsened early in 1926 when the *Prins Valdemar* capsized and blocked the harbor for over a month, from January 10 to February 29. This was of immediate consequence: passengers and cargo remained locked in Miami. Some fifty vessels held up in the Atlantic went aground on reefs while attempting to get closer in. As a result, forty-five million feet of much-needed lumber for construction remained out at sea.

Another sign of the bust was the unfavorable attention that Florida began to receive in the national newspapers concerning complaints on real estate frauds. There were also reports of investigations into the complaints. Enthusiasm among land purchasers

13. Schooners jam Bayfront to load building lumber supplies during the Boom. (Photo dated 1925.)

was very much dampened. Arrival of Federal investigators to inspect the courthouse records and scrutinize the profits of certain speculators, the remarks of northern business experts in the summer of 1925 that the Florida boom had passed its peak, and the inquiry of the National Better Business Bureau into fraudulent promotions further curtailed land sales. By the summer of 1926, bank deposits had fallen sharply as had revenue stamps for deeds. These two factors, coupled with heavy withdrawals and the failure of buyers of property to make payments, triggered the failures of some banks. In the spring and summer of 1926, the mass exodus of speculators signaled that the boom was over.

The hurricane that struck Miami in September 1926 ended any hope of revival. On Friday, 17 September, increased winds signaled a hurricane that arrived soon after midnight. By the time that the hurricane had passed by late Saturday afternoon, Miami Beach lay under two to four feet of sand and Miami lay devastated. In the Sunday papers around the country the hurricane made front-page headlines, such as "South Florida Wiped Out in Storm."[21] Mayor E. C. Romfh declared that "Miami was almost back to normal."[22] Others tried to make light of the "Big Blow" and closed their eyes to the impact on real estate values. Cheery words were forthcoming from Miami boosters. Purchasers who had paid one-fifth down on lots, however, began to default on payment of the balance.

Migrant Influx

Waves of immigrants have at one time or another been a factor in the growth of Greater Miami. The first wave was of black migrants from the Bahamas, who became the core of the labor force in the first few decades of the twentieth century. Then there was the massive influx of refugees from Fidel Castro's Cuba to Miami and the rest of Florida beginning in December 1961. In November 1965, when Castro opened the port of Camarioca, five thousand more Cubans flocked to Miami. It is estimated that by 1970 more than three hundred thousand Cubans had settled in Dade County and represented 22 percent of the population of the county. Between 1 December 1965, and 1 February 1970, a total of 182,375 refugees arrived on twice-daily freedom flights Monday to Friday. They continued to show up at the rate of 2,800 a month.[23] Cuban refugees were processed in the old Miami Daily News Tower, which was then renamed the Freedom Tower. The incursion of refugees, at first from Cuba and later from other parts of Central America and the Caribbean, enabled Greater Miami to grow from a provincial city to a cosmopolis. There was, in addition, a steady stream of predominantly Jewish elderly who fled the Snowbelt for Sunbelt Greater Miami, specifically Miami Beach, from the 1940s and onwards.

The Shapers of Growth

In a special "Dade at 150" issue, the *Miami Herald* newspaper published lists of "The Most Influential People in Dade's History" that it had requested from four experts. The only persons to appear on all four lists were Julia Tuttle and Carl Fisher, while the names of Henry Flagler, George E. Merrick, and Everest George Sewell surfaced on three lists.[24] An alternate list could be drawn up to take into account the growth factors described in the previous pages, based on the criterion of identifying those who exerted a major influence on the growth of Greater Miami. The names on this list would include Richard Fitzpatrick, the founder of Dade County; Julia Tuttle, George Merrick, and Glenn Curtiss, the successful builders of dream cities; Henry Flagler (helped by John Sewell) and Carl Fisher (with the Lummus Brothers and John Collins), the predominant developers; James Deering (Vizcaya) and Hugh Anderson (who with Roy Wright made Biscayne Boulevard a gateway to Miami), who added a singular feature to the city; and the revolutionary leader Fidel Castro, whose conquest of Cuba sent a half-million of the island's inhabitants to Miami.

Framework of Development

WHAT were the forces that shaped the growth and pattern of Greater Miami's communities? These forces can be identified as legislative, physical, political, social, and economic thrusts. The legislative and physical drives are described in this chapter. Political, social, and economic catalysts are depicted in Chapter 5. Legislative forces were Florida's distinctive municipal incorporation process, the singular local governance structure of Greater Miami, and the manner in which the physical growth of the city was managed and controlled. Governance of Greater Miami centered on the drive for metropolitan government that eventually bore fruit in the late 1950s. Physical growth of the city was managed through physical planning and zoning. Environmental regulation, however, was not effective until it was introduced in the mid–1970s.

Municipal Incorporation

A major influence in the development of Greater Miami was Florida's municipal charter process. The process was the dominant force in the creation of communities during the nineteenth and first half of the twentieth centuries. Establishment of municipalities was superseded by the introduction of metropolitan government in 1957. A municipal charter is the basic law that defines the organization, powers, and functions of the municipality and delineates its major administrative procedures.[1] Communities embarked on the charter process because incorporation as a municipality provided certain corporate powers and privileges. These included, first, authority to regulate and improve streets, pavements, and sidewalks; establish markets; lay sewer lines; prevent and abate nuisances; protect public health; control undesirable activities; support public education and libraries; establish a police force; and, second, empowerment to borrow money and issue bonds. Later, incorporation also meant municipal autonomy in zoning, liquor licensing, and law enforcement, particularly regarding gambling.

Governance

Before the establishment of metropolitan government in Dade County in 1957, there were many local governmental units. These were the twenty-six municipalities, the county commission, the Board of Public Instruction, the Dade County Port Authority, and the Little River Valley Drainage District. Furthermore, there were multicounty organizations that had some jurisdiction over Dade County, such as the Central and Southern Florida Flood Control District, the Everglades Fire Control District, and the Florida Inland Navigation District. The number of local units compared favorably with other metropolitan areas of comparable size that averaged over one hundred twenty local governmental units each.[2] The major issue in Greater Miami at mid-century was a governance system unable to cope with pressing issues. Among these were the rapid population growth of the area, public demand for services, and irregular municipal boundaries that included "islands" of unincorporated territory.

By the middle of the 1950s, Dade County had become the most populous county in Florida with a growth rate among the highest in the country.[3] The growth was due to suburban development in the unincorporated areas rather than in the municipalities. Population of the municipalities grew at a reduced rate from 1930 to 1960. While the rate was about 70 percent in both the 1930s and 1940s, it decreased to just over 50 percent in the 1950s. On the other hand, the increase in the unincorporated areas of the county during the same decades was dramatic. The rate ranged between 164 percent and 256 percent (Table 2). Although the unincorporated areas contained just under 30 percent of the Greater Miami population in 1950, these areas accounted for 60 percent of the total population by 1960.

Problems that arose from this growth and population distribution could not be managed by a county system established in an agricultural era and by a Florida legislature that met only every two years in Tallahassee. The state legislature severely constrained the actions of the county and municipal governments. For example, the county budget was prepared by a budget commission appointed by the Governor. Also, efficiency in public service was hampered by duplication of identical governmental functions. These were carried out both by the county government and by twenty-six mu-

"Dade County is a governmental paradox—successful professional management entwined with high levels of political fragmentation. This paradoxical situation has led to failures of the combined political entities to work together to create a stronger and more cohesive infrastructure, strengthen the County's economic base, and protect important human and environmental assets."
David B. Hertz, *Governing Dade County*, 16.

TABLE 2 Municipal Population Censuses and Decennial Changes

Area	Year of Original Charter	1900 Number	1910 Number % Change	1920 Number % Change	1930 Number % Change	1940 Number % Change	1950 Number % Change	1960 Number % Change	1970 Number % Change	1980** Number % Change	1990 Number % Change
Dade County	1836	4,955	11,933 140.8%	42,753 258.3%	142,955 234.4%	267,739 87.3%	495,084 84.9%	935,047 88.9%	1,267,792 35.6%	1,625,781 28.2%	1,937,094 19.1%
Unincorporated Areas			3,274	6,460 97.3%	10,872 68.3%	11,674 7.4%	41,596 256.3%	109,805 164.0%	352,146 220.7%	537,277 52.6%	799,084 48.7%	1,036,925 29.8%
Total Municipalities		1,681	5,473 225.6%	31,881 482.5%	131,281 311.8%	226,143 72.3%	385,279 70.4%	582,901 51.3%	730,515 25.3%	826,697 13.2%	900,173 8.9%
Municipalities											
Miami (city)	1896	1,681	5,471 225.5%	29,571 440.5%	110,637 274.1%	172,172 55.6%	249,276 44.8%	291,688 17.0%	334,859 14.8%	346,865 3.6%	358,548 3.4%
Homestead (city)	1913			1,307	2,319 77.4%	3,154 36.0%	4,573 45.0%	9,152 100.1%	13,674 49.4%	20,668 51.1%	26,866 30.0%
Florida City (town) * [Detroit (town), 1908]	1914			355	452 27.3%	752 66.4%	1,547 105.7%	4,114 165.9%	5,133 24.8%	6,174 20.3%	5,806 −6.0%
Miami Beach (city)	1915			644	6,494 908.4%	28,012 331.4%	46,282 65.2%	63,145 36.4%	87,072 37.9%	96,298 10.6%	92,639 −3.8%
Coral Gables (city) *	1925				5,697	8,294 45.6%	19,837 139.2%	34,793 75.4%	42,494 22.1%	43,241 1.8%	40,091 −7.3%
Hialeah (city)	1925				2,600	3,958 52.2%	19,676 397.1%	66,972 240.4%	102,452 │ 53.0%	145,254 41.8%	188,004 29.4%
Opa-locka (town/city)	1926/1927				339	497 46.6%	5,271 960.6%	9,810 86.1%	11,902 21.3%	14,460 21.5%	15,283 5.7%
Country Club Estates / Miami Springs (town)	1926 / 1930				402	898 123.4%	5,108 468.8%	11,229 119.8%	13,279 18.3%	12,350 −7.0%	13,268 7.4%
South Miami (town/city) * [Larkins (town), 1899]	1926/1927				1,160	2,408 107.6%	4,809 99.7%	9,846 104.7%	11,780 │ 19.6%	10,944 −7.1%	10,404 −4.9%
Miami Shores (town) (village)	1922 / 1932				612	1,956 219.6%	5,086 160.0%	8,865 74.3%	9,425 6.3%	9,244 −1.9%	10,084 9.1%
North Miami (town) [Arch Creek (town), 1903]	1925/1927				520	1,973 279.4%	10,734 444.0%	28,708 167.4%	34,767 21.1%	42,566 22.4%	49,998 17.5%
Golden Beach (town)	1928				36	83 130.6%	156 88.0%	413 164.7%	849 105.6%	612 −27.9%	774 26.5%
North Miami Beach (city) [Fulford (town/city), 1926/1927]	1931					871	2,129 144.4%	21,405 905.4%	30,544 │ 42.7%	36,553 19.7%	35,359 −3.3%
Biscayne Park (city) (village)	1931 / 1932					500	2,009 301.8%	2,911 44.9%	2,717 −6.7%	3,088 13.7%	3,068 −0.6%
Surfside (town)	1935					295	1,852 527.8%	3,157 70.5%	3,614 14.5%	3,763 4.1%	4,108 9.2%
El Portal (village)	1937					305	1,371 349.5%	2,079 51.6%	2,068 −0.5%	2,055 −0.6%	2,457 19.6%
Indian Creek (village)	1939					#	44	60 36.4%	82 36.7%	103 25.6%	44 −57.3%
Sweetwater (town/city)	1941						230	645 180.4%	3,357 420.5%	8,251 145.8%	13,909 68.6%
North Bay Village (city)	1945						198	2,006 913.1%	4,831 140.8%	4,920 1.8%	5,383 9.4%
Bal Harbour (village)	1946						224	727 224.6%	2,038 180.3%	2,973 45.9%	3,045 2.4%
West Miami (town/city)	1947						4,043	5,296 31.0%	5,494 3.7%	6,076 10.6%	5,727 −5.7%
Bay Harbor Islands (town)	1947						296	3,249 997.6%	4,619 42.2%	4,869 5.4%	4,703 −3.4%
Virginia Gardens (village)	1947						235	2,159 818.7%	2,524 16.9%	2,098 −16.9%	2,212 5.4%
Hialeah Gardens (city)	1948						11	172 1463.6%	492 186.0%	2,700 448.8%	7,713 185.7%
Medley (town)	1949						106	112 5.7%	351 213.4%	537 53.0%	663 23.5%
Pennsuco (town)	1949						133	117 −12.0%	74 −36.8%	15 −79.7%	#
Islandia (city)	1961							#	8	12 50.0%	13 8.3%
Key Biscayne Village	1991										#

Source: Bureau of the Census Population Censuses

Notes: # Not reported

* Parts detached in 1930

** Annexations by Homestead, North Miami Beach, South Miami, and Sweetwater (part detached also)

│ Revised count since 1970 census

Municipal Changes: Miami city [Areas annexed, 1925; parts detached, 1932; corporate limits extended, 1937]

Hialeah city [Limits reduced, 1927; extended, 1932; part detached, 1933] nicipalities of unequal size and uneven income distribution. Services included the fields of tax collection and assessment, police and fire personnel training, jails, traffic courts, criminal records and investigation bureaus, and building and zoning activities. Except for the large municipalities of Miami, Miami Beach, Coral Gables, Hialeah, and Homestead, the remaining incorporated areas lost most of their original strength as cohesive, independent units because of the rapid growth of the suburbs in the unincorporated parts of Greater Miami (Figure 14).

Was the Miami "metropolitan experiment" a success? Many scholars have given their views on this question. Edward Sofen, for example, believes that the environmental and political conditions, and the functional consolidation of health, hospital, school, and port activities, made the experiment in metropolitan government in Dade County successful.[4] In a comprehensive evaluation, Richard Langendorf concluded that the charter reform of 1957 was in the end a procedural rather than a structural reform. Changes in governance evolved over time more through court interpretations, political actions, financial capabilities, and the commitment of leaders in the county. He derived his conclusion from an extensive analysis of metropolitan federalism in Dade County. His evaluation used twenty-four criteria in the areas of administrative effectiveness, equity, efficiency, and citizen response.[5] Langendorf makes the point that sweeping generalizations are impossible to make owing to the dynamic and complex character of Greater Miami and the variety of rigorous criteria in evaluation. On balance, however, he considers the experiment a success. Reinhold Wolff, on the other hand, considered "Metro" government, as it had been introduced in Dade County, not to be the textbook solution to the needs of the average multicity area. It was an answer born of historical coincidence rather than economic and social logic.[6] In the view of another scholar, Parris Glendening, the Dade County Charter of 1957 includes all the major features of the reform model (described in Appendix B). He adds that it ". . . is the only government currently in existence that has adopted this combination of reforms (and) affords an excellent opportunity to test many of the reformers' beliefs."[7] Glendening suggests that three instrumental factors influenced the reform campaign and the resultant form of metropolitan government in the atypical environment of Greater Miami: a greatly increasing population, especially in the unincorporated areas; a relatively low rate of governmental disintegration, as indicated by the good reception given to previous reorganization proposals and actions; and the lack of effective countywide political organizations. Dade County, though, persists in confounding

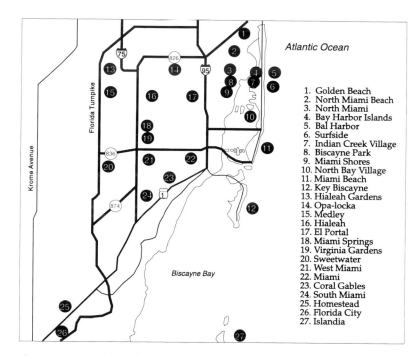

1. Golden Beach
2. North Miami Beach
3. North Miami
4. Bay Harbor Islands
5. Bal Harbor
6. Surfside
7. Indian Creek Village
8. Biscayne Park
9. Miami Shores
10. North Bay Village
11. Miami Beach
12. Key Biscayne
13. Hialeah Gardens
14. Opa-locka
15. Medley
16. Hialeah
17. El Portal
18. Miami Springs
19. Virginia Gardens
20. Sweetwater
21. West Miami
22. Miami
23. Coral Gables
24. South Miami
25. Homestead
26. Florida City
27. Islandia

the best minds and continues to flourish despite views that it ". . . seems unlikely that Metro will survive the new urban politics of the 1980s without fundamental structural revision."[8] U.S. District Judge Donald Graham abolished the old system of electing commissioners in 1993. He imposed a redistricting scheme on racial and ethnic lines. While the political theater changed with the elections under the new rules, it remains to be seen how far the basic metropolitan structure will alter.

Management of Development

Planning and Zoning. Planning in Florida may have begun relatively late, but within a few decades it has advanced to the most progressive in the country. Despite the provisions of the federal State Zoning Enabling Act of 1926, it was not until 1939 that Florida's cities and towns were granted the power to prescribe and enforce zoning regulations governing the construction, location, and use of buildings and other structures.[9] During the 1930s, however, there were three jurisdictions, each with its own zoning code. Not until the end of 1960 did the Dade County Planning Department present a preliminary land use plan for Greater Miami.[10] The plan's policies were aimed at containing the rapidly spreading sprawl, developing downtown city centers, establishing a new focus in the growth area in the southern portion of the county, developing the islands in Biscayne Bay, and developing Homestead for agricultural and related activities. Dade County produced its first master plan in 1965. On the one hand, it called for the protection of the islands in Biscayne Bay but not the Everglades. On the other hand, this plan also contemplated construction of a Seadade deepwater port and oil refinery, and the construction of three causeways across the bay. Only in 1969, when a state enabling act was passed, did counties and municipalities acquire the authority to adopt and amend master plans. These were to become the first generation of comprehensive plans to guide future development. The enabling act also provided municipalities with the power to adopt and enforce zoning regulations. Under the Community Redevelopment Act of 1969 cities were empowered to improve rundown areas of their downtowns.[11] Comprehensive planning, however, tended to be permissive and infrequently used.[12] By the early 1970s, it became obvious that the state's planning and regulatory system was not adequate to the challenges of booming population growth, a fragile ecological system, and local government's lack of capacity to respond to problems.[13] As Figure 15 shows, most of these problems persist today.

A major hole in the growth management system was closed when a new act was introduced in 1975.[14] The intent, purpose, and scope of the 1969 law was thereby amended. The new act represented a major departure from the old frontier mindset and provided the foundation for the state's current planning laws.[15] To guide and control future development, the 1975 act instituted specific requirements for a planning process to establish and carry out comprehensive planning procedures and stipulated that certain content areas be covered in planning.

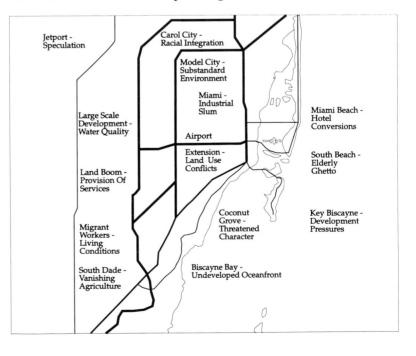

15. Dade County growth problems, 1978. Many of these problems persist today.

In 1975, the Comprehensive Development Master Plan for Metropolitan Dade County superseded the 1965 general land use master plan. Two years of intensive collection of data, analysis, and citizen involvement went into the 1975 plan. Special features of the planning process included six citizen task forces and numerous public meetings to assess community aspirations. The 1975 plan was adopted by the County Commission and was intended to be the official guide for managing growth and development of the metropolitan Dade County area. Three aims were to be achieved: first, to direct and achieve coordinated and harmonious development; second, to provide adequate community facilities; and third, to protect the ecological balance of the environment. A new direction became clear; in the 1975 plan, emphasis shifted sharply from growth and development toward conservation. Further measures of the plan were designed to decrease densities, to concentrate specialized and diversified activities around centers, to prohibit further drainage of wetlands, to protect Biscayne Bay that was designated a national park in 1980, to preserve the aquifer recharge areas, to protect agricultural areas, and to obtain dedication requirements from developers for schools and open space. The three-part plan encompassed metropolitan development policies, an environmental protection guide, and a metropolitan development guide.

Between 1979 and 1983, two major studies dealing with the East Everglades and Biscayne Bay led to changes in the comprehensive plan and the land use plan. The Biscayne Bay Management Plan of 1985 was remarkable in that it included the water's edge as a matter of concern, sought to prevent the further walling off of the bay, and established a review process for development along the shoreline.[16] Other significant developments in the field of planning that were of relevance to Greater Miami during the 1970s and 1980s were the establishment of the South Florida Regional Planning Council,[17] the Dade County Metropolitan Transport Authority,[18] and the state safe neighborhoods program, which enabled some local municipalities in the county to improve selected localities.[19]

Despite the intentions of the comprehensive plan, the problems of growth in Greater Miami continued. Statewide, there was a recognition that the 1975 comprehensive planning legislation, unfortunately, assured neither the quality of local plans nor their implementation.[20] A complete overhaul of the 1975 law was required. In 1985, the comprehensive planning act was amended to cover the preparing, adopting, and carrying out of local government comprehensive plans. The law was retitled to include the term "Land Development Regulations."[21] All local governments were now required to compile into one document all their land development regulations that carry out the comprehensive plan, as well as to adopt comprehensive plans according to a specified format of goals, objectives, and policies. Among other significant legislative changes were declarations of levels of service standards and concurrency requirements. For any project, service standards were to be met before development orders could be issued. Similarly, concurrency requirements were to be in place before development could be approved. Local plans were also required to be consistent with the applicable regional policy plan and to comply with the state plan. According to a former Florida Secretary of Community Development, the state plan "comprises no less than a revolution in the approach to planning the state's growth."[22]

The latest Dade County Comprehensive Development Master Plan (CDMP) contains eleven separate plan elements. These address both the incorporated and unincorporated areas. The latter areas are emphasized due to the many areawide responsibilites of the County. Each of the twenty-six municipalities has also produced its own comprehensive plan. The twenty-seventh municipality, Key Biscayne, was created after the completion of the planning process and is included in the county's plan. It is now in the process of preparing its own comprehensive plan. The new county master plan left essentially unchanged the pattern of land use and urban growth adopted in the 1975 plan. In the new plan, short-term development is to be directed within the Urban Development Boundary and future growth within the Urban Expansion Area. A major challenge is the over three hundred thousand new residents that have flooded into western Dade County during the 1980s. The influx has crammed roads, jammed classrooms, and led to the filling in of thousands of acres of fragile Everglades.[23] Overall, the growth of Greater Miami's population brought additional strains on water supply, garbage collection, and the justice system.

The CDMP envisions limited development in the Big Cypress Area of Critical State Concern and the East Everglades, wellfield zones, and many environmental protection subareas. Besides land use, the other plan elements are traffic circulation; mass transit; port and aviation facilities; housing; conservation of natural resources, aquifer recharge and drainage; potable water, a sanitary sewer system, and solid waste treatment; recreation and open space; coastal management; intergovernmental coordination; and capital improvements. Dade County also has under consideration the inclusion of traditional neighborhood developments in its comprehensive plan. These types of developments are conceived as mixed-use land use areas that seek to discourage urban sprawl and recapture the atmosphere of pedestrian-oriented developments of the past. Other approaches to development include houses with zero lot-lines on wide and shallow properties.[24]

Environmental Regulation. By 1980, almost half the Dade County population lived in the unincorporated areas. Most new development was located on the western fringes of the urban territory, where the fragile ecosystem of the Everglades has become endangered by the encroachment of new subdivisions. Beginning in the 1960s, development was and continues to be challenged by environmentalists. Growth was slowed to consider ecological issues. Major projects, such as the proposed jetport in the Everglades and a proposed oil refinery in the southern part of the county, were rejected. Environmental protection came in the form of the creation of the Biscayne National Monument, the John Pennekamp State Park, and the Bill Baggs–Cape Florida State Park.

By the beginning of the 1970s, it was obvious that the state's regulatory system was not adequate to the challenges of a fragile ecological system. After the drought of 1970–71, the Florida legislature passed several landmark laws in 1972 aimed at handling growth and the threats to the state's land and water resources. The principal legislation aimed to protect natural resources, to reverse the deterioration of water quality, to make the optimum use of limited water resources, and to encourage orderly and well-planned development. The protection of coastal resources was added as a concern in 1978, and assistance to local governments in their conservation efforts in 1989.[25]

Several significant procedures were introduced in 1972. The Water Resources Act of 1972 (Chapter 373) made all waters of the state subject to regulation. It marks the dramatic turnaround in Florida's approach to the environment. The practice of the 1940s, when the Corps of Engineers had a free hand in the planning and building of drainage facilities, was now superseded. Now a state department of natural resources and six Water Management Districts (WMD) would be involved. This 1972 Act was also a major landmark environmental law. It focused on the management of surface and ground water, the prevention of damage from floods and excessive drainage, and provisions to minimize degradation of water resources by the discharge of stormwater.[26] A law was also passed that required the establishment of a list of environmentally endangered lands that should be selected for purchase.[27] Concern over long-term orderly development, then, required the protection and control of natural resources, purchase of endangered land, and regulation of land use by planning. Acquisition of 570,000 acres of land in the Big Cypress Swamp area was the most extensive of the land purchases. The purpose was to protect the watershed that supplies water to the communities on the southeast coast and the land for the Everglades National Park. Two other significant programs initiated in the early 1970s were the Development of Regional Impact (DRI) and the Areas of Critical State Concern (ACSC), but these lacked state policy to direct their efforts. Further legislation introduced during the decade was aimed at the prevention of pollution, the management of energy resources, and the reclamation of land.[28]

The environmental developments in Greater Miami and in Florida were part of a national trend. In 1969, Congress passed the National Environmental Protection Act (NEPA), which established a new policy on environmental protection.[29] Other federal environmental legislation enacted during the 1970s included the Clean Water Act, the Safe Drinking Water Act, the Solid Waste Management Act, the Resource Conservation and Recovery Act, the Toxic Substance Control Act, the Coastal Management Act, the Wild and Scenic Rivers Act, and the Flood Disaster Protection Act. In Dade County, the Department of Environmental Regulation (DERM), established in the early 1980s to control pollution, saw its role expanded. Its mandate now extended to other areas of environmental planning, including Biscayne Bay, wetland management, control of industrial and agricultural waste, well field protection, and acquisition of valuable hammocks and pinelands. In 1989, President George Bush signed a bill to add 110,000 acres to the Everglades National Park. The purpose was to restore the original natural water flow and establish a permanent western boundary for development in west Dade.[30] With a projected seventeenfold increase in population,[31] this part of the county is the area where the conflict between environmental concerns and urban growth is at its highest. The increase is projected to be from 13,064 residents in 1970 to over 230,500 by the year 2000. It is also the district where the most amendments to the comprehensive plan were submitted during the 1980s. A reflection of the mounting commitment to the environment was the 56 percent to 40 percent approval given by Dade County voters in 1990 to a two-year tax to buy and maintain environmentally sensitive lands so that precious undeveloped tracts of the county's landscape can be left undisturbed.[32]

Political, Social, and Economic Backdrop

AJOR influences on the growth and development of the city of Greater Miami were national and international events, local social changes and tensions, diversification of the city's population, and the formation of an internationally oriented urban economy. Major national and international events that framed the development of the city begin with Florida's admission to the Union, followed by the various wars and their aftermaths, Prohibition, the Great Depression, and Fidel Castro's revolution in Cuba. Social changes and tensions include the growth of the city's population, racial disturbances, and crime. The area's economy grew from an agricultural base into one largely dependent on tourism and international banking and the activities of multinational companies.

National and International Events

Union and the Civil War. The move to statehood for Florida began with the Constitutional Convention, which sat from 3 December 1838 to 4 January 1839. Later that year—by a vote of 2,065 to 1,961—a state constitution was approved. Continued opposition initially prevented the territory from becoming a state until finally President John Tyler signed a bill to admit Florida to the Union on 3 March 1845. Florida seceded from the Union on 10 January 1861 and joined the Confederate states in the Civil War that followed. Events in Florida had only secondary military and economic importance during the Civil War. Federal ships intermittently blockaded the coast of Dade County. In the period of Reconstruction (1865–1877), Florida and the other secessionist states were placed under the authority of the Union government with a small army of occupation. No federal troops were stationed in South Florida, perhaps because the population was so sparse.

The results of the election of 1876 brought to an end the period of Reconstruction. The next quarter-century became known as the era of the developers. Federal and state governments now disposed of large tracts of land to transportation and land companies. This contrasted with the decade of 1866–1876, when state land was reserved for homesteaders—freedmen and immigrants from the North.

The Spanish-American War. During over two centuries of Spanish control, Cuba and Florida were historically associated. Havana was the principal source of all things Spanish, while Florida was then little more than a military outpost. In the second half of the nineteenth century, Cuba was an important market for Florida. The state received immigrants from the island and, in the last decades of the century, political refugees. Anticipating conflict with Spain over the independence of Cuba, the War Department announced on 5 April 1898 that batteries and home guards would be stationed in Miami and other East Coast cities. War was declared on 25 April by the Teller Amendment. On the 19th and the 25th of May, when General Wade visited Miami, he turned the small town down as a campsite because "the city was no place for 7,500 troops in the summer."[1] Florida East Coast Railway officials went ahead with plans for the camp, anyway; but use of a crude bucket system and drinking from surface wells led to a high incidence of typhoid fever, and apart from the luxurious Royal Palm Hotel, the city offered no attractions for the men. Just over a month later, the soldiers were ordered to Jacksonville, and on 12 August the War ended.

World Wars. In 1917, on 6 April, the United States entered World War I against Germany. Five of the thirty-five aviation schools established nationwide were in Florida, and two of the five were at the Curtiss and Chapman fields in Greater Miami. By the end of the War on 11 November 1918 (Figure 16), 200 officers and 300 enlisted men had trained at Curtiss Field, the only Marine Corps school. A naval training base at Dinner Key closed, probably in 1919, owing to the protest from the residents of Coconut Grove.

The entry into World War II by the United States following the attack on Pearl Harbor on 7 December 1941, ushered in a new era for Florida. German U-boats extended their devastating war against the North Atlantic shipping to Florida. They sank the tanker *Pan Massachusetts* south of Cape Canaveral on the night of 19 Febru-

16. Armistice Day Parade in front of the Ponce De León Hotel. (Photo dated 1931.)

ary 1942. As the Nazi submarines struck repeatedly at vulnerable merchant ships up and down the coast within the following week, frightened tourists fled Miami by the thousands. By then, the city was under a blackout. Oil from sinking ships found its way onto the beaches and into Biscayne Bay, adding to the tourists' unpleasant experiences. In May the Mexican tanker *Portero de Llano* was torpedoed south of Fowey Rock; a week later, the *Faja de Oro* was also hit off the Florida Keys. People in all types of boats went to the rescue of survivors of the wrecks that piled up on the coral reefs. By the end of February, the FBI had picked up twenty-nine German, Italian, and Japanese aliens who were found in possession of guns, cameras, and binoculars suspiciously near the Opa-locka Naval Air Station.

Florida's large areas of flat and unoccupied land and its good weather led to the conversion of the state into a vast military training school, offsetting the loss of tourism. Also, the normal rate of growth of the agricultural industry was greatly accelerated. Eventually 85 percent of the hotels on Miami Beach turned from accommodating tourists to housing enlisted men training in the newly launched Officer Candidate School. By 1 April 1942, the Army Air Corps was using thousands of hotel rooms on Miami Beach, where one-fourth of the officers and one-fifth of the enlisted men trained.[2] Into the remaining rooms and in apartment houses crowded the families of soldiers, many of which came to like the area and returned after the War. The University of Miami provided classroom instruction, and Pan American World Airways gave in-flight training. At the University, young Englishmen were trained in celestial navigation. Hotels on Biscayne Boulevard were turned into quarters for the Navy's Submarine Chaser Training Center, which attracted candidates from many nations. A Lighter-Than-Air Station, the second largest in the nation, was installed south of Miami. The unfinished fifteen-story Roosevelt Hotel became the Lindsey Hopkins Vocational School for wartime crafts. After the War it was turned into a technical "skyscraper school."[3] Through-out the War the wounded were flown directly from the various battlefields to Miami, where the Miami-Biltmore Hotel in Coral Gables was turned into a large veterans' hospital. Miami became a manufacturing area for military equipment and also a crossroads for military personnel bound for Africa, Europe, and the Orient. Pan Am, National, and Eastern airlines flew cargo to India and Persia via South Africa, Dakar, and Ascension Island.

At the end of the War, Miami had become one of the country's leading ports of entry, a position it has maintained as its economy has continued to diversify.[4] Economic growth was accompanied by a mass migration to Miami of men who had trained or recuperated in the area during the War. They returned drawn by the sunshine, the informal lifestyle, the availability of land for housing with out-door living—and perhaps the glamor. The men and their families bought houses on land made available by developers who cut down the pines and palmettos south of South Miami and north of North Miami. Other suburban communities, such as Miami Shores and Miami Springs, also grew. Home purchase was eased by the mort-gage insurance policy of the federal Housing Agency.

Prohibition. Prohibition began in Dade County in 1914. Three years later the Florida legislature approved the prohibition of the manu-facture, sale, and use of alcoholic beverages. Florida voters ratified Prohibition in 1918 and it became effective in 1919. A year later, after the passage of the Eighteenth Amendment, the nation was officially dry. The east coast of Florida, however, became a lead-ing area in the country for rum-running and also the smuggling of aliens and narcotics. Many factors proved propitious for turning the area into a bootlegger's paradise, or, as the epithet had it— one of the "leakiest spots" in the country. Proximity to supplies in Cuba and the British West Indies, the long coastline with many inlets, and the indifference of local authorities to enforcement were among the factors facilitating illegal profits.[5] The greatest part of the annual liquor imported into the United States came through Florida, with Homestead serving as the de facto distribution center for liquor and aliens. In 1928, the United States Coast Guard made a serious effort to break up the illicit traffic through a blockade of the Miami–Fort Lauderdale coastline, but the blockade was abandoned at the end of the season.

The Great Depression. By 1930, it was clear that the land market had failed to recover from its collapse in 1926. Assessed value of real estate in Florida had dropped from $623 million to $441 million. Operating revenues of railroads fell from $91 to $46 million, with the Florida East Coast and Seaboard railroads going into receivership in 1931. The reported income of corporations dropped from $815 to $84 million.[6] During the Depression of the 1930s, suits filed in court to collect judgments on unpaid claims became an everyday affair. Heavy withdrawals and failure of buyers of land to make payments produced failures among the smaller and more recently organized banks. Notices of land to be sold for delinquent taxes at public auction took up pages and pages in newspapers. The *Miami Herald* went as far as to headline "Miami Facing Lean Winter with Bond Maturities and Interest Greater Than Present Budget."[7] The City of Miami faced financial disaster in its municipal finances in the 1930s, given the high level of bond indebtedness incurred for public services after the expansions and speculative developments of the boom era in the 1920s. The City's expansion occurred through several annexations. Its territory had expanded from two square miles in 1900 to forty-three in 1925. In 1931, Miami de-annexed territory to reduce its area to thirty-four square miles, cut back on services, and abandoned some municipal programs.

President Franklin D. Roosevelt's New Deal Program enabled Florida to cope economically and financially with the Great Depression. On 21 July 1932, the Emergency Relief and Construction Act was passed by Congress. This act authorized the Reconstruction Finance Corporation (RFC) to lend $300 million to the states. The Federal Emergency Relief Agency, established under the New Deal Program, enabled 16,000 persons in Miami to receive assistance. By early 1933, one out of five families in Florida was on relief. In addition, the Civilian Conservation Corps helped to improve Matheson Hammock Park and to transform the Greynolds' rock pit property into a park. Under the Public Works Administration (PWA), many new public buildings were constructed, including Florida's first public housing project, Liberty Square. The Works Progress Administration (WPA) allowed the performance of useful labor to substitute for direct relief. Thus unemployed artists could create artworks for public buildings, writers could prepare a *Guide to Miami and Environs*, and unemployed actors and musicians could work on various projects in their field. By June 1938, the WPA in Florida had completed many projects.[8] One was the timber Village Hall in Biscayne Park that is still in use today and has been designated a historic structure.

Among the signs that Miami was on the way to recovery was the increase in tourists from Latin America and the northern United States. Pan American's "Flying Clippers" were bringing in thousands of tourists from Latin America. Signs in Spanish appeared in shop windows. Eastern Airlines, along with the newer airlines National and Delta, brought in many visitors. The majority, however, still came by the new streamline diesel trains. In Miami Beach, new hotels and apartment buildings in the Moderne style showed a phenomenal growth. Despite the Great Depression, Miami Beach in the mid- to late 1930s experienced a great surge in new hotel building. The number of hotels on Miami Beach increased from 291 in 1942 to 382 in 1955. The entire city of Greater Miami also saw increased tourism.

In the postwar atmosphere of the 1940s, a surge in real estate development and residential construction occurred, mainly in suburban municipalities, eight of which incorporated in the first five years after the war. The suburban municipalities experienced enormous growth in the 1940s, with an increase in population of 142 percent, surpassed by the even-larger increase of 164 percent in the unincorporated areas during that ten-year period.[9] Construction became an important activity in Dade County.

The Cuban Revolution. Fidel Castro, the revolutionary leader, overthrew Fulgencio Batista in January 1959. Cubans began to flee to Miami. On 17 April 1961, members of the Cuban exile invasion force, some of whom lived in Miami, participated in the aborted invasion at Playa Giron (Bay of Pigs), at the southern end of Matanzas Province. This force was known as the 2506 brigade, named after the brigade number of Carlos Rodriguez Sanatana, who had died in a training accident.[10] The Cuban Missile crisis of October 1962 brought units of all the armed forces to South Florida to set up antimissile installations. Fortunately, the crisis passed without incident.

Social Changes and Tensions

Population Growth. The first territorial census in 1825 estimated that there were only 317 persons in South Florida. Early cen-

TABLE 3 Dade County Population Growth Census Data

Census Date	Dade County Pop.	Proportion of State Population	Florida State Pop.	County Decennial Increase	State Decennial Increase
1830	—	—	34,730	—	—
1840	446	0.8%	54,477	—	56.9%
1850	159	0.2%	87,445	−64.3%	60.5%
1860	83	0.1%	140,424	−47.8%	60.6%
1870	85	0.0%	187,748	2.4%	33.7%
1880	257	0.1%	269,493	202.4%	43.5%
1890	861	0.2%	391,422	235.0%	45.2%
1900	4,955	0.9%	528,542	475.5%	35.0%
1910	11,933*	1.6%	752,619	140.8%	42.4%
1920	42,753**	4.4%	968,470	258.3%	28.7%
1930	142,955	9.7%	1,468,211	234.4%	51.6%
1940	267,739	14.1%	1,897,414	87.3%	29.2%
1950	495,084	17.9%	2,771,305	84.9%	46.1%
1960	935,047	18.9%	4,951,560	88.9%	78.7%
1970	1,267,792	18.7%	6,789,443	35.6%	37.1%
1980	1,625,781	16.7%	9,746,324	28.2%	43.6%
1990	1,937,094	15.0%	12,937,926	19.1%	32.7%

Source: Bureau of the Census.
Note: Dade County originally included the areas that are now Palm Beach and Broward counties.
*Excludes Palm Beach County, 1909
**Excludes Broward County, 1915

suses, however, were incomplete and unreliable. During the first half of the nineteenth century, there were quite a few discrepancies between population figures reported by various visitors and the figures of the United States census reports. For example, the area of Biscayne Bay was abandoned by settlers in 1840 after the Indian attacks, yet the census reports a population of 446 people for that year. It should be recalled that Dade County then included a vast region, as described previously, and that the population was scattered over this large territory.

The county census data from 1860 and 1870 (see Table 3), reveal a drop of 83 in the already small population after the Third Seminole War (1855–1857). There was an increase of only two persons after the Civil War (1861–1865). During the decades from the 1870s to the 1920s, Dade County grew explosively. Growth reached a peak between 1890 and 1900 when the population grew from 861 to 4,955—almost a fivefold increase. If Palm Beach County had not been carved out of Dade County, Dade's population would have registered an additional 5,577 inhabitants in 1910, to yield an increase of 253.4 percent instead of 140.8 percent.

Similarly, if Broward County had not been cut out, the population increase in Dade between 1910 and 1920 would have been an additional 5,135—or an expansion of 301.3 percent instead of 258.3 percent.

There is a general perception that the population of Dade County increased dramatically after World War II. This is indeed the case if one uses absolute numbers. Over one-quarter of a million new people were added to the county's population between 1940 and 1950. In terms of relative growth, however, the census data show a steady, even growth of around 85 percent in each decade from 1930 to 1960, compared to the dramatic decennial increases of over 230 percent in the period between 1910 and 1930 (Figure 17). Since 1960, the population growth rate of the county has declined each decade, as has the county's proportion of the state's population. Without the Cuban refugee influx during the early 1960s and the Mariel boatlift in 1980, the increases no doubt would have been smaller. In absolute numbers of people, however, Dade County continues to be the largest in Florida. It has 1.9 million people, or 15.0 percent of the state's population, followed by Broward County, with 1.3 million population (9.7 percent of the state's population) and Palm Beach, with approximately 1.0 million people (7.4 percent of the state's population).

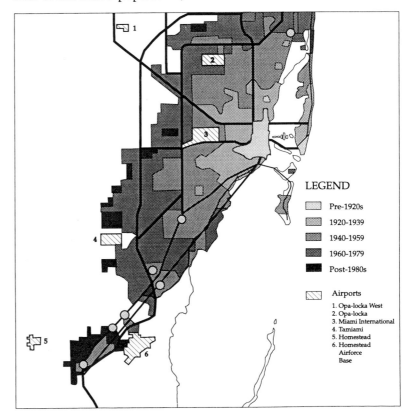

17. Urban growth in Dade County, pre-1920s to post-1980s.

Social Disturbances. Decades of segregation flared into violence with the Carver Village bombings in 1951. Integration after the Civil Rights Acts of 1964 did not relieve the social stresses, however. Dade County's first race riot occurred in Liberty City during the Republican Convention on Miami Beach in August 1968. Overtown was undergoing "urban renewal," which, combined with the routing of Interstate Highway 95 through the center of the area, led to the dislocation of black communities and the devastation of Overtown.[11] Displaced residents moved to Liberty City, which overflowed with residents, and also to Opa-locka.

The deep discontent among the black population erupted on 17 May 1980, after an all-white jury in a trial failed to find four Miami police officers guilty. The accused had allegedly beaten to death a black businessman, Arthur McDuffie, while attempting to arrest him. There was widespread burning and looting of property in the black areas. After these disturbances in 1980,[12] another police killing in December 1982 of another black man, Nevell Johnson, instigated another riot, this time mainly in Overtown. There were also riots in some black areas on 16 January 1989, just before the Super Bowl in Miami, after motorcyclist Clement Lloyd was shot by a police officer. Lloyd's passenger on the motorcycle, Allan Blanchard, later died from the accident. Greater Miami remains on the edge of a racial cauldron simmering with discontent.

Tourism and Crime: Miami, the New Casablanca. Illegal activities are nothing new to Miami. During the 1920s, racketeering became widespread, and during Prohibition, rum-running was pervasive. By the 1940s illegal gambling was rampant. Marijuana, in the 1970s, and cocaine, in the 1980s, were the illegal drugs that came through Greater Miami. Money laundering flourished as well. As it became widespread, many Federal operations were set in motion to control the flow of illegal cash.[13]

By the 1980s, two major threads in the historical development of Greater Miami—tourism and crime—reached new levels. Tourism in Miami had a severe setback in 1982 when the economies of Venezuela, Brazil, Argentina, and other Latin American countries went into a crisis. A major impact was on the condominium market in Greater Miami, which since then has never really recovered. The TV series that was to put Miami on the national and international tourist scene was, strangely enough, *Miami Vice*, which premiered in 1984. Miami as a city then began to appear in the "What's Hot" columns across the nation. The area had "turned the corner." Pop artist Christo's wrapping of eleven Biscayne Bay islets in pink plastic brought millions of visitor dollars to Miami. In the late 1980s,

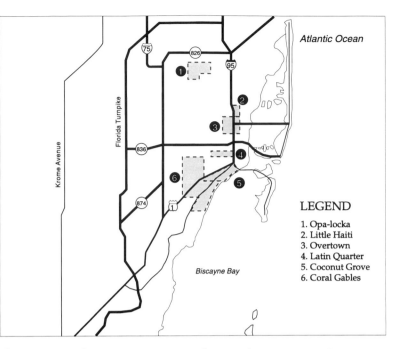

18. Distinctive districts of Greater Miami.

Atlantic Ocean

Florida Turnpike

Krome Avenue

Biscayne Bay

LEGEND

1. Opa-locka
2. Little Haiti
3. Overtown
4. Latin Quarter
5. Coconut Grove
6. Coral Gables

the Art Deco district in Miami Beach again became a tourist mecca. Record numbers of passengers arrived in Miami to board the increasing number of cruise ships that used Miami as their home port. Other districts, such as Coral Gables and the Latin Quarter in Little Havana, also became tourist centers (Figure 18).

Examples of the prevalence of crime were the charges against police officers, mainly drug-related, such as the "Metro Eight" (1981), the "River Cops" (1987), and the "Mercado Case" (1989).[14] Miami, with 621 murders in 1981, had the dubious honor of being the "homicide capital of America."[15] Two years later, the new drug "crack" appeared on the streets. In 1987, marijuana and cocaine seizures were now measured in tons.[16] Crime, which had been a concern over the decades, reached new heights with the "cocaine wars" of the late 1980s. Despite this, Greater Miami moved from a decade of fire to one of hope in the 1990s. Suddenly the battered city became Paradise Found, "one of the most fascinating cities in the world,"[17] and realized it could successfully absorb "exiles and refugees" and handle "growth and environment."[18]

Diversified Community

A correct theoretical classification of Greater Miami's diverse population requires a consistent set of criteria: culture, race, and ethnicity. Major population groups are the white Anglos, the black African-Americans, and the Latinos. Jews and Creoles form minority clusters. These groups are delineated primarily by language, race, and religious criteria. The Latino group has white and black racial components. Each of the population groups, in addition, is made up of different ethnic entities. Latinos, for example, consist of Cubans, Nicaraguans, Colombians, Venezuelans, Panamanians, and others. The once-dominant white Anglo community shrank from 48 percent of the total Greater Miami population in 1980 to 30 percent in 1990. At the same time, the black community expanded from 17 percent to 21 percent. A peak of 35 percent had been reached by the black population in 1910 from 26 percent in 1900.[19] The Latino community, the majority being Cubans, has been a significant component only since 1960 when it formed barely 5 percent of the county's population. Since then, the proportion has increased dramatically to 25 percent in 1970, 36 percent in 1980, and 50 percent in 1990.[20] Black Latinos make up about 3 percent of Greater Miami's population.[21] Between April and September 1980, more than one hundred twenty-five thousand Cubans fled to Florida in what became known as the Mariel boat lift. More than fifty thousand Marielitos were accommodated in tent cities in the Orange Bowl parking area and on public land under the I-95 highway.

A discernible geographical pattern has emerged in Greater Miami in the last decade of the twentieth century (Figure 19). Areas in which three groups constitute the majority—blacks, Latinos, and Anglo whites—can be identified. Black communities are found concentrated north of downtown Miami in Overtown and Liberty City with pockets in South Dade. Up to 1980, Latinos dominated only Little Havana and the city of Hialeah. Little Havana, originally known as Riverside, is the area west of downtown Miami between S.W. 8th Street and Flagler Street. The area from S.W. 12th to 17th Avenues has now been designated by the City of Miami as the "Latin Quarter." By 1990, seven cities in the northwest and the west areas of Dade County had a majority of Latinos. These were Miami, Hialeah, West Miami, Hialeah Gardens, Sweetwater, Medley, and Virginia Gardens.[22] Large numbers of Nicaraguans have concentrated in East Little Havana, which is becoming known as "Little Managua," and Sweetwater.[23] Anglo whites were clustered on the eastern fringe of the county along the northern and southern coasts and on the barrier islands. The southwest suburbs of Greater Miami are currently a mix of Anglo and Latino whites. The first Jewish immigrants located themselves in South Beach, also in Shenandoah, west of downtown Miami. They were replaced by Cubans in the 1960s. Most Jews that settled in South Beach were elderly retirees. Miami Haitians have created a vibrant community in the Edison-Little River area that is now known as "Little Haiti."

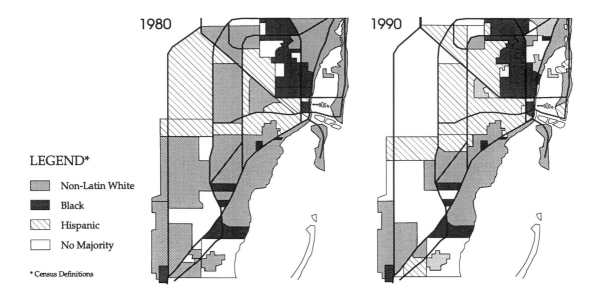

1980   1990

LEGEND*

▦ Non-Latin White

■ Black

▨ Hispanic

☐ No Majority

* Census Definitions

19. Spatial pattern of Greater Miami's cultural and racial majorities, 1980 and 1990.

The Black Community. Soon after the founding of the City of Miami, a section of city's northwest sector, about 15 percent of the city's area, became known as Colored Town.[24] In this segregated area the black employees of Flagler's company built their shotgun shacks. In 1920, many Bahamians immigrated to Greater Miami to seek employment in hotels, restaurants, and laundries. Bahamian neighborhoods were created in Colored Town/Overtown, and Coconut Grove. Other segregated black areas arose in Goulds, South Miami, and Liberty City.

In 1900, William Johnson and William Randolph, both blacks, homesteaded land in an area now known as Goulds. Randolph wanted other blacks to have a piece of land and either sold his land cheaply or gave it away. Sim Lewis, who was white, established a homestead on 80 acres west of Randolph and later added another 40 acres north of his original claim. By 1910 William H. Cauley owned a large expanse of tomato fields, a general store, a packing house, and a hotel for his workers at Goulds.

By the early 1930s, most of the black population of over twenty-five thousand was crowded into the 350 acres of Colored Town/Overtown located northwest of the central business district over the railway tracks. "Colored Town" has had many names, but Overtown remains the most persistent. Culmer has been used as a formal name in grant applications, for example. The commercial center was on Avenue G (now N.W. 2nd Avenue). The area was the cradle of business culture and entertainment for black residents, visitors, and tourists. During the heyday after World War II, when as Fats Waller put it, "the joint was jumping," world-famous entertainers such as Billie Holliday, Lena Horne, Louis Armstrong, Nat King Cole, Ella Fitzgerald, and the Ink Spots performed in the local nightclubs. This was Miami's "Little Broadway."

There were few places where blacks could own land and live. Besides Overtown, there was the small community of Coconut Grove, Brownsville (N.W. 41st Street to N.W. 53rd Street west of 27th Avenue), and a subdivision established by a white real estate man, Floyd W. Davis, roughly N.W. 62nd Street and 17th Avenue. Marshall Williamson came to Larkins in 1912 and bought land, eventually owning property from S.W. 64th Street to S.W. 66th Street between S.W. 62nd and 65th Avenues. He was the first black to buy land in the area. In 1926, the South Miami City Council set aside this expanded tract for blacks. There were also pockets of black communities in Perrine, Homestead, and Florida City.

Late in 1933, the limited-dividend Southern Housing Corporation submitted an application to President Roosevelt's new Public Works Administration for slum clearance and low-cost housing for Miami's blacks. The Reverend John E. Culmer was at the helm of the Negro Civic League in initiating the slum clearance program. New housing was to be at Liberty Square. This federally financed housing project was approved by the Housing Division of the PWA project in 1934. As Miami's elite wanted it located five to six miles from the city core, the project was located at N.W. 62nd Street between 12th and 14th Avenues. The 243-unit project was completed in 1937. It became the nucleus of a new and rapidly growing black ghetto that eventually became the fifteen-square-mile area now known as Liberty City.

At the beginning of the century there were many black businesses in Colored Town/Overtown. One business that continues today is the *Miami Times* newspaper. It was established in 1923 by Henry E. S. Reeves. A prominent resident of Overtown was Dr. William A. Chapman, a pioneer doctor who also held many positions in community organizations. His house, built in 1923, is designated an historic site. It is used now as the Ethnic Heritage Children's Folklife Education Center. Other black immigrants from various parts of the Caribbean have added to the ethnic diversity of Greater Miami. It is estimated that there are thirty thousand Jamaicans and smaller numbers from other islands living in the area. In addition, as many as fifty thousand, or 40 percent, of the Cubans arriving in the Mariel boat lift were black.[25] In 1980, thousands of refugees from Haiti began to arrive in their flimsy boats and continued off and on to arrive in various numbers during the decade. It is estimated that at the end of the 1980s, Haitians in

Greater Miami numbered one hundred fifty thousand. The exact number is hard to come by as many Haitians are illegal immigrants.

Latinos. In December 1965, the federal government began and subsidized two "Freedom Flights" daily. Soon thousands of Cubans began to arrive in Miami.[26] The district around S.W. 8th Street attracted the inflow of refugees because it offered inexpensive housing, close access to work in the downtown area, the availability of Catholic schools, and good public transportation. The district was formerly a middle-class Anglo and Jewish neighborhood. It also contained a small Cuban colony of refugees who had fled the overthrow of the Machado government in 1933.[27] By the mid–1970s, it became obvious that there was not only an influx of refugees from Cuba, but also a major stream of Latino immigrants from elsewhere. During the 1980s, Cubans still arrived in significant numbers to seek a new life in Greater Miami. They came in the thousands as tourists who did not return to Cuba, and by rafts (usually inner tubes) at increasing rates, reaching a high point of 3,000 for the year 1993.[28] Over the decades, the dominance of Cubans has declined from 83 percent of the Latino population to 66 percent in 1990.[29] The proportion of Mexicans and Puerto Ricans has remained small, while the size of the Nicaraguan and Colombian population has increased. Nicaraguans flooded into Miami disillusioned with the Marxist revolutionary Sandinista regime. At the end of the 1980s, the number of Nicaraguans living in Greater Miami was estimated to be over seventy-four thousand.[30]

In 1973, Dade County began to adopt bilingualism in a series of ordinances. These were rescinded in 1980 because of anti-Cuban backlash. There was another reversal in 1993 when a new multiethnic and racial county commission was elected. This commission, in turn, repealed the English-only ordinance. In early March 1977, the Cubans of Miami held their first Calle Ocho festival. From a "small" crowd of one hundred thousand in 1977, the festival has grown to be a huge party that attracted a million people in 1993.

The Jewish Community. When large numbers of Jews first arrived in Greater Miami in the 1920s and 1930s, anti-Semitism restricted their residential location severely.[31] Miami Beach, more specifically South Beach, was one of the few resort areas in the country open to Jews. By 1940, one-fifth of the permanent population of Miami Beach was Jewish. This proportion rose to one-half in 1947. After World War II, Jewish immigration to Greater Miami from the country's northeast cities, primarily New York, began. The total

Jewish population of Dade County increased substantially each decade, from 8,000 in 1940 to a high point of 268,000 in 1980, declining to 202,000 in 1990. South Florida's diversified community now includes the largest Jewish population concentration in any major U.S. metropolitan area.[32] The 650,000 Jews who live in South Florida represent 17 percent of the region's population. It is the second largest Jewish community in absolute numbers after metropolitan New York City. As many Jews were drawn to settle near other Jews, the Jewish community became concentrated in the southern part of Miami Beach. In the 1980s, there was a shift of the Jewish population from South Beach as significant numbers migrated to Broward and Palm Beach counties.

The Elderly. In Greater Miami the elderly age group cuts across all cultural, racial, and ethnic groups. Thus it is not surprising that this group is as diverse as the population as a whole. Elderly persons are a significant factor in the growth of the area, nearly one-fifth of the residents being sixty years of age or over compared to one-tenth nationally. The greatest growth in this age group in Greater Miami occurred after World War II. While still substantial, the growth rate has declined from 128 percent in the 1950s, to 76 percent in the 1960s, and 41 percent in the 1970s.[33] The largest concentrations of elderly residents are in Miami Beach, North Miami, and North Miami Beach.

Formation of an Internationalized Economy

Manufacture of coontie starch, shipping live green turtles to Key West and New York, and bartering with the Seminole Indians was the core of the early economy of the area. The Indians came in their canoes from their camps on the edge of the Everglades, collecting the wreckage from shipwrecks that supplied settlers with a part of their needs. Coontie starch making was the only way to make money in Dade County in the 1850s. Starch was the basis of the Indian diet. The Indians had the secret of washing the ground-up roots of the palmlike plant (*Zamia Intergrifolia* or *Floridana*). Settlers in the area soon developed mills to grind the plant to pulp, then dried it in the sun on cloth-covered frames.[34] Starch making finally disappeared and so did the coontie industry in 1925.

In the 1870s, settlers became involved in the growing of pineapples, oranges, lemons, and limes as these fruits could survive the transportation to the main market, Key West. By the early 1900s, Miami's specialties for the national market were avocados and mangoes.[35] Around 1920 the pineapple era began to wane on account of competition from Cuba, depletion of the soil, and the shift in land use. Historically, agriculture was the dominant component of the area's economy. It was superseded in importance in the early twentieth century by traditional and beach-oriented tourism and, later in the century, by business tourism.[36] An important component of the area's economic base has been the provision of services for retirees who have migrated into Greater Miami from elsewhere, particularly the Northeast.

In 1978, the federal International Banking Act amended various banking regulations and statutes. These amendments were introduced to allow the federal government to regulate participation by foreign banks in domestic financial markets. The most significant provision, as far as Greater Miami was concerned, was authorization of interstate branching by foreign banks to the same extent that states authorize branching by domestic banks. A Florida law made branch banking in the state subject to the Florida banking code, effective 1 January 1978.[37] By June of that year the fourteenth Edge Act bank, branches of national banks chartered in other states solely to finance international trade, opened in Greater Miami. Larger financial reserves thus became available to fuel economic expansion in the city.

There were several significant factors in the emergence of Greater Miami as an international banking and trade center in the 1980s. These include United States multinational corporations, foreign bank branches, and the Free Trade Zone. In addition, foreigners invested in Florida on an unprecedented scale. At the end of 1982, the Insurance Exchange of the Americas, similar to Lloyd's of London, began operation. By the early 1980s, there were 130 banks engaged in international operations compared to none in 1977. By 1989, there were 24 Edge Act banks with headquarters here. Also, there were 38 foreign banks in Greater Miami, more than any other city in the United States.[38] International deposits constituted almost 25 percent of all the deposits in banks and savings and loans in Dade County.

The Arab oil embargo of 1973 reminded Floridians of their vulnerability to fuel shortages. Florida has no coal, little oil, almost no water power, and no major refinery facility. In 1972 and 1973, the Florida Power and Light Company started the nuclear generator at Turkey Point on Biscayne Bay, eighteen miles south of Miami. During the recession of the early 1970s, the worst since the 1930s, unemployment rose and construction projects stopped.[39] The end of the recession for Miami was manifested when the Omni International Complex opened in 1977.

Greater Miami's image of the 1980s as a hub for drugs, guns, and fast money appears to have faded by the early 1990s. The city is now seen as the Latin American headquarters for large American, Euro- pean, and Asian companies. It is estimated that at least one-quarter of the city's economy is directly tied to international commerce and tourism. Miami has transformed itself from a languid resort town to a pulsating center of international trade—"the capital of Latin America."[40] Location and easy transportation make the area a logical base for international companies. Only New York's John F. Kennedy International Airport moves more foreign passengers and cargo than Miami's Interational Airport, the tenth busiest in the world.[41] Greater Miami has also become the most popular place in the United States to film commercials. The number of national and international fashion photographers, television producers, and moviemakers working in the area has increased fivefold during the 1980s.[42]

In 1991, the global business was needed to offset the losses of the city's largest corporations. Bankruptcy led to the collapse and disappearance of long established names such as Amerifirst, Eastern Airlines, Pan American World Airways, and the city's largest savings and loans company, CenTrust. The losses were com- pounded by a construction bust and an office and condominium glut. Paradoxically, in the same year, leading business and finan- cial journals began to describe Greater Miami as "one of North America's hottest business cities." This status was attributed to the city's diverse economy, the rapid new business growth, a healthy wholesale and retail trade, and expanding bank deposits.[43] Greater Miami had emerged as an international city.

Interaction among political, social, and economic forces and the facets of incorporation, physical planning and zoning, and environmental control led to the melding of the disparate communities. Greater Miami emerged as an international city with a special character all its own. As was shown previously, this was aided by the area's natural advantages, developments in transportation, and drainage of swampland.

The theme of Part II is set within the framework of the urban history depicted in Part I. Architectural images of Greater Miami are the focus. There are many ways to describe the architecture of a city. Francesco Milizia's theory, in which the city is conceived with its architecture, is adopted here as it is the most applicable.[1] Urban artifacts, according to Milizia, can be ordered into three categories: the form and organization, or architectural style, of individual buildings; classes of buildings (private and public); and the location of building types in the city.

In the first category, two broad classifications of styles in the architecture of Greater Miami are distinguished. These are, first, the various historic styles that were prevalent from the nineteenth century up to the end of World War II. Second are the distinctly modern styles that prevailed after the War. Greater Miami's different historic and modern styles of architecture are described in Chapter 6.

The second category of Greater Miami's architecture covers the private and the public classes of buildings. Private buildings as a class consist of single-family dwellings, apartment structures, and hotels. Although hotel buildings have some semipublic spaces, their predominantly private characteristic calls for their inclusion in the class of private buildings. The class of public buildings contains the remaining building types—including various commercial edifices, community buildings, educational buildings, and government structures. Greater Miami's notable historic-style private buildings are depicted in Chapter 7. Distinguished public buildings are described in Chapter 8. Chapters 9 and 10 depict the city's modern-style private and public buildings respectively.

The third category pertains to the location of building types, or the area of Greater Miami where the building stands. In the following chapters, location of an architecturally important historic-style building is delineated by the specific community in which the building is located: Miami, Miami Beach, Coral Gables, Coconut Grove, and North or South Dade. By definition, the International Modern style of architecture shuns locational influence or local context; consequently, the third category, location, is not applied to the modern-style buildings described in Chapters 9 and 10.

Part II

Greater Miami's Historic and Modern Styles of Architecture

Architectural Styles

ARCHITECTURAL style as the form and organization of a building is the special characteristics that distinguish a building. The characteristics that make up a style are a special combination of the building's particular features. These include mass; composition of external building elements such as roofs, porches, and windows; use of exterior materials; and the type of construction used. Buildings with a resemblance of special characteristics are placed together in the same class of architectural style, of which there are a number.

In Greater Miami, two broad classes of architectural style—the historic and the modern—can be distinguished. It is not possible to define a clear-cut boundary between the two classes as they overlap in time. Historic styles dominated before World War II, however, and the modern styles after the War. The major types of historic styles are the vernacular, Mediterranean, and Moderne, while minor ones are the Mission, Pueblo, and Moorish styles.[1] Types of modern styles are modernist, or International Modern, and South Florida Progressivist. The Moderne style is included as a historic style as it prevailed from the mid-1920s to the early 1940s, though it was also part of the modern movement. It should be noted that the Southern Californian style is included in both the historic and the modern classes. Classification of historic and modern styles covers the city's distinguished buildings but does not attempt to categorize all structures in Greater Miami (Figures 20–22). Many buildings, particularly houses built after 1945, have no discernible architectural style.

Vernacular: Wood Frame

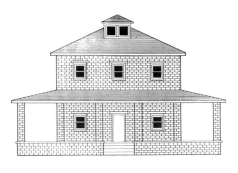

Vernacular: Masonry

Mediterranean

Mediterranean Revival

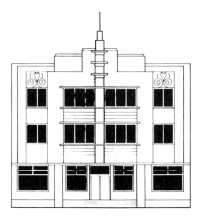

Moderne: Art Deco

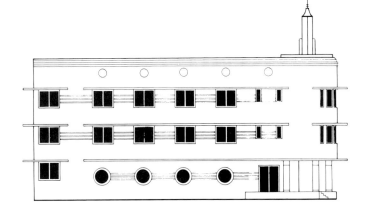

Moderne: Streamline

20. Greater Miami's major historic styles of architecture.

Mission

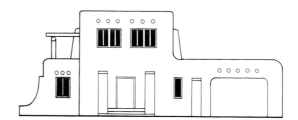

Pueblo

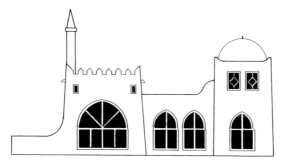

Moorish

Southern Californian: Bungalow

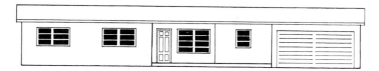

Southern Californian: Ranch

21. Greater Miami's minor styles of architecture.

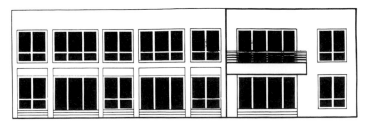

International Modern: Residential

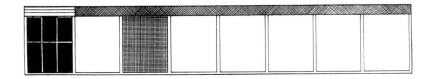

International Modern: Commercial

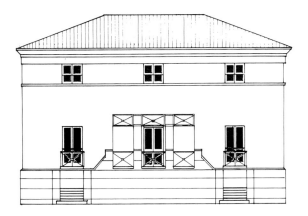

South Florida Progressive

Vernacular (1850–1920s)

South Florida had a distinct vernacular architecture in response to local climatic conditions and the limited choice of building material. Porches and roof overhangs provided the necessary shade from the intense sun. Large wall openings were specially arranged to allow cooling breezes to flow through the building. Structures were raised off the ground both to cool the building and to avoid floods during tropical storms. Local pine was used extensively as a building material. It proved resistant to termites and moisture, although driving a nail in the hardy wood was difficult. Oolitic limestone gave buildings an identifiable attribute. In addition, the background of the early settlers—whether from the deep

South, the urban Northeast, or the Bahamas—shaped the vernacular architecture of South Florida.

Wood Frame. Vernacular buildings, evolved initially by carpenters rather than architects, used local materials and improvised adaptations of imported forms and details. Most of these types of buildings were constructed between 1880 and 1920, but a few of them remain from the early days of Dade County. The buildings have a rectangular form and are of one or two stories, the construction being of a wood frame variety. The whole structure is raised on wooden or masonry piers to allow breezes to flow underneath the building and keep it cool. Roofs, which are covered with wooden shingles, are of a hipped or gable type, with the gable end facing the street. Eaves with exposed rafters have overhangs to provide shade. In earlier buildings, roof overhangs were broad and were often supported by wooden brackets. If the gable or hipped roof was steep enough, an attic was fitted underneath. After 1920, gable roofs had lower pitches and hipped roofs became rare. Where porches were not covered by the main roof, a shed type of roof was used, supported by wooden posts. Open, deep porches with balustrades of wood are a distinctive feature of the vernacular building. The predominant wall facing material was horizontal weatherboard siding, while vertical boards and battens were sometimes used, particularly in the earlier buildings. Windows in the earlier buildings were the double-hung wood-sash type, usually long and narrow, and were placed to take advantage of the prevailing breezes. Rooms were generous in size and had high ceilings. As buildings were improved in the 1930s and later, these windows were replaced by aluminum awning or jalousie types. When exterior weatherboard walls were resurfaced, stucco was often used to create a different effect. Wood roof shingles were replaced by composition or asbestos shingles of various colors and shapes.

A variation of the vernacular style is the Bahamian or Conch (1896–1920s) wood frame type, which is a two-storied structure with a low gable roof. The gable is usually perpendicular to the front and rear facades. A major characteristic of this style is the wood balustraded porch that runs the full front of the building, and sometimes around the side, on both stories. Furthermore, the construction of the building is of the "balloon" wood frame type, rather than the original cross-braced system of heavy timbers employed by shipbuilders turned carpenters. The Bahamian or Conch-style house is still found in the Charles Avenue neighborhood of Coconut Grove. There are a few left in the Culmer-Overtown area as well.

Masonry. Vernacular masonry building has similar characteristics to the wood frame type, except that it is constructed with masonry instead of wood. Three kinds of masonry were used: imported hollow clay or terra cotta tile, locally made cement block, and oolitic limestone and keystone. Rusticated cement blocks became popular because they did not require other surface finishes. Most commonly found is the porous, textured oolitic limestone, which could be used as structural, facing, or decorative material. Quarried locally, oolitic limestone is unique because of the disintegrated coral and other sealife formations that it contains. Keystone, on the other hand, is more porous than limestone, more closely resembles coral rock, and is characterized by visible coral formations and shells in the stone. It became a popular material during the 1930s and 1940s. This stone is quarried in the Florida Keys. As thin slabs, the stone is used as a surface covering or decorative accent. Keystone is often dyed a shade of pink or green.

Mediterranean (1915–1930s)

The sources of the Mediterranean style are from the countries of Italy and Spain, and to some extent of France and North Africa as well. In South Florida, the style is sometimes mistakenly called Mediterranean Revival. There was no such revival of an earlier style, however, as South Florida Mediterranean was in the process of being created. This influence was derived from two sources. For one thing, South Florida architects at the time either traveled to southern Europe to absorb the local architecture, or drew upon their own imagination for inspiration; for another, the Spanish Colonial Revival style, popular in southern California at the beginning of the century, spread across the country, including Greater Miami. Ornate Spanish Baroque style received national prominence in the 1915 Panama Pacific International Exposition at San Diego, and in various publications.

The first traces of the Mediterranean style locally have been attributed to August Geiger, who designed the Miami City Hospital ("the Alamo") of 1915 and the Miami Beach Municipal Golf Course House of 1916. The architectural characteristics of these buildings, however, are more in the Southern California style; the elaborate applied decoration is inspired by the architecture of Mexico, New Mexico, and Texas, rather than that of Spain itself. In Florida, the roots of the Mediterranean style are most likely to be found in Saint Augustine. In Greater Miami, the Mediterranean trend was established from two sources. Inspiration came from the design of the Vizcaya palazzo, completed in 1916. This style replaced classicism.[2] Then there were the design contributions of the architect Richard Kiehnel, which will be described in later chapters.

South Florida buildings in the early Mediterranean style (1915–1930s) generally have distinctive characteristics. Facades are asymmetrical, with articulated wall massing and varied rooflines. Roof tiles are terra cotta on low-pitched hipped roofs with little or no eaves overhang. Walls are rough stucco, sometimes specially aged to yield a weathered effect. Windows often have canvas awnings with wrought-iron grilles and railings. Arched door and window openings are common, as are balconies or upper-story terraces that are supported by wood brackets. The arches, perhaps the most recognizable feature of the Mediterranean style, can take a variety of shapes, from semicircular to segmental, pointed, or with Moorish elaborations. Windows vary in size, may be grouped or randomly placed, but are usually of the casement type. Doors are of wood with panels, sometimes glazed, and most often are intricately carved. Decoration, with Spanish Baroque as the most popular kind, is applied around doorways, windows, and cornices. The decorative materials most often used are glazed ceramic tiles, terra cotta, and oolitic limestone. Decoration can also take the form of classically derived details such as pediments, twisted columns, and ornamental parapets at gable ends. Favored Mediterranean features include loggias, courtyards, and patios. Interiors often have beamed ceilings, floors of terra cotta tile, and adorned mantels over fireplaces.

In Coral Gables, the Mediterranean flavor was captured in many ways. These included subtly pitched roofs with handmade tiles in terra cotta, ocher, and sienna colors. Walls were finished in stucco with surfaces sometimes artifically weathered. They were painted in pastel colors, mainly with coral rock and/or brickwork features for diversity. Round arches, with the occasional pointed Venetian arch, were used to form arcades and loggias. Columns frequently culminated in capitals freely borrowed of the classical orders. Wrought ironwork and decorative tiles were other features. In awnings, colors and patterns complemented the basic mass of the building.[3]

Mediterranean Revival, 1980s–present. During the Depression years of the 1930s, the building industry stagnated. The Mediterranean style lost impetus and was gradually abandoned. There was a revival of the Mediterranean style in the 1980s that continues today. Of particular note is the ordinance passed by the City of Coral Gables in 1987, providing certain bonuses to developers of properties in the city's downtown area if a Mediterranean style is used in the proposed building.[4] The Mediterranean district is bounded by Douglas Road, Eighth Street, Le Jeune Road, and Santander, with a western projection around Biltmore Way up to Anderson Road. In Dade County, a truly Mediterranean Revival style manifested itself in the late 1980s and early 1990s. The Mediterranean look is becoming increasingly popular. Residential buildings in this Revival style are large houses or villas with separate but connecting buildings, each with their own hipped or gable roofs. The major features continue to be red tiles and arched windows. There are many variations, though, in the treatment of wall openings. A covered entry is common. External stucco-covered walls are often painted a pastel color. Internally there are usually an expanded family room, a kitchen, and a den.

Moderne (1925–1948)

The Moderne style was a product of new ideas derived from the movements in modern art and architecture at the beginning of the twentieth century. Sources of inspiration were not sought in the past but in the design styles of movements such as Cubism, Futurism, and De Stijl. On the whole, Moderne buildings in Greater Miami are structures that have a simple geometric, generally cubic mass with smooth wall surfaces, flat roofs, and parapets. Hotels and apartment buildings on Miami Beach often have front porches and courtyards that face the ocean breezes, and most are three or four stories high. Hotels went up mainly along Ocean Drive, but the ones not on the seafront were within a short walking distance of the beach. When apartment buildings began to be constructed, these followed the style of the hotels but were located further inland to the west. The early period of Moderne, from the mid-1920s to the early 1930s, is noted for distinctive features. An integrated design of voluptuous applied Art Deco decoration and facade details was applied to the basic geometrical mass of the building. In hotels, the signs were always an integral part of the facade scheme. During the 1930s, massing became more important, with the emphasis on aerodynamic shapes that led to the emergence of the Streamline style. The Moderne style, then, can take either the Art Deco or the Streamline form.

Art Deco Moderne (1925–mid-1930s). Art Deco as a term was derived from the short title for the Exposition Internationale des Arts Décoratifs et Industriels Modernes, held in Paris in 1925. Contemporary with the Jazz Age, the Art Deco style became widely used in Europe. It could be found in building interiors and artifacts such as light fittings, radios, ornaments, and furniture, as well as in jewelry, typography, and graphics. The dual inspiration of the style was drawn from the fashions for exotic and sensuous images and materials and the creations and ideas of the Futurists, Cubists, and Surrealists.[5] The style was redefined for the United States at the popular world fair, "Century in Progress," held in Chicago in 1933–1934. In architecture worldwide, the image-making qualities of Art Deco made it the most widespread style in movie theaters. The style was also used in institutional and commercial buildings. Nowhere, however, is there the concentration of Art Deco hotels and apartment buildings that there is in Miami Beach.

The Art Deco Moderne architectural style is distinguished by the angular forms of the buildings and, in general, the use of a vertical composition in the facades. Masts, flagpoles, and finials, most pronounced at entryways, emphasize the vertical dimension. Sometimess facades are stepped—that is, the facade planes are staggered back from the center—to establish a rhythm across the facade. Originally, features on the exteriors were painted in bright colors that stood out against neutral colored walls. Applied decorations on the surfaces of the external walls are of a geometric or abstract organic form. The decorations are in bas-reliefs, stucco panels, etched glass, or murals. The zigzag figure was popular as it could represent many symbols, from a stylized wave, to electricity as the modern source of power, to Egyptian or Aztec designs. Themes are of a nautical, tropical, or historic nature. Motifs in use are fountains, waves, palm trees, flamingos or others from Native American or Egyptian sources. The discovery of Tutankhamen's tomb in 1921 created a wide interest in Egyptian art.

Streamline Moderne (mid-1930s–1948). Streamline Moderne represents the later development of the Moderne style in the 1930s, the period when the emphasis on streamlined industrial products passed into architecture. The idea of streamlining derived from scientific observations of movement. Industrial designers, in particular, were interested in shapes that encountered minimum resistance when in motion. Their designs of airplanes, trains, and ocean liners resulted in forms reflecting speed and efficiency that soon became symbols of modernity. In architecture, the application of detail became less important than the massing of the building. Streamline Moderne facades achieve their sleek look through many devices, from round building corners to windows that pierce the corners and "wrap around" the front and side facades. The faces of buildings have a horizontal composition accentuated by the window arrangement. Linear, sometimes wavy, bands or "racing" stripes also add to the feeling of horizontality. These bands are applied or incised onto the wall surface. The aerodynamic effect is increased by means of cantilevered slabs and window, or "eyebrow," canopies. A modern appearance was achieved through new materials such as glass block, chrome, stainless steel, neon lighting, and terrazzo. Much of the played-down decoration is in the form of bas-reliefs and applied ornamentation. In Miami Beach, sunbursts and geometric floral patterns are popular motifs on facades. The external walls have a white or off-white background with accents in sea green, sunny yellow, and flamingo pink. In the area's Streamline Moderne buildings, nautical symbols from the luxury liners of the 1930s are very visible. Features such as porthole windows, tubular pipe railings, flagpoles, and sundecks were used. Windows are of the casement type to allow for sea breezes to be scooped in while simultaneously providing uninterrupted views.

A variation of Streamline Moderne was Depression Moderne, an austere style used mainly in public buildings. Classical elements were used in decoration, which was spare in comparison to the other Moderne styles.

Mission and Pueblo

Mission and Pueblo are two separate but related styles with similar heritages. The Mission style was derived from early Spanish mission churches in California, while the Pueblo style was inspired by the adobe houses of Native Americans of Arizona and New Mexico. These styles are distinctive for their uncomplicated forms, flat roofs, and little to no applied decoration.

Mission (1910s–1930s). The unpretentious scale and inexpensive construction of the Mission style made it a popular form in moderate-income housing developments and small apartment structures. Buildings are simple in shape, with flat roofs obscured behind parapets. The tops of parapets are curved or flat and are finished with a simple stucco moulding or with a single row of sloping tiles. Rainwater from the flat roof drains through cylindrical tiles, known as scuppers, which pierce the parapet in various patterns. Door, window, and front porch openings are often arched. The porch arch sometimes extends over a carport or garage entrance located on one side of the front of the building. Exterior surfaces are of stucco, often roughly textured, and windows are either of the casement or the sash type. Striped awnings over windows are customary. Ornamentation is simple, confined to parapet moldings or scuppers, and occasionally niches with urns and carved stonework. Hialeah was the earliest residential area in the Greater Miami area to use Mission-style architecture extensively.

Pueblo (mid-1920s). In the Pueblo style, flat roofs are hidden behind parapets. These have irregular profiles of hand-molded shapes. The uneven aspect is continued in the rough surfaces, the soft and rounded corners, and the variable lines of the external walls. Where walls are thick, they sometimes taper upwards. Concrete block or wood frame form the structure of the house. Parapets are pierced by projecting wood beam ends, or logs, to simulate Pueblo construction. Beam ends are not usually exposed but are attachments to the exterior of the building. Also, the original Pueblo sun-dried mud surface is expressed locally in the textured stucco finish. The Pueblo style, although it was intended to be the architectural theme of the development of Miami Springs, prevailed only during the mid-1920s.

Moorish (late 1920s)

Strictly speaking, the Moorish architecture of Greater Miami is not a style. The style was a fantasy creation of the developer of Opa-locka, Glenn Curtiss, and his architect, Bernhardt Muller of New York. They were inspired by the *One Thousand and One Tales from the Arabian Nights.* Domes, minarets, pointed or other shaped arches, and crenellated parapets are features borrowed from Islamic architecture. Other characteristics drawn from this source are colorful glazed geometrically patterned tiles and cracked stucco, as well as symbols such as crescent moons and stars. Flat roofs are hidden behind parapets that are pierced by scuppers.

Southern Californian (1910s–present)

Bungalow (1910s–1930s). The Bungalow style was an import from southern California. During the first two decades of the twentieth century, the Bungalow style was most popular among the middle-income group across the country. Externally, exposed structural members, unfinished surfaces, gable roofs, and plentiful porches were combined in an assortment of models. Internally, there were space-saving conveniences. Low maintenance requirements were reflected in the use of natural finishes and rough textures.[6]

Adaptations to local South Florida conditions included covering the exterior walls of the house with horizontal weatherboard or wood shingles, or occasionally stucco. Oolitic limestone was used for the porch walls and also chimneys and exposed foundation walls. The common Greater Miami bungalow has a wood frame structure. It is one-story, sometimes one-and-a-half stories. Its profile is low, with a broadly pitched gable roof, overhanging eaves, and dormer or attic windows. The most popular form of roof was the gable. In this type the ridge of the roof of the main building is perpendicular to the street with a separate lower gable over the porch. Otherwise, the ridge is parallel to the street. A dormer window opens in the side of the roof. A distinguishing feature of the style is the deep porch, the roof of which is supported by masonry piers. The piers take a variety of forms, depending on the creativity of the builder. Masonry piers taper upward. They can also consist of a combination of a lower half of stone and an upper half of a wood post (or posts). When the piers were broad with a thickset appearance, they were called "elephantine." Because air circulation and cross-ventilation are so important, large sash windows are positioned carefully. In the attic space, dormer windows or louvered outlets are used. The Bungalow type was concentrated in the Edgewater, Buena Vista, and Little Havana areas.

The Belvedere Bungalow style is characterized by its two-story mass and multiple roof gables. The second floor, or "belvedere," is smaller than the first floor and is usually used for the master bedroom. Belvedere bungalows were very prominent in the Lawrence Estates Subdivision, a development of the Tatum Brothers that was built close to Miami and near the Miami River.

Ranch (1940s–present). Building contractors introduced the early Californian Ranch style in the mid-1940s. Boxlike or rectangular houses are differentiated externally by low sloping roofs, light-colored stucco walls, shaded windows, and initially, by extensive wood trim. In the 1970s, the style was developed further, adding internal features such as entry halls, kitchens expanded to hold an eating space, and second bathrooms.

Modernist or International Modern (1945–present) [7]

The term International style was coined in America in 1931.[8] It denoted the modern movement of rationalist architecture in Europe. Nationally, only a few buildings were designed in this style before 1945. After World War II, the style was accepted widely. During the unprecedented economic growth era of the 1950s and 1960s in the United States, the style became predominant. It was virtually the only style of architecture used in commercial buildings. The modernist-style buildings are characterized by clearly articulated features. These include abstract geometric forms and clean lines without decoration. The reinforced concrete or steel-frame structures exhibit large areas of glazing (the external walls often being

"**Modern environments and experiences cut across all boundaries of geography and ethnicity, of class and nationality, of religion and ideology . . . .**"
Marshall Berman, *All That Is Solid Melts into Air: The Experience of Modernity*, 15.

The global turbulence of 1968 was a harbinger of change. At 3.32 p.m. on the 15th of July, 1972, the modernist prize-winning Pruitt-Igoe development in St. Louis was demolished with dynamite as it had become an uninhabitable environment. In the same year the influential populist *Learning from Las Vegas* by Venturi, Scott, Brown, and Izenour was published.

David Harvey, *The Condition of Postmodernity*, 38.

fully glazed). Open, rather than cellular, floor plans make for free-flowing and airy interior spaces. In its glass form, the curtain wall, a skin or outer membrane of a building that carries no structural weight, became the most ubiquitous feature of office buildings.[9] The aims of modernist architects were many. They wanted to design buildings with a new kind of space and form. They strove for a machine-inspired aesthetic. In particular, in the search for a universal aesthetic, they sought to break completely from the past by eliminating historical allusions.

In the 1960s, antimodernist and counterculture movements arose. These changed the International Modern style considerably during the stormy decade of the sixties. Some hold that there was more than change involved and go so far as to declare the demise of modernism. Moreover, whether the changes represent revision or reaction is debated. Here the account presented by a widely published author of books on contemporary architecture, Charles Jencks, will be adopted.[10] To simplify, it can be said that Modern architecture developed into new versions. These are Late Modern, which was established from the late 1960s and onwards, and Postmodern, introduced in the early 1970s after the emergence of "postmodernism" between 1968 and 1972. Since the 1980 Venice Biennale exhibition, some form of consensus in the designs of leading international architects is evident. The presentation, organized by Paolo Portoghesi, displayed the work of seventy architects from around the world. These designs share conventions that, according to Jencks, can be described as Postmodern.

Modern architecture, from the 1920s until the early 1960s, can be categorized as Early Modern or High Modern. Early or Classic Modern is epitomized by the architecture produced by the Bauhaus architects and their followers. An influential Early Modernist was Le Corbusier, a key figure in Congrès Internationaux d'Architecture Moderne (CIAM). This group created an international climate of architectural ideas that lasted until the 1950s.[11] High Modern architecture is a variation on Early Modern in the use of new materials such as plastics, for example, and less glass. Architects and builders in the 1960s became critical of the excessive use of glass. New York's World Trade Center building, for example, was a precursor of the changes to come—the facade was dominated by steel columns rather than glass.[12]

A major developer informed Moshe Safdie: "We feel that postmodernism is over. For projects which are going to be ready in five years, we are now considering new architectural appointments."

Safdie, "Skyscrapers," 30.

Late Modern architecture takes the ideas and forms of the Modern movement to an extreme. The nature and the technological image of a building are exaggerated to please aesthetically or to amuse. The architecture may be playful, self-ironizing, and irreverent pastiche.[13] Common devices that are used in the Late Modern style to create an element of dissonance are skewing grids to intersect at odd and imaginative angles, to represent imperfection; juxtaposing volumes in vehement opposition to one another; or providing blank white walls that are relieved only by the play of shadows. Another is the creation of boxlike buildings with large holes in them. Among the major types of exaggeration are sculptural form, 1920s revivalism, and a second–Machine Age aesthetic.

Postmodern architecture, in contrast, represents a split from the previous era. It is not, however, a total rejection of the Modern tradition. In a Postmodern building, the architectural vocabulary of the Modern style is combined with elements of another architectural language. For example, a few Modern elements, such as large plate-glass windows, are used together with traditional forms—for instance, a colonnade or sculptural group. Among the other architectural languages that have been combined with the Modern are neovernacular, historical revivalist, metaphorical, and contextual. It is not a question of copying slavishly from these other languages, however. The Biennale's title announced that "The Presence of the Past" meant that everything old was not entirely new again, but that it was not entirely old anymore either. Postmodernism calls for inclusion and participation, pluralism is its salient characteristic.[14]

South Florida Progressive Styles

During the early 1990s, there were signs that South Florida architects were searching for a local style of design. This exploration has taken the form of progression beyond modernism in all its forms. The basic idea is that the city should express its history, and that its buildings should be manifestations of its culture. Two styles that have emerged are the neoclassical and the Fusionist. As the search for a progression is still at its initial stages and remains undefined, there are very few examples of the Progressive styles.

Rolando Llanes: "I'm trying to consolidate that language [the vernacular, the Mediterranean, and Art Deco] into one . . . ."

Rafael Portundo: "Context is a continuing quest . . . how you address the street, how you deal with it when the fabric is nondescript." Quoted in Beth Dunlop, "Shaping the 90s," 11.

Neoclassical. In the neoclassical style, the search is for a new interpretation of the classical tradition of architecture. Explicit references to the past are made to emphasize a concern for continuity.

Fusionist. The Fusionist style seeks to avoid eclecticism and attempts a synthesis of elements from the local vernacular, Mediterranean, and Moderne styles.

Architectural Styles of the City of Greater Miami

The identification and depiction of the historic and modern architectural styles found in Greater Miami completes the first category, form and organization of individual buildings. This category is essential to depicting the architectural images of the city. In the next four chapters, the city's most notable private and public buildings will be described. As there are hundreds of notable buildings in Greater Miami and it is not possible to describe them all, only a selected few can be included in this book.[15] The choice of which buildings to include here was based on the recognition that a particular building has received. For historic-style buildings, recognition took two forms: official designation of one kind or another and the consensus of informed persons or groups that the building is noteworthy.[16]

For Modern-style buildings, recognition takes two forms. Some buildings receive an architectural award in annual statewide or local programs. The statewide program has been organized by the Florida Chapter of the American Institute of Architects since the 1950s, with award-winning buildings published in the *Florida Architect* magazine. The local awards program is separate from that at the state level, and arrangements for it are made by the Florida South Chapter of the American Institute of Architects. Records date from 1981. Significantly, both the state and local programs use nationally renowned architects to form a jury or panel to select which submissions are to receive awards. Another form of recognition for modern buildings is given to edifices that meet certain other criteria. For example, the architectural critic of the *Miami Herald*, Beth Dunlop, selects notable buildings for review. Some buildings receive notice through a feature in an architectural journal. Other buildings have been illustrated in *A Guide to the Architecture of Miami* by a Committee of the Florida South Chapter of the American Institute of Architects in 1963. Finally, the projects of nationally and internationally renowned architects are a focus of attention.

The complexity of the selection process is further complicated by the fact that architecture as a public art generates widely different responses arising from different aesthetic orientations. The differences are illustrated in the 1987 Florida South Chapter of the American Institute of Architects (FS/AIA) Awards Program. The 1987 program was unusual: instead of the conventional architectural jury, members of the FS/AIA as well as the public, represented by readers of the *Miami Herald*, were invited to vote on the buildings submitted for an award. In addition, the *Miami Herald*'s architecture critic, Beth Dunlop, compiled her own list without knowing the results of either the AIA members' or the public's selections. The single Miami building to make all three lists was Bayside. On two other lists—the public's and the architects'—the only buildings in common were the Museum Tower, the Douglas

Entrance, and the Woodruff House. It would appear that the architects favored Modern-style buildings with strong geometry and crisp lines, whereas the public leaned toward buildings that "were lush, rich, tropical houses."[17] Although there were many methodological problems with the exercise, the differences in choices among the readers', the architects', and the architecture critic's are evident. It should also be pointed out that the buildings represent only one particular year and, further, that many architects—many distinguished local architects—had no submissions that year.

An analysis of the architectural styles of Greater Miami buildings that have received an architectural award reveals a general pattern favoring modernist architecture since World War II. The notable buildings that dominated the 1950s and early 1960s, and persisted with lesser force through to the 1980s, were in the Early or Classic Modern style. The major form of modernist architecture in the city of Greater Miami, however, is the High Modern style, which appeared in the mid-1960s and has prevailed until today. Late Modern appeared in the early 1980s; by the end of that decade, it began to challenge the High Modern style. Postmodern made a token appearance in the mid-1980s but has remained an insignificant architectural style in Greater Miami. Given the confusion and disagreement as to the meaning of Postmodern, the reader is referred back to the definition given earlier in this chapter. As yet there are only a few examples of South Florida Progressive-style buildings.

Throughout the decades, the architecture of Greater Miami has also been distinguished by its tropical use of color. In Miami Beach the keystone was tinted green, blue, and pink. Vizcaya was originally light red (a ripe papaya color), yellow (a lemon cream color), and peach. The Biltmore Country Club was a peachy yellow tone.[18]

A singular characteristic of the architecture of Greater Miami is the dominance of modernist architecture. This is reflected in the choices of a panel of well-known architects. Except for the vernacular-style Coral Gables House, the buildings they selected as representing the best of Miami's architecture in 1981 were all in the Modern style.[19] Despite the commanding presence of modernism, a contemporary form of the wood vernacular style has remained as a persistent minor theme throughout the second half of the twentieth century.

The friction between the two contrasting approaches, the Modern and the vernacular, is captured in a 1958 interview of the proponents of each style.[20] Lester Pancoast responded thus to the question in what direction American architecture was headed:

"Architectural techniques and thinking in this country are becoming more and more inspired by modern technology, leading us toward a day when factory-produced buildings, or pieces, thereof, will be flown to their sites and outmode what we now call prefabrication. I think that this can result in a scientific aesthetic which many of the world can share." To the question "Do you prefer the word modern or contemporary applied to your own work?" he replied, ". . . contemporary [is] more complementary. Its implication is that it is appropriate to the times; modern's implication is anything since 1935." In contrast, Alfred Browning Parker responded, "I would prefer neither. I would be very happy if some of the things I have designed and built would in future years be called architecture. I think that's enough." The two architects held different and opposing views as to whether architecture was becoming the first "international" art. Pancoast expressed an appreciation for regional sensitivities, saying that "eventually there may be common factors in architecture for all people, not overriding these special sensitivities but underlying them." Parker's response was that he resented the efforts of the Bauhaus adherents "to apply one, pat formula to all buildings in all places. . . . The international school results in what I call 'americanned' architecture, and I hate to see this happening to our country."

At the beginning of the 1990s, the architecture of Greater Miami is being influenced by the thoughts and works of some young architects.[21] Abandoning the modernist style, these architects seek to create a South Florida Progressive approach. Representatives of these young architects, and their works in Greater Miami, are Michael Kerwin of Spillis Candella and Partners and his involvement in the design of the University of Miami Physics Building; Maria de la Guardia and Teofilo Victoria, in their stunning concept for the Ca'Ziff in Coconut Grove; Jorge Hernandez and his elegant design for a villa at Cocoplum in Coral Gables; Suzanne Martinson, with her thoughtful approach to the Greenberg House in South Dade and the renovation of the Art Deco Miami Shores theater with Thorn Grafton; Luis and Jorge Trelles, in their sensitive composition for a private residence in Coral Gables and the classically inspired Atrio House in Old Cutler Bay; Rafael Portundo and his delightful scheme for a private residence in Gables by the Sea; and Rolando Llanes, for his study of the Colonnade and other work. For a tenth, notable young architect, Mark Schimmenti, there are no local examples of his work. A striking exhibition at the Center for the Fine Arts in early 1993 displayed the work of many of these young architects, as well as designs by other promising architects. Together with the projects, built or proposed, of internationally known architects, the exhibition underscores Greater Miami's architectural richness.

Despite the intrusions of High, Late, and Postmodern styles and the initiatives shown by the South Florida Progressivist architects, the Classic Modern style is alive and well. There are two clear signs. The first is that in September 1992, the youngest architect to receive one of Florida's highest architectural prizes was Roney Mateu.[22] It is the Award of Honor for Design awarded by the Florida Association of the American Institute of Architects for a consistently excellent body of work. The award is not given every year. Mateu's preference for the clean geometry of modernism is evident in the simple and timeless shapes he uses in the design of commercial and residential buildings. The second indication of the persistence of the Modern style is that the only architectural award given for a Greater Miami building in the 1992 statewide program was bestowed on the Fiorentino Residence.[23] Dan Williams's design of cubical volumes punctured by rectangular openings accentuated by tubular railings is in a Classic Modern style.

chapter 7

Historic-Style Private Buildings

T H E class of private buildings consists of three major building types: single-family dwellings, apartment houses, and hotel buildings. The proportion of these building types differ from community to community. In Greater Miami some communities have only the single-family building type. Others also have some apartment houses. Yet others have a varying proportion of houses, apartments, and hotels. Furthermore, the architectural style of buildings within each type is different from locale to locale. As this chapter is organized by community, it conveys a sense of location of the different types of Greater Miami's historic private buildings. The buildings selected for description are historic-style notable structures built between the mid-nineteenth and mid-twentieth centuries.

Miami

Single-family dwellings. A structure in Dade County that survives from the last century is the one-story Fort Dallas barracks (Figure 23). The 1849 building was originally William English's plantation slave quarters before it became an Army barracks. After 1891, it was used by Julia Tuttle for storage. In 1925, the Daughters of the American Revolution had the coral rock vernacular building moved, stone by stone, to its present location in Lummus Park. Also from the last century is the oldest-known (1858) wood vernacular home still standing in the county, the William Wagner House (Figure 24). It was moved from its original location, now known as the Highland Park Subdivision. Dade Heritage Trust, to whom the house had been donated, relocated the structure when it was endangered by the construction of Metrorail. The Trust restored the much-altered house in 1978. A typical structure built

23

24

by the Dade County pioneers, it provides a good idea of the first houses in the area. Early houses were simple rectangular shapes with vertical butt-jointed boarding on frames, made from hand-hewn lumber with mortise-and-tenon joints, and with steep gable roofs. Later, imported milled lumber was used and porches were added. Another surviving private building from the nineteenth century is the Royal Palm Cottage (Figure 25). It is one of about thirty Royal Palm Cottages built by Henry Flagler to accommodate the managerial rank of the labor force that was constructing the Royal Palm Hotel nearby. Flagler's houses were frame vernacular with steep gable roofs, horizontal sideboarding, and a front porch with simple support posts and turned wooden balusters. They were located along 1st and 2nd Streets. The City bought the sole existing house in 1979, relocated the structure a short distance south of the river to Fort Dallas Park, and restored its exterior.

In what is today downtown Miami, there were Victorian-style

23. Fort Dallas barracks, Lummus Park, 404 N.W. 3rd Street, Miami. 1849.

24. Wagner House, Lummus Park, 404 N.W. 3rd Street, Miami. C. 1858. The house was moved to its present location in Lummus Park in 1979.

25. Royal Palm Cottage, Fort Dallas Park, Miami River at S.E. 1st Avenue, Miami. 1897. The cottage, one of the last thirty built by Henry Flagler for the Royal Palm Hotel workers, was moved to its present location in 1979.

26. Typical Miami cottages. (Photo dated 1905.)

25

26

residences of the well-to-do (Figure 26). These early residences have now all disappeared. There remain, however, some notable historic-style houses in the neighborhoods to the south, west, and north of the downtown area. A distinctive subdivision south of the Miami River was the Brickell Addition, which was opened in 1905. The erection of palatial houses on the scenic bayfront property along Brickell Avenue led to the thoroughfare being called "Millionaires' Row." The large residences in varied styles were built mostly before 1920 and have now been replaced by high-rise condominiums. There were some fine residences. Among them was the Villa Regina/Briggs Residence (pre–1920s) with its classical details. Still standing is the Villa Serena/Bryan Residence (1911–1915) with its broad overhanging eaves, abundant windows, and central courtyard—all designed in response to local climatic conditions. In contrast to the architectural style of these two villas was the New England–shingle manner of the Mitchell–Bingham Residence (1919–1922).

To the west of the Miami River, the neoclassical Warner Residence is a fine example of the elegant houses that were built in the area. A striking feature of the exterior of the building is the two-story Doric colonnade, which runs the full length of the front face and continues around on the side facades. Special features in the interior are the central staircase and the elegantly crafted wood details. The Warner family ran the first floral business in Miami from the downstairs level of the house. It remained open until the 1970s.

There are many fine examples of the Bungalow style in the many neighborhoods of Miami. These include Highland Park, Allapattah, the Brickells' Riverside, and the Tatum Brothers' Lawrence Estate Park (the last two now part of Little Havana). Not only in these communities was the Bungalow style dominant, but also in the northern suburbs of Buena Vista and Edgewater, as well as in Miami Beach.[1] The future of the large collection of bungalows in Little Havana is extremely uncertain, given the pressures for redevelopment, as is that of the eclectic collection of Mission, Mediterranean, and Moderne-style homes on S.W. 11th Street.[2] Mission- and Spanish-styled houses are prevalent in the Grove Park subdivision, which was a Tatum Brothers development. It is located between N.W. 7th Street and the Miami River around S.W. 17th Avenue. In Shenandoah in the southwest part of the city, some fine residential streets are also to be seen.

North of downtown Miami, in Culmer-Overtown where the black community was concentrated, the modified wood Conch houses and narrow, long shotgun houses were the most common dwelling types.[3] This area, the cradle of black culture in Miami, is intended to become the Historic Overtown Folklife Village, a symbol of Dade County's black heritage, with the restored Chapman and reconstructed Dorsey houses.[4] Further north, along the bayfront and in Lemon City, Buena Vista, and Little River, are many small subdivisions that have houses in a variety of styles. In Buena Vista, some fine Mediterranean-style homes can still be seen, interspersed with Bungalow-style and Moderne buildings. Buena Vista, along with the neighborhoods of Morningside and South River, have been designated by the City of Miami as historic districts.

In the Morningside area, the John Nunnally House (1925) is a very good example of the high quality of the development that took place during the 1920s and later.[5] This area was originally known as Bay Shore and was first platted in 1922. Buildings in various styles including vernacular, Mediterranean, Mission, and Moderne, are to be found in the area. Many of these structures were designed by well-known architects—V. N. Nellenbogen, Phineas Paist, Kiehnel and Elliott, and Robert Law Weed among them. There is also a house designed by Miami's first woman architect, Marion Manley. Villa Paula (1926) is an example of an architecturally notable single-family residence in Miami that is not located in a historic district. The one-story house, originally the home of the Cuban consul, is a variation on the Renaissance style. Although the facade has a symmetrical composition, arched openings, and a balustraded parapet, the coupling of column and pier in the porch is a distinctive element.

Hotels. Most magnificent of the private buildings in Miami was the Royal Palm Hotel, although it was constructed in haste. It had a splendid location at the mouth of the Miami River, with views of Biscayne Bay, well-landscaped gardens, and a peripheral waterfront road (Figure 27). It was an impressive five-story hotel that had 350 guest rooms and many amenities. The Beaux Arts–style building featured a French mansard roof with a row of dormer windows. There was, also, a grand entrance portico at the center of the north facade. The portico, which was five bays wide and two stories high with classically derived columns, was the focal point of a palm-lined pathway through the hotel grounds. Miami's first grand hotel had a short life, opening in January 1897 and closing after the 1928–29 winter season. Unfortunately the building was torn down in June 1930.

There was a varied array of styles in other hotels. On Flagler Street and 2nd Avenue (now the site of the Alfred I. Dupont Building) was the Halcyon. Gralynn, a former private residence, was

27. Royal Palm Hotel, Miami.
1897. (Demolished a few years
after the 1926 hurricane.)

on S.E. 1st Avenue, where it was relocated from N.E. 6th Street and the Bay. The Halcyon Hotel (1905–1906) was a large five-story structure with turrets and a neoclassical portico. In contrast, the Gralynn (1908) was a three-story wood frame vernacular building. In 1916, the neoclassical-styled, eight-story McAllister Hotel on Biscayne Boulevard became the first medium-rise hotel in downtown Miami. It was designed by Walter DeGarmo.

Miami Beach

The notable private buildings in Miami Beach are located mostly in what is known as South Beach, the area south of Dade Boulevard. Among the first buildings on the beachfront were bathing casinos that serviced northern tourists seeking the sun. Then followed hotel buildings, concentrated on Ocean Drive and Collins Avenue. Afterwards apartment houses began to cluster west of Washington Avenue. Estate villas were located on the beachfront north of Dade Boulevard and also along North Bay Road.

In the first decade of Miami Beach's existence, the architectural style of many grand hotels and imposing residences was "Mediterranean Eclectic."[6] This style was a mix of Spanish Colonial Baroque, Tuscan Villa, and Venetian Gothic. The Mediterranean Eclectic style continued during the 1930s, but in a more sedate fashion.

Art Deco and Streamline Moderne styles were used in Miami Beach primarily between the mid–1920s and the early 1940s. The Moderne styles were adopted and used so extensively because architects sought an appropriate expression for resort architecture.

In addition, the images of fantasy and romance in the styles were attempts to delight tourists and seasonal residents and lift their spirits during the despondency of the Depression. Modern and dazzling styles, together with modest construction costs, were prime attractions for the new clientele of middle-income visitors.

Miami Beach has some fine examples of single-family residences in Art Deco style. The style, however, is more visible in the dominant hotel and apartment buildings. In the Art Deco District there are 871 standing buildings, but only a few of the most notable examples of the hotel and apartment buildings can be described here. Those selected are the designs of the principal architects Albert Anis, L. Murray Dixon, Roy France, Henry Hohauser, and Anton Skislewicz.[7] Both Dixon and Hohauser were responsible for several apartment buildings. They are better known, however, for the many outstanding Moderne hotels they designed. Between them they completed twenty-eight hotel designs in just over a decade (Dixon from 1936 to 1947 and Hohauser from 1935 to 1948). The high point in Dixon's output came in 1939, when he designed seven hotels. Hohauser's major accomplishment was eight hotels in 1936.

A hectic period for Moderne was the 1930s. Perhaps the 1990s will be the same for the Modern styles. In June 1993, leading architects, consultants, government officials, and residents convened to create a master plan for the South Pointe district. The initiative came from the owner of thirty-five acres of prime property in the area, Thomas B. Kramer, who wanted to create a cosmopolitan waterfront development founded on the latest urban design theories. By this time, South Pointe was already graced by a flurry of projects by prominent local architects. It may turn out to be the major location for the new architecture of Greater Miami.

Hotels. The Brown/Star was the first hotel on Miami Beach when it was built in 1915. Carl Fisher's Lincoln Hotel followed in 1916. Within a decade there were well over a hundred hotels. Among the first grand ones was Fisher's Flamingo Hotel, which opened on New Year's Eve, 1921 (Figure 28). It was a multistoried structure designed in the Beaux Arts classical tradition with a symmetrical arrangement of the building forms—a taller central section and lower wings on either side. The hotel established a standard for adorned public spaces, exotic landscaping, and services for guests. Services varied from the practical, such as a laundry and shops, to entertainment attractions ranging from speedboats to polo matches to gondola rides around the new islands in Biscayne Bay. After the success of the Flamingo, other grand hotels were opened, such as

28

29

30

Stoltz's Fleetwood (Figure 29) and Fisher's Nautilus (Figure 30). The latter was a six-story luxury hotel with Spanish decorative elements designed by New York architects Schultze and Weaver, their first commission in the area. In 1968, the Nautilus was torn down to make way for a new nursing school and paramedical building for the Mount Sinai Medical Center.[8]

Hotels in Mediterranean Style. An early hotel in the Mediterranean style was Robert Taylor's design for the Madrid, built in 1923. Another early resort hotel is the three-story George Washington. The building, designed by William P. Brown in 1924, has arched and elliptical window openings, twisted columns, two rooftop spires with decorative plaques, and a pediment parapet. The nine-story Floridian Hotel, later renamed the Biscaya and demolished in 1987, was designed by S. D. Butterworth in 1925. It had a monumental staircase up to its second-floor entrance, was lavished with Baroque details, and was noted for its square colonnaded rooftop tower. The eight-story Roney Plaza Hotel, with its Spanish-inspired tower building, went up in the same year (Figure 31). The architectural firm of Schultze and Weaver used the same tower motif in its conception of the Roney Plaza Hotel. The firm was also responsible for the design of the Miami Daily News Tower in downtown Miami and the Miami-Biltmore Hotel in Coral Gables. All three buildings are visually connected one to the other from the observation deck of each tower. These towers were a modified rep-

31. Roney Plaza Hotel, main entrance, Miami Beach. 1925. Architects, Leonard Schultze and S. Fullerton Weaver of New York. (Building later demolished.)

lica of the Giralda Tower of the Cathedral of Seville, Spain (Figures 32–35).[9]

Another large Fisher hotel was the six- to eight-story Boulevard (1925), designed by W. F. Brown. A fourteen-story hotel, the Blackstone, was designed by Kingstone Hall in 1929 and remodeled by V. H. Nellenbogen in 1934. One of the largest hotels in the Mediterranean style is the Edward Hotel designed by H. Maloney in 1935. The five- to six-story structure covers most of the block on which it is located. Arched openings on the first two floors, a monumental staircase to the second-floor entrance, spacious terraces, and the ubiquitous red roof tiles are major Mediterranean features. It featured a solarium, a roof garden for dancing, and a private swimming pool. The Hotel Edison (Figure 36) shows that the architect Henry Hohauser was master of both the Mediterranean and the Moderne styles.

Hotels in Moderne Style. The Surf Hotel (1936), designed by Henry Hohauser, is a superb example of the Art Deco Moderne style (Figure 37). The building has a cubic mass painted white, a stepped facade, vertical configuration, and fairly extensive decorative bas-relief friezes. Because of the symmetrical composition of the facade, the two full-length friezes on either side of the entry door are mirror images of each other. This effect is repeated in the two slightly smaller friezes at the top center of the building. It also appears in the two full-length friezes at the corners of the first floor. Ground-floor friezes have stylized plant life themes, whereas each of the

The original tower in Seville and its Greater Miami imitations.
32. Giralda Tower, Seville, Spain.
33. Miami-Biltmore Hotel tower, 1200 Anastasia Avenue,
Coral Gables. 1925–1926. Architects, Leonard Schultze and
S. Fullerton Weaver of New York.

34. Miami Daily News Tower (later renamed the Freedom
Tower), 600 Biscayne Boulevard, Miami. 1925. Architects,
Leonard Schultze and S. Fullerton Weaver of New York.
35. Roney Plaza Hotel tower, Miami Beach. 1925. Architects,
Leonard Schultze and S. Fullerton Weaver of New York.
(Hotel later demolished.)

36. Hotel Edison, 960 Ocean Drive, Miami Beach. 1935. Architect, Henry Hohauser.

37. Surf Hotel, 444 Ocean Drive, Miami Beach. 1936. Architect, Henry Hohauser.

top two friezes depicts a nude figure and a flamingo. Flamingos also highlight a central decorative panel. The focal point of the composition is a large frieze at the top and center of the facade. It portrays stylized plants and two profiled nude female figures, along with the popular sun motif.

Another choice Art Deco Moderne design is the three-story Hotel Webster (1936), also designed by Henry Hohauser (Figure 38). The plain surface of the geometric facade is offset by a vertical central plane, which is framed by a border of incised decorative molding. Between the windows of the second and third floor, in the center of the front facade, is a plaque with elaborate vegetation motifs. Scalloped arches characterize the first-floor arcade. A striking Art Deco Moderne–style hotel building is the three-story Cavalier (1936) by Roy F. France (Figure 39). Its geometric stepped-back facade is elongated in character. Verticality is emphasized by the fluting of the two central pilasters, by the incised decorative friezes, by the proportion of the windows, and by the stepped-back framing of the outer windows on the second and third floors of the facade. The lettering of the hotel's name at the top of the central plane of the building is unified into the total design.

Typical Art Deco interior details and materials are exemplified

38. Hotel Webster, 1220 Collins Avenue, Miami Beach. 1936. Architect, Henry Hohauser.
39. Cavalier Hotel, 1320 Ocean Drive, Miami Beach. 1936. Architect, Roy F. France.

38

39

in the lobby of the Waldorf Towers (1937), designed by Albert Anis. Details include the attractive terrazzo floor, resplendent ceiling light fixtures, a fine mirror over the fireplace, and glass block beneath the window. A unique feature of the hotel's exterior is the symbolic circular tower that crowns the rounded corner of the three-story building. Against the darkness of the night sky, the drum-shaped tower's silhouette is graced by a line of blue neon encircling the roof eaves of the tower.

The front facade of the Neron Hotel (1940), unfortunately demolished in 1982, was designed by Hohauser as a mixture of Art Deco Moderne and Streamline Moderne features (Figure 40). Its two-story facade had a symmetrical composition. Both the front wall and the parapet had stepped planes. The central vertical structure over the double entry doors was accentuated by the streamlined masthead. This vertical feature contained a glass block panel in front of which was displayed the hotel's name. Flagstaff finials graced either side of the masthead. The typical wraparound corner windows had cantilevered "eyebrows" or sunshades. Other features were the octagonal porthole windows on either side of the entry doors and the horizontal raised bands, or "racing stripes," above and below the second-story windows. Decoration was confined to a

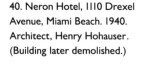

40. Neron Hotel, 1110 Drexel Avenue, Miami Beach. 1940. Architect, Henry Hohauser. (Building later demolished.)

41. Cardozo Hotel, 1300 Ocean
Drive, Miami Beach. 1939.
Architect, Henry Hohauser.

small vertical frieze of organic patterns placed below the masthead,
and the fluted molding on the two end parapets.

Hohauser's three-story Cardozo Hotel (1939) best distinguishes
the Streamline Moderne–style buildings, particularly those on
Ocean Drive (Figure 41). The two facades of the L-shaped building have a very strong horizontal and sleek emphasis, brought
out even more strikingly by the cantilevered sunshades that extend over and between the windows. On the Ocean Drive facade
the horizontality is broken by central vertical accents. Major em-
bellishments are two concentric ornaments at the top of two of
the vertical wall panels, and the keystone used for the porch columns and balustrade. Other adornment is furnished by the window frame in the center of the two upper floors. The Governor
(1939) is another exceptional illustration of the Streamline style
(Figure 42). It is a Hohauser-designed building. Features are its
stepped-back facade, cantilevered sunshades, rounded corners, applied decoration in stylized wave insets and floral reliefs, vertical
fluting, and flagstaffs. Of particular note is the Art Deco lettering of the hotel's name on the marquee, a stainless-steel canopy
projecting above the entrance to the building. One of Hohauser's
finest design efforts and the embodiment of the Streamline style is
the Greystone (1939) on Collins Avenue (Figure 43). The three-
story building has a stepped-back facade with racing stripes and
a stepped parapet. It features rounded corners with wraparound
windows and window "eyebrows." Vertical elements are the masthead with signage and twin flagpoles threading through decorative
semicircular discs. Another Hohauser creation, the Streamline Mo-

42. Governor Hotel, 435 21st
Street, Miami Beach. 1939.
Architect, Henry Hohauser.
43. Greystone Hotel, 1920
Collins Avenue, Miami Beach.
1939. Architect, Henry
Hohauser.

42

43

44. Century Hotel, 140 Ocean Drive, Miami Beach. 1939. Architect, Henry Hohauser.

derne Century Hotel (1939), resembles the design of the Neron (Figure 44). Both buildings are two-story. Each has a front porch, and both have a symmetrical facade composition with a central vertical emphasis. The front facade of the Century is dominated by the central striped mastlike structure. A three-dimensional effect is created by continuing features around the corner of front and side facades. On the second story this effect is achieved by the wrap-around windows, "eyebrows," racing stripes, and porthole symbols on the top corners, all of which continue around three sides of the building. The nautical motif is repeated in the "portholes" of the low wall separating the front porch from the sidewalk. It appears also in the "half-portholes" and the stylized waves that frame the entry doors.

Another good example of a Streamline Moderne–style hotel is the Berkeley Shore (1940) by Albert Anis (Figure 45). The building is three stories high with a symmetrically composed front facade that has stepped-back planes. Its facade, dominated by a futuristic central structure, consists of a vertical cylinder that rises over the entry doors and penetrates through several horizontal cantilevered fins on its way skyward. The stepped parapet softens the geometrical shape, as do the two large cast plaques, with their stylized organic forms, placed above the upper windows. A front porch is set three steps up from street level. The Plymouth Hotel (1940) exemplifies the Streamline Moderne style's fascination with science fiction and Buck Rogers movies (Figure 46). It has a rocketlike

Historic-Style Private Buildings 123

structure or pylon at the corner of the L-shaped edifice. Anton Skislewicz designed the hotel. The building consists of two three-story wings. These are joined by a four-story drum structure, with a towering pylon at the corner of the L. Apart from the cantilevered window canopies, a horizontal band above the upper windows, and the vertical fluting on the front of the polygonally shaped pylon, there are no other features to relieve the otherwise austere front facade. In the rear of the drum structure there was a breakfast room that overlooked the patio and swimming pool. Cove lighting and a panoramic Ramon Chatov mural of a tropical paradise characterize

45

the interior of the circular lobby. Another Chatov mural, featuring
an agricultural scene, is above the green Vitrolite fireplace in the
lobby of Hohauser's Colony Hotel (1935). Skislewicz's other hotel,
the Breakwater (1939), is noted for its roof deck and the Neptune
mosaic at the bottom of the swimming pool. The pool is shared
with the adjacent Hotel Edison (1935). A memorable feature of the
Breakwater is its vertical tower. This landmark has double-faced
signage in blue neon that glows afar at night. The flamingos and
palm trees etched on the glass of the lobby windows are fine examples of the tropical imagery that architects integrated into their
designs.

Trademarks of the hotels designed by L. Murray Dixon on Collins
Avenue are the finials, pointed ornaments at the top of tower structures or other high points of the buildings. The Tiffany (1939) has
a curved metal finial on top of the hotel's masthead, which in turn
sits on a futuristic finned cylinder (Figure 47). At the Tudor (1939),
Dixon placed a "rocket needle" at the pinnacle of the masthead that
also bears the hotel's name (Figure 48). On the top of the ziggurat
tower of the Palmer House (1939), there is a hexagonal glass-and-
metal lantern capped by a chrome sphere (Figure 49). Next to the
Palmer House is the Kent (1939); the triangular masthead bear-
ing the hotel's name is topped by aerodynamically shaped railings
and a rocketlike finial (Figure 50). The now demolished Senator,
built in 1939, had the simplest structure. The tower consisted of a
square shaft that sat on a base resembling classical types. Dixon's
penchant for sculptured roof towers is highlighted in his Adams
Hotel (1938). This hotel building has a futuristic structure on its

roof to hide the elevator machinery. The structure is formed by a
deeply fluted cylinder topped by another smaller cylinder that is
embellished with vertical fins (Figure 51).

Roy F. France designed an admirable example of the high-rise
hotel building type in the St. Moritz (1939). This ten-story hotel
building has a typically asymmetrical facade. There is a vertical
component slightly left of center (looking at the facade from the
street) and a horizontal segment to the right. A flagstaff finial and
an upright fluted panel emphasize the vertical aspect, while the
projecting broad linear panels highlight the horizontal appearance
of the building (Figure 52). Placement of the building is unusual

47

48

49

50

51

Miami Beach finials by L. Murray Dixon, architect.
47. Tiffany Hotel, 801 Collins Avenue, Miami Beach. 1939.
48. Tudor Hotel, 1111 Collins Avenue, Miami Beach. 1939.
49. Palmer House Hotel, 1119 Collins Avenue, Miami Beach. 1939.
50. Kent Hotel, 1001 Collins Avenue, Miami Beach. 1939.
51. Adams Hotel tower, 2030 Park Avenue, Miami Beach. 1938.

52. St. Moritz Hotel, 1565 Collins Avenue, Miami Beach. 1939. Architect, Roy F. France.

52.

in that it is situated back from the street toward the ocean on an artificial mound. Other illustrations of the high-rise type are the Dixon-designed Raleigh (1940) and Victor hotels (1937). The finest, however, were the Sands (1939), by Roy F. France; the Senator (1939), by Murray Dixon (Figure 53); and the New Yorker (1940) by Henry Hohauser (Figure 54). All three, regrettably, have been demolished.

53. Senator Hotel. 1201 Collins Avenue, Miami Beach. 1939. Architect, L. Murray Dixon. (Building later demolished.)

Hotels in Transitional Modern Style. A Moderne-Modern style of architecture was apparent in the hotels built during the 1950s and 1960s. These hotels were high-rise buildings, often of fifteen stories or more, and were fully air-conditioned, enabling the hotels to operate year round, whereas the hotels on South Beach had to close during the hot months from May to November. The new hotels were built along the oceanfront north of Lincoln Road, replacing the palatial mansions of wealthy industrialists and others. Three high-rise hotels next to one another on Collins Avenue can be considered transitional buildings between the Streamline Moderne style and the Modern style: the Ritz Plaza by Murray Dixon, the Delano by Robert Swartburg, and the National, also by Dixon (Figure 55). The buildings are modernist in style except for their articulated skylines. The sculptural roof tower that crowns each differs strikingly from its counterpart. The National has a silver cupola over Moorish arches; the Delano, a four-winged headdress structure; and the Ritz Plaza, cubic blocks topped by an embellished cylinder. Five hotels north of the Ritz Plaza also mark the passage of Moderne to Modern. These are the Marseilles (1946) by Robert Swartburg, the South Seas and the Richmond, both built in

54. New Yorker Hotel, 1611 Collins Avenue, Miami Beach. 1940. Architect, Henry Hohauser. (Building later demolished.)

55

55. High-rise hotels, Miami
Beach. From left to right: *Ritz
Plaza Hotel*, 1701 Collins Avenue.
1940. Architect, L. Murray
Dixon. *Delano Hotel*, 1685 Collins
Avenue. 1947. Architect, Robert
Swartburg. *National Hotel*, 1677
Collins Avenue. 1940. Architect,
Roy F. France.
56. Shelborne Hotel sign, 1801
Collins Avenue, Miami Beach.
1954. Architect, Igor Polevitzky.

56

1941 and designed by L. Murray Dixon, and the Raleigh (1940),
also by Dixon. A little farther along Collins Avenue there is also the
high-rise Shelborne (1954), designed by Igor B. Polevitzky (Figure
56). It is probably the last transitional building between the Moderne and the International styles. The severe geometry of the
horizontal window bands and the vertical wall planes is relieved
by the impressive signage on the roofline.

A major difference in architectural styles between the 1920s–
1930s and the 1950s–1960s lies in the height of buildings. In
the earlier period, three- to four-story (with the occasional seven-
story) low-rise structures were common in contrast to the later
period's ten- to fifteen-story high-rises. Another distinction is that
in the Moderne hotels of the prewar era, decoration was heaped
on the facades and lobbies, but rooms were rather functional. In

the postwar modernist-style hotels, facades were stark. Conversely, the interiors were lavishly provided with "Hollywood"-set lobbies, and "starlight" ballroom rooftops. Services were wide-ranging, included coffee shops, drugstores, and access to bathing pavilions.[10] Modernist-style hotels were set back from the street and had driveways and sometimes porte cocheres. These new features reflected the motorized age. The most widely known of these hotels is the crescent-shaped Fontainebleau (1953) designed by Morris Lapidus.[11] His firm also designed the adjacent Eden Roc (1955) and the nearby Americana (1957) hotels.

Apartment Buildings in Mediterranean Style. H. Hastings Mundy's Palm Gardens apartment building (1923) is a striking illustration of a Mediterranean-style structure (Figure 57). The two-story complex consists of a courtyard flanked by buildings that have very low, sloping, hipped roofs. Semicircular arches support balconies that have patterned balustrades of semicircular barrel tile. Upper windows are framed by pointed arch moldings, and the corners of the buildings are accentuated by twisted column pilasters. Another fine example of a Mediterranean-style apartment house

57. Palm Gardens Apartments, 752 Meridian Avenue, Miami Beach. 1923. Architect, Harold Hastings Mundy.

is the three-story Amsterdam Palace (1930). Henry La Pointe, the building's architect, designed an open courtyard defined by a lower colonnade and upper galleries (Figure 58). The medieval-style front facade features an archway entrance with a set of tall wooden doors that lead into the courtyard behind. Other attributes are the asymmetrically placed arched windows and balconies. On the raised entrance terrace there is a kneeling nude statue by the Los Angeles sculptor V. K. Vuchinich.

On Espanola Way is the "Spanish Village," the block between Washington Avenue and Drexel Avenue, created by Robert Taylor for N. B. T. Roney in 1925 (Figure 59). The group of apartment and hotel buildings is distinguished by an arcade, red tile roofs, asymmetrically placed turrets, and hidden courtyards. Facades have arched windows, pilasters with classical capitals, and grillework. Originally there were other Mediterranean features such as balco-

58. Amsterdam Palace Apartments, 1116 Ocean Drive, Miami Beach. 1930. Architect, Henry La Pointe.
59. Espanola Way, Miami Beach. 1925. Architect, Robert Taylor.
60. Royal House Apartments, 1201 Pennsylvania Avenue, Miami Beach. 1936. Architect, Henry Hohauser.

nies and wooden trellises. Renovation of the buildings began in 1986 when the ground-floor spaces were converted into shops.

Apartment Buildings in Moderne Style. Royal House (1939) is a small two-story Moderne building designed by Henry Hohauser (Figure 60). The symmetrical front facade presents a balanced contrast between the vertical center component and projecting horizontals on either side. The center component itself consists of a sequence of vertical elements. At the bottom an entry door is surrounded by a glass block panel. The panel is topped by a narrow window in a wall plane edged by pilasters. The ensemble is capped by a simple decorative pattern of fluting and bosses (raised ornaments). A cylinder surmounted by a futuristic rocket-shaped finial crowns the whole vertical structure. Horizontal elements in the facade are formed by widely projecting slender slabs above the windows and entry door, linear bands above the upper windows and along the top of the parapet, and incised lines on either side of the center component.

An intriguing design is that of Roy F. France's apartment buildings (1935) on Pennsylvania Avenue (Figure 61). He created a "mirror-image" visual impact by placing two identical buildings facing each other across a narrow courtyard. The buildings are each two-story with long cantilevered slabs or "eyebrows" to shade the raised front porches and lower windows, and shorter "eyebrows"

60

61

above the upper windows. The long, narrow projecting bands or racing stripes, accentuated by color, and the straight parapets give the buildings a sleek look.

Two splendid examples of the Moderne style are the Penn Terrace (1936) and the Ed Lee (1936) Apartments on Pennsylvania Avenue (Figures 62–63). Both were Henry Hohauser creations. Penn Terrace is a three-story cubic structure with a symmetrical front facade. Recessed, cantilevered balconies, three projecting narrow horizontal fins, vertical fluting on either side of the entry doors, and the rounded corners of the parapet relieve the otherwise geometric facade. There is no applied decoration on the facade as

62

63

there is on that of the nearby Ed Lee Apartments. The decoration on this three-story building consists of horizontal moldings on either side of the doors, a stucco plaque above the entry doors depicting stylized plants, and cantilevered circular segmental slabs that recede in size as they progress toward the parapet. Another contrast is the asymmetrical composition of the facade and the application of colored accent stripes. Both buildings feature a common stylistic attribute, wraparound windows.

Coral Gables

The most notable feature of the historic-style private buildings in Coral Gables is the prevalence of the Mediterranean style. Many different architects were involved in the design of the architecturally distinguished single-family houses in this community. The most prolific was George Merrick's cousin, H. George Fink, who was associated with the Coral Gables development from 1921 to 1928 after having worked for Carl Fisher in Miami Beach from 1915 to 1921. In Coral Gables, Fink's designs for private buildings included many single-family dwellings, an apartment building, and a hotel in the City's downtown area. The cousins traveled to Spain together in 1924 to study Spanish architecture. George Fink received a tribute from King Alphonso XIII for his contribution to the "Spanish Arts in America" and was also made a don, the equivalent of a British knight. Two other prominent architects also designed buildings for George Merrick. Walter DeGarmo, the first registered architect in the State of Florida, was one. The other was Phineas Paist, who came initially to work on Vizcaya for F. Burrell Hoffman and stayed on to become Merrick's supervising architect for the Coral Gables development. Head of the landscaping was Frank M. Button, who came from Chicago to take charge of a department that eventually totaled 130. The landscaping staff was responsible for the extensive planting designed to complement and reinforce the architecture of the buildings. Merrick's uncle Denman Fink, a nationally renowned painter and illustrator, played a magnificent role in supporting and promoting the dream of the City Beautiful. Merrick designated him "Artistic Advisor" to the Coral Gables development.

Single-Family Vernacular-Style Houses. On Coral Way is the Merrick House, now renamed the Coral Gables House (Figure 64). It was built in 1899 by the Reverend Solomon Merrick and his son George. In 1906, the wood structure was replaced by a plantation house designed by Mrs. Althea Fink Merrick, George's mother. Elevated from the ground, the house had a wide veranda that wrapped around the first-floor rooms. The design was in the local traditional manner. So was the use of local oolitic stone for the external walls and of Dade County pine for the woodwork throughout the house. In viewing the house today, one can see several classically inspired features that depart from the vernacular: the columns that support

64. Merrick House, 907 Coral Way, Coral Gables. 1906. Designer, Althea Fink Merrick.

65. Ricketts Residence, 1251 Coral Way, Coral Gables. (Photo dated 1923.)

the porch; the entranceway, which is defined by a set of double columns and by a pediment above on the shed roof of the porch; and the conspicuous second-floor window, a Palladian motif consisting of an arched central opening flanked by two smaller, square-headed openings. In the 1920s, Althea Merrick again remodeled the family home and added a garage with servants' quarters.[12] After the collapse of the land market, Althea and her daughter Ethel added five bathrooms. They changed the name of the house to Merrick Manor and began to take in paying guests until Ethel's death in the mid-1960s. In 1977, restoration work on the house began a year after the City of Coral Gables had acquired the property.

On Coral Way there are a few other rock-style houses, among them the Ricketts Residence (Figure 65). Another is Poinciana Place, built by George Merrick in 1916 for his bride Eunice Peacock, the daughter of R. Peacock, a Coconut Grove pioneer. It was Merrick's second house. The first was the family home he built with his father and subsequently altered by his mother as just described. George Fink's own one-story home is another rock house on Coral Way. It was named Casa Azul (Blue House) and was built in 1924. Except for the blue glazed roof tile, the building followed local traditions.

Wood frame houses and front porches characterize the Bahamian heritage of the homes in the MacFarlane neighborhood, bordered by Oak Avenue and Grand Avenue, Brooker Street and U.S. 1. The neighborhood was declared historic in 1989.[13]

66. Merrick Residence III, 832 South Greenway Drive, Coral Gables. (Photo dated 1925.)
67. View from the golf course of the Miami-Biltmore Hotel, 1200 Anastasia Avenue, Coral Gables. 1925. Architects, Leonard Schultze and S. Fullerton Weaver of New York.

Mediterranean Style. In addition to vernacular-style houses H. George Fink also designed residences in the Mediterranean style. Three houses that were built in 1924 are noteworthy. The first was constructed for Doc Dammers, the City's first mayor, best remembered as the "wheeling and dealing" land sales agent for George Merrick. The Dammers House has a fine symmetrical facade, with double-column arches that frame the first-floor openings and the wrought iron balconies on the second floor. The second was a house for George Merrick, his third house (Figure 66). Fink varied from the pure style in using an irregular form and a combination of textured stucco and exposed coral rock. The third was the Grasso House, which is relatively small. Facade features are an arched gateway, applied decoration, and an inclined tile parapet.

Arguably one of the finest of the Coral Gables Mediterranean residences is the Pape House (1926), designed by Frank Wyatt Woods. It has arched openings, a central tower, and entrance portal. Attached to the multisided building are a walled garden and a porte cochere. Elaborate applied decoration allows the Maxwell House (1926), designed by John and Coulton Skinner, to surpass other Mediterranean-style buildings for embellishment. The ornate entrance portal is framed by Corinthian pilasters topped by a Baroque pediment that is dominated by a cartouche and the pair of classical urns that anchor the pediment above.

H. George Fink also designed an apartment building, the Bennett Apartments (1925). It was modeled on a small Venetian palazzo. The building underwent many changes through the years. It was closed and condemned by the City before the building was renovated in 1975. Another notable apartment building is the Venetia (1925), designed by Martin Hampton.

Hotels in the Mediterranean Style. The Miami-Biltmore Hotel[14] is the most prominent and the best-known building in Coral Gables (Figure 67). Its fifteen-story tower, topped by a three-stage cupola, was designed by Schultze and Weaver. With its imposing struc-ture, the Miami-Biltmore can be seen for miles around and is used as a landmark by boaters on Biscayne Bay. On the north facade, the entrance, the hotel tower projects slightly forward from a cen-tral ten-story block. This in turn is flanked by obliquely placed seven-story wings, each terminated by a six-story building. When seen from any angle, the building presents a complex mass with hipped roofs at different levels descending from the center. The main entrance, identified by a three-story Baroque portal, is on the second floor at the center of the building. It is reached by a ramped roadway that enables vehicles to pick up and drop off passengers. The south facade, which faces the golf courses, features an arcaded loggia and patio (Figure 68). Otherwise, the composition of this facade is a variation of the north frontage. The smaller Country Club building, with its tall arched openings attached to the west side of the hotel building, is reminiscent of an Italian Renaissance palace. The south facade features a second-floor terrace and elegant loggia that formerly led to the dining salon.

From its opening on 15 January 1926 until the late 1930s, the 400-room Miami-Biltmore Hotel was one of Florida's fashionable hotels for the country's elite. Not only did it offer the finest in

67

68

69

68. South terrace loggia,
Miami-Biltmore Hotel.
69. Country Club arcade,
Miami-Biltmore Hotel.

accommodation and gourmet dining but it also staged the best in entertainment, ranging from big-name dance orchestras to unsurpassed sports facilities, including two eighteen-hole golf courses, up to twenty tennis courts, and equestrian events. Water extravaganzas were held in an enormous swimming pool measuring approximately 150 feet by 225 feet, then the largest in America. The epitome of luxury was the authentic gondolas that were available to transport hotel guests down the Coral Gables Waterway to Biscayne Bay, to Tahiti Beach. Here guests could relax under thatched huts and coconut palms, swim in salt water, and imagine themselves in the exotic South Seas. Tahiti Beach was rebuilt after the 1926 hurricane and opened to the public. When it closed in the early 1970s, the site became the present exclusive Cocoplum development.

In 1942, the War Department purchased the Miami-Biltmore and the following year the building was reopened as a 1,200-bed hospital, named the Pratt General Hospital, in 1946. Following the War, the facility continued as a Veterans Administration (VA) Hospital until 1968. When the building was vacated by the VA, the citizens of Coral Gables rallied together to prevent the empty building from being razed. After years of negotiation, the federal government eventually deeded the property to the City of Coral Gables in 1973. The Biltmore Country Club building, which is adjacent and attached to the Miami-Biltmore Hotel, was renovated and opened as the Metropolitan Museum and Art Center, with a restaurant, in the late 1970s (Figure 69). The hotel building itself was renovated and opened as a 286-room luxury hotel, its original use, in January 1987. Because of the economic recession of the late 1980s and early 1990s, the hotel was closed for a few years.

In Coral Gables the first hotel was the Inn at Coral Gables, built by the Coral Gables Corporation. The company realized the need to accommodate and entertain the potential land buyers who began to respond to the exceptional advertising operation launched by George Merrick. By the beginning of 1925, three new hotels were opened—the Cla-Reina, the Antilla, and the Casa Loma—to meet the demand from visitors. The San Sebastian Hotel was opened in May 1926. The Miami-Biltmore, however, remained the premier hotel.

The Inn at Coral Gables (1922), designed by Hampton and Ehmann, was modeled on a Spanish tavern, with a central courtyard that one entered from the street through an arcaded loggia (Figure 70). The Inn, later renamed the Coral Gables Lodge and Hotel, became a home for retired performers of the Musicians' Club before the building was demolished in 1972. A distinctive characteristic of the Cla-Reina/La Palma Hotel (1924), an H. George Fink creation, is the large courtyard between the two wings of the building (Figure 71). Also of note are the twisted columns and decorative arches that frame the two entrance doors. Features of the Antilla Hotel (1925) were the corner tower building with its tall, semicircular, arched opening and arcades that ran around the

70. The Inn, 303 Minorca Avenue, Coral Gables. 1922. Architects, Martin L. Hampton and E. H. Ehmann. (Building later demolished.)

71

72

top of each side of the tower (Figure 72). It had a spacious loggia
with an outdoor terrace above it shaded by striped awnings. The
architect was Lee J. Wade. The building was demolished in 1960
to make way for the undistinguished Chateaubleu Inn. Another
Hampton and Ehmann design was the elegant Casa Loma Hotel
(1925). It was a U-shaped three-story building with an entrance
loggia fronted by an arcade of semicircular arches (Figure 73). On
the roof of the loggia was an outdoor terrace. The hotel, located
next to the Miami-Biltmore, was converted into a nurses' residence in 1943 and was finally demolished in 1972. Today the site

73

71. Cla-Reina/La Palma Hotel, 116 Alhambra Circle, Coral Gables. 1924. Architect, H. George Fink.
72. Antilla Hotel, 1108 East Ponce de Leon Boulevard, Coral Gables. 1925. Original architect, Lee J. Wade. (Building later demolished and replaced by the Chateaubleu Inn.)
73. Casa Loma Hotel, 1224 Anastasia Avenue, Coral Gables. 1925. Architects, Martin L. Hampton and E. H. Ehmann. (Building later demolished.)
74. San Sebastian Apartment Hotel, 333 University Drive, Coral Gables. 1926. Architect, Phineas Paist.

74

is the parking lot of the restored Biltmore Hotel and Country Club complex.

Besides building the Antilla Hotel, the Coral Gables Corporation also constructed the San Sebastian Apartment Hotel (1926). Its purpose was to provide housing for the company's employees. Originally, the three-story building contained seventy-two apartments and seventy hotel rooms (Figure 74). The University of Miami purchased the building in 1939 for student dormitories and office space. When the University sold the building in 1967, it reverted to an apartment building. The architect, Phineas Paist, dealt with the design problem of a long unbroken front facade by means of five projections: a central five-bay entrance structure, two three-bay corner "pavilions," and a three-bay projection with a gable roof between the center and each of the two corners of the facade.

The Sevilla Hotel was known as the King Richard Inn during the 1960s. It was renamed the Hotel Place St. Michel in 1979. Originally an office building, it was converted to hotel use soon after its construction in 1926. The building, by Anthony Zink, is noteworthy for its framed entrance on Alcazar Avenue and the arched windows on the first floor of both street facades (Figure 75). Above the arched entrance doorway there are three heraldic shields and, on the second floor, three scalloped arches. Internally, the first-floor rooms have beautiful Spanish tiles and vaulted ceilings.

75. Sevilla Hotel/Hotel Place St. Michel, 146 Alcazar Avenue, Coral Gables. 1926. Architect, Anthony Zink.

Foreign-Style Villages. George Merrick signed a contract with the American Building Corporation in 1925 to develop large tracts of land in Coral Gables. His intention in the new development was to vary from the predominant Mediterranean style. The deed included the requirement that "villages" of various styles be built. These were to be the Italian, Javanese, Italian Country, Neapolitan Baroque, Mexican, African Bazaar, French Eighteenth-Century, Persian Canal, Venetian Country, Florida Pioneer, and Tangier villages.[15] Because of the land boom bust, only seven villages were constructed, and in these fewer dwellings than planned were built —only forty in all. The villages, which are scattered throughout the city, were constructed between 1925 and 1927 and designed by different architects.

The villages provide Coral Gables with a unique quality that can still be seen today. France provided the inspiration for three of the developments: the French Normandy or Provincial Village, the French City Village, and the French Country Village. In the French Normandy Village, the fifteenth- and sixteenth-century-type houses, designed by John and Coulton Skinner, are two-story (Figure 76). Buildings have steep roofs that provide additional living space in their attics. Exteriors have exposed horizontal and vertical timber framing, are painted brown, have stucco-covered infill panels, mullioned windows, chimneys, and shingle roofs. Typical eighteenth-century-style elegant homes are the pattern for the French City Village designed by Mott B. Schmidt (Figure 77). The houses are two stories with porches, courtyards, and kitchen gardens, all enclosed with graceful walls. Stucco facades are dominated by attractive moldings and French shutters and doors. The eighteenth century was also the source of ideas for the French Country Village designed by architects Frank Forster, Edgar Albright, and Philip L. Goodwin (Figure 78). They were inspired by the country farmhouse estates of that century. Exteriors of the large two-story houses have the distinctive red brick accents, steep red tile hipped roofs with dormer windows, chimneys, and mullioned windows of their French models. In the interiors there are high ceilings. The houses generally have four bedrooms, servants' quarters, and large backyards.

Other countries that stimulated design themes for villages were Italy, China, and South Africa. The Italian Village, by Frank Wyatt Woods, consists of a two-story villa type of house that is built up to the sidewalk (Figure 79). Entrance doorways, really portals, are reached by a few tiled steps. Stucco walls and red barrel-tile gable roofs complete the picture. Houses in the Chinese Village, designed by Henry Killam Murphy, are distinguished by their

76

77

78

79

80

81

Seven Coral Gables Villages.

76. French Normandy Village, 400 block of Viscaya Avenue. and LeJeune Road, Coral Gables. 1926–1927. Architects, John and Coulton Skinner.

77. French City Village, 1000 block of Hardee Road, Coral Gables. 1925–1926. Architect, Mott B. Schmidt.

78. French Country Village, 500 block of Hardee Road, Coral Gables. 1925–1926. Architects, Forster Albright and Goodwin.

79. Italian City Village, Monserrate Street, Altara Avenue, Palmarito Street, Coral Gables. 1926. Architect, Frank Wyatt Woods.

80. Chinese Village, 5100 block of Riviera Drive, 5100 block of Menendez Avenue, Castania, Maggiore, Sansovino Avenues, Coral Gables. 1926–1927. Architect, Henry Killam Murphy.

81. Dutch South African Village, 6000 block of LeJeune Road, Riviera Drive, Maya Avenue, Coral Gables. 1925–1926. Architect, Marion Sims Wyeth.

82. Colonial Village, 4000 block of Santa Maria. These homes back onto the Riviera Golf Course, Coral Gables. 1925–1926. Architects, John and Coulton Skinner.

82

brightly colored trim in red, yellow, and green. Other attributes are their decorative gates, carved wooden balconies, intricate lattice balustrades, and curved roofs covered with highly glazed tiles (Figure 80). Further Chinese features are the walls, with openings filled with cast concrete made to look like bamboo, that join the residences, together with the various animal sculptures perched on roofs that are considered symbols of protection and good luck. The manor houses developed in the middle of the eighteenth century at the tip of Africa are the pattern for the Dutch South African Village (Figure 81). In architectural history the style is better known as the Cape Dutch style. Plans of the two-story houses, by architect Marion Syms Wyeth, are either U-shaped, or in the form of an L. An entrance hall leads into an inner hall, which normally serves as the dining room. On the facades the two paramount features are the central gable and the entrance doorways. The central gables can take various forms—pedimented, curvilinear, and scrolled, for example. The entrance doorway is framed by pilasters with a tall fanlight that lights up the entrance hall above the door. Roofs are steep with gable ends, the walls are stucco (in contrast to those of the original South African models that are limewashed sunburnt bricks), and the chimneys twisted. Pioneer Village, sometimes called the Colonial Village, is a reminder of the antebellum Deep South (Figure 82). The mansions, designed by John and Coulton Skinner, are in the Greek Revival style. Two-story porticoes with tall, slender white pillars and wide porches distinguish these mansions. Slate gable roofs and white picket fences are common features. Internally there are a large hall, spacious rooms with vaulted ceilings, guest suites, and servants' quarters.

Coconut Grove

Single-Family Residences. As Coconut Grove is one of the oldest settlements in Greater Miami, it is not surprising that many of its notable private buildings are in the vernacular style. The oldest houses are frame vernacular. There is Ebenezer Woodberry Frank Stirrup's Key West–style home (1897) on Charles Avenue (formerly Evangelist Street), heart of the Bahamian settlement. Then there is the prototypical Barnacle, designed and built by Ralph Middleton Munroe in 1891 (Figure 83). The Barnacle is built on a hammock close to the bay water's edge. Its structure reflects Munroe's knowledge of ship design and boat construction. The original house was a framework arrangement, with lumber that came mainly from shipwrecks. Originally, the house was raised eight steps off the ground, bolted to the foundation, and built to withstand the storms. Munroe made subsequent alterations to the

83. The Barnacle, 3485 Main Highway, Coconut Grove. Originally constructed in 1891 as a one-story house; raised in 1908 to accommodate a second story below. Designer, Ralph Middleton Munroe.

house to accommodate the changing needs of his family. Most dramatic was the transformation in 1908, when he lifted the entire house and built a new first floor underneath. For climatic reasons, a wide shady veranda runs around all sides of the house except the hot west side. Inside, the corner rooms open onto a central octagonal-shaped dining room. The volume of this room extends into the hipped roof to allow hot air to escape to the outside through a skylight and clerestory windows. These are operated by ropes and pulleys. This system allows the prevailing breezes in summer to flow through the windows of the outer rooms, to the central dining room, and upwards and out through the rooftop openings. In this way the house is kept remarkably cool. Unfortunately, the foremost and proven principles of shading and cooling used by Ralph Munroe in the Barnacle were not followed extensively in the design of future houses in Greater Miami, particularly after World War II. In 1973, the Munroe family sold the Barnacle to the State of Florida, which has preserved the building in excellent condition as an historic site.

Noteworthy of the masonry vernacular-style buildings in Coconut Grove is the Brisbane House (1903) with its many windows. This building was moved from its South Bayshore location to its present location on Tigertail Avenue and is now the home of the headmaster of the Ransom Everglades School. The Anchorage (c. 1908), another masonry vernacular house, has wide roof overhangs and porches but also features a central courtyard, stucco exterior, and Cuban tiles. Originally named Marymount, the house was designed by the boat builder Carry Huntington. He sold it to William Jennings Bryan, three times an unsuccessful presidential candidate but very successful in selling real estate in Coral Gables. There were other residences in Coconut Grove, also with characteristics derived from various styles. Kiehnel and Elliott's Cherokee Lodge (c. 1917), for example, included English cottage attributes.

Kampong (Javanese for cluster of houses) is a complex of geometrical masses, stucco exteriors, Javanese decorative elements, stone gateway, and tile roofs. Built in 1928, it was designed by Edward C. Dean. In 1991, a campaign was launched to purchase the nine-acre property adjacent to the Kampong, which is part of the National Tropical Botanical Garden.[16]

Vizcaya was the most magnificent private residence in Greater Miami. The villa, with its formal gardens, was the winter home of James Deering, a vice president of the International Harvester Company. Because he suffered from pernicious anemia, he chose to winter in South Florida's warm climate. He was also attracted to the area because his father lived there and owned 180 acres of land. Construction of Vizcaya (Basque for 'elevated place') began in 1914, and the villa was completed in the short time of two years, no doubt because of the presence of a one-thousand-strong work force. The formal gardens were finished later. James Deering spent every winter from 1916 until his death in 1925 at his bayside villa. In 1952, the Deering estate sold the property and donated the villa's period furnishings to Dade County. The restored villa and gardens were opened to the public and have become a prime attraction in the area.[17]

The architecture of the seventy-room Vizcaya villa combines features from sixteenth- and seventeenth-century Italian Renaissance villas (Figures 84–85). Three designers were responsible for the creation of the entire complex: F. Burrell Hoffman, Jr., was the principal architect who produced the overall design of the building, Paul Chalfin was the associate architect who fashioned the interiors, and Diego Suarez planned the formal gardens. The building takes the form of a square with outer wings of rooms arranged around a central courtyard that affords cross-ventilation to the rooms. At each outside corner of the square the wings project forward to acquire a tower shape; on the bayside, they increase in height to accommodate the guest bedrooms. Entrance to the villa is through loggias on three sides of the building. The main entrance is on the street and west side. Two other entries are from the formal gardens on the south side and from Biscayne Bay on the east side. The finish on the building's exterior is stucco. Corners, cornices, and the frames of door and window openings are in cut and carved stone. Hipped roofs are covered with red tiles. There are many other facade attributes, including balconies, pediments, and loggias. The exterior also features a grottolike pool on the north side. On the bayside is the villa's most dramatic feature—a wide terrace that overlooks a large stone barge at the water's edge. The formal gardens are an extension of the villa and are conceived as

Vizcaya, 3521 South Miami
Avenue, Coconut Grove.
Building 1916–1917, gardens
1921. Architect, F. Burrell
Hoffman, Jr.; interior
designer, Paul Chalfin;
landscape designer, Diego
Suarez.
84. Vizcaya, from the air.
(Photo dated 1934.)
85. Vizcaya, bayfront.

84

85

outdoor rooms with walls of vegetation. The vast gardens contain several interesting elements. These vary from geometrically shaped hedges, water stairway, casino, maze garden, theater garden, statuary walks, canals, bridges, greenhouses, a yacht house, to a tea house, and even a secret garden. Inside the villa the first floor contains the formal state rooms, the second floor the family rooms, and the mezzanine between the floors comprises the servants' quarters. In the basement are the utility and service areas, as well as a billiard room, a smoking room, a bowling alley, and access to the swimming pool. All the modern conveniences of the time were also included, for example, central heating, a central vacuum-cleaning system, fire sprinklers, refrigeration, and two elevators.

The Village of Vizcaya was a cluster of outbuildings that accommodated the staff. The buildings once included living quarters for the superintendent, chauffeur, boat captain, boat engineer, chief engineer, garage man, fishing guide, and married and single servants. There were also workshops for the carpenter, the painter, and the blacksmith, together with a supply house. Other buildings housed the storekeeper's office; a garage, machine shop, and pit for the Packard and other luxury cars; and a laundry and walled drying yard. A farmyard with a central watering trough, stable, carriage house, dairy, and chicken coop completed the services in the Village. The buildings form a harmonious ensemble despite their different shapes and sizes. They have remained almost intact and in excellent condition. The Dade County Parks and Recreation Department now uses the buildings as offices. Entrance to the Village is through a gatehouse from South Dixie Highway or Miami Avenue.

Vizcaya and El Jardin (The Garden) are the earliest known buildings in Greater Miami rendered completely in Mediterranean style. El Jardin was a mansion built in 1918 as the winter home of John Bindley, President of the Pittsburgh Steel Company (Figures 86–87). Kiehnel and Elliott, the architects of the mansion, designed the building around a central garden courtyard with galleries on the first and second floors. The front or street facade presents a solid, private appearance, whereas the rear or bayfront view presents a more open image. Colonnaded loggias on the first and second floors dominate the bayfront facade. The central mass of this facade is flanked on either side by slightly projecting corner pavilions. Arches are a major theme in both the courtyard and the exterior facades. Intricate cast-stone ornamentation appears throughout, particularly around and above the entrance doorway, the frieze, and the second-story loggia. Low pitched roofs, with generous overhangs, are covered in red Spanish tile; and the stuc-

86

El Jardin/Carrollton School, 3747 Main Highway, Coconut Grove. 1917–1918. Architects, Kiehnel and Elliott.

86. El Jardin, east front. (Photo dated 1938.)

87. El Jardin, gatehouse. (Photo dated 1993.)

87

coed exterior walls are painted a pink color. The garden motif was extended into the ten-acre bayfront site with the planting of tropical trees, rose gardens, and orchid houses. In 1961 the building was purchased by the Sacred Heart Convent, and it is now the Carrollton School.[18]

There are other residences with Mediterranean-style features in Coconut Grove. Rock Reef House (1926), with its arched openings and tiled roof designed by Walter DeGarmo, is one. Another is the Cole House (c. 1923) with its decorative water fountain. In 1955, the Coral Reef Yacht Club bought the house, made several additions, and since then has used it as its clubhouse.

Inns. Two of the three notable inns in Coconut Grove were built in the vernacular frame style. Bay View House, known as Peacock's Inn for the owners Charles and Isabella Peacock, was a long two-story wooden building built from lumber washed up on the beach from shipwrecks (Figure 88). There were porches on both levels around three sides of the building. A steep gable roof, covered with shingles, featured dormer windows. The Inn was opened in 1883 and became the center of community life. A room in the building served as the post office while Charles Peacock served as postmaster. In 1902 the inn closed due to his ill-health, and the building was demolished in 1926. The site is now a park.

About 1913 the Sunshine Fruit Company built the Sunshine Inn and cottages to accommodate potential customers for land in its Coconut Grove subdivisions. Many additions were made subsequently to the Inn's original frame vernacular building. It served first as Gulliver Academy and now the Vanguard School. Built in 1922, the El Dorado Inn is Spanish in both name and style. It was once an exclusive inn with eight cottages. The inn is now a residence and law office, and the cottages are private homes.

88. Bay View House/Peacock Inn, 2820 McFarlane Road, Coconut Grove. The site is now Peacock Park. 1882–1883. (Building later demolished.)

North Dade

Single-Family Houses. Residences of architectural interest in North Dade are clustered in Miami Shores and Morningside (Figure 89). There are houses of interest in other communities, however. In El Portal, for example, there are two residences worthy of notice. The El Portal house (c. 1910), whose first owner may have been Charles Finch, is a fine illustration of early wood frame vernacular architecture, as evidenced by the front-end gable roof, the horizontal weather boarding, and the sash windows. Porches on the first and second floor were altered from their original form. The second residence is the Sherwood Forest House (1925), one of the best cases of an English Tudor–style house in the area. It is the only survivor of developer D. C. Clarke's dream of a beautiful and picturesque subdivision. He began it in 1925, but the development ended soon after with the collapse of Miami's land boom.

Significant Miami Shores residences are all in the Mediterranean style. The Spears/Harris house (1925) has undergone few alterations. It is noted for its arched openings, the one-story porch, second-floor balcony with iron balustrade, and barrel tile gable roofs. Also virtually unchanged is the Tyler Residence (1926). Its front facade is distinguished by a large arch and casement window, arched openings, and barrel tile gable roofs (Figure 90). There are exposed wood rafters in the eaves and exposed wood beams in the living room. A T-shape distinguishes the Tyler house from the rectangular form of the Spears/Harris house and the L-shape of

89

the Riach/Rapp Residence (1925) and the Camp Residence (1927). Along the length of each of the two wings of the L-shaped Camp house is an arcaded loggia that opens out to a courtyard (Figure 91). The main entrance of the house is at the bottom of the tower that joins the two wings. Designed by Walter DeGarmo, the Camp house is an excellent example of the intention of the developers, Shoreland Company, to create a thematic group development. Twenty-five residences, all designed in the Mediterranean style, make up the group. DeGarmo, with Phineas Paist, designed a more classical house in the Pedineilli Residence (c. 1925). It is a two-story rectangular building with a simple, symmetrically composed front facade. On the side of the house is a terrace defined by urns on pedestals; other classical traits are a pediment and unfluted Corinthian columns. In addition, the house has a porte cochere and an enclosed sunroom.

Apartment Buildings. The Shoreland Company also intended to construct several hotels and apartments as part of its general plan for Miami Shores. Grand Concourse Apartments (1925–1926) was the only major building of this type constructed before the collapse of the land market (Figure 92). The architect, Robert Law Weed, designed this building with two wings, each of two stories. These meet at a four-story entrance structure. The shapes of window openings vary from rectangular to arched to semicircular. On the first floor of the entrance structure is a portico with an arcade that consists of three pointed arches separated by decorative octagonal masonry piers. On the other side of the entrance structure is a hexagonal stair tower, also with pointed arches. Weed was also responsible for the design of many other buildings in Miami Shores.

South Dade

Single-Family Residences. Nearly all the architecturally notable residences located in the various South Dade communities are in the wood vernacular style. These residences, although the least known in Dade County, are among the best preserved and finest examples of the style.

In South Miami along Sunset Drive, now declared a state historic and scenic road, there are three significant houses in the vernacular style. The first two, one-story structures, appear almost the same as when they were built. These buildings are the Jordan/Foster/Wheeler/Dorn House built by Robert Urwin in 1910, and the Thomas House (1932), designed by Robert Finch Smith (Figure 93). The Laesch/Bartram House, the third building, is unusual in that it was built as a two-story wood frame structure in the early 1900s but was extensively renovated by H. George Fink in 1927 to produce a Mediterranean-style house. Of particular note is the decorated frame around the entrance doorway. The Richards/Erwin Homestead (1890) was built originally in local vernacular style but has been altered considerably.

South Miami is exceptional as it contains buildings in other architectural styles besides the vernacular. The first of what may be regarded as "imported" vernacular in South Miami is the Robert Frost Winter Home. It consists of two small, one-story cottages of wood that were shipped from New England and assembled on the South Miami site in 1942. An entry courtyard forms the space between the cottages. One cottage was used for sleeping and the other for reading and writing by Robert Frost, America's poet laureate and a four-time Pulitzer Prize–winner. During his annual winter stay, Frost gave readings of his poetry at the University of Miami until 1960. Another "imported" building is the Greek Revival Cornell Residence. It was built in Monroe County, Georgia, in 1860 and was moved to South Miami in the 1950s. The Sollett/Hagner House, known as Stonegate, has a novel Mediterranean style. It was begun in 1923 by Oliver Sollett and was incomplete when it was severely damaged by the 1926 hurricane. It was not until 1946 that the structure was completed by Casper Hagner. Typical features are the semicircular arched windows and tile roofs. What makes this large house distinctive is the exposed oolitic limestone walls. Other atypical characteristics are the horseshoe shaped central arch and the words "WELCOME TO A SUNLIT HOME" formed by heads of nails on the wooden front door. The sole example of a Bungalow-style house, in modified form, is the Wheeler House (1914) with its shallow hipped roof and porch with sloped masonry piers.

93. Doc Thomas/Tropical Audubon House, 5530 Sunset Drive, South Miami.

94

Designated an Historic Highway in 1974, Old Cutler Road is the location of very different structures, each significant in its own way. In 1899, Maude Richards, eldest child of pioneer Adam Richards and the granddaughter of William Wagner, married Charles Seibold. The couple bought a forty-acre property on Old Cutler Road. As the house on the property was built sometime in the 1890s, this makes it one of the oldest existing dwellings in the county. After Seibold died in 1910, Maude later married Charles E. Black. The Seibold/Black House is a one-and-one-half-story wood frame vernacular structure. It has a steep pitched main gable roof, a smaller gable roof with a dormer window, and front and rear porches. Although the house has been changed considerably over the years, the pioneer character still shines through.

There are two other notable vernacular-style buildings on Old Cutler Road. These are the simple Richmond House, built in 1896 by S. H. Richmond and his wife Edith, and Richmond Cottage, an inn they opened in 1900. In 1916, Charles Deering, brother of James, purchased the Richmond property, and eventually the whole of Cutler, to form his 360-acre estate. He razed what remained of the town of Cutler, except for the Richmond buildings. These he linked with his own mansion, designed by Phineas Paist and Frank Hogdon and completed in 1923. The large two-story mansion has an eclectic Mediterranean style with arched openings, both semicircular and pointed, arcaded loggias on the first and second floors facing Biscayne Bay, a barrel tiled gable roof, and a bell

95

tower and tall chimney. The ceiling of the south side porch is inlaid with seashells.[19]

Silver Palm and Redland still contain many pioneer homes built at the beginning of this century in vernacular style (Figure 94). Each house has one or more notable attributes. A distinguishing feature of the Lindgren House (1912) is the large bay window and decorative railings of the porch and deck. A wraparound porch and multiple hip and gable roofs are the special qualities of the Mobley/Wood House (1910 [Figure 95]). Then there are the multiple gables of the Mindermann House (c. 1915) and the coral

96

rock facing of the Coral Rock House. This facing was added in 1945 to the original 1913–1915 one-story frame building, formerly a lab for citrus canker research. An outstanding porch and dormer windows distinguish the Dan Roberts House (1926). The Walton/ Blanco House (c. 1919) is more like an English cottage with its vast hipped roof, towering stucco chimney, and multipaned windows. In Homestead, the Tropical Palm Lodge with its eighteen rooms is unusually large for a vernacular frame construction (Figure 96). It was built by the renowned horticulturist Colonel Henry Wallace Johnston in 1912.

No doubt the most extraordinary construction in Dade County is Coral Castle. Massive coral rocks weighing many tons were chiseled, carved, and moved by unknown engineering means by the Latvian immigrant Edward Leedskalnin to build his unique rock structures and garden. His creation, built during the 1920s and 1930s, was originally located in Longview. He moved all the structures to their present location in Homestead in 1939, loading and unloading by himself, refusing all help. Ostensibly he labored in the hope that his young fiancée, who had left him years before, would return to the remarkable home he had made. As it turned out, his hope went unfulfilled and in that sense he worked for a lifetime in vain. Nevertheless he did leave behind him evidence of the breadth of human ingenuity.

97. Richmond Cottage (*left*), partially demolished by Hurricane Andrew, and Charles Deering Mansion (*right*), S.W. 167th Street and Old Cutler Road, Old Cutler. 1900 and 1923.
98. Drake Lumber Company Boarding House, 13425 Coconut Palm Drive (S.W. 248th Street), Princeton. C. 1904–1912. Demolished.

97

98

Hotels. Three hotels of noteworthy architectural value in South Dade are all in the wood frame vernacular style. The impressive two-story inn, Richmond Cottage (1900), is connected perpendicularly to the simple two-story Richmond House by a gabled addition (Figure 97). Wide verandas run around three sides of the inn structure on both the first and second floors. The original roof was a steep pitched-gable type with three dormer windows. In Princeton the Drake Lumber Company Hotel/Boarding House (c. 1904–1912) was originally located on South Dixie Highway with Drake's Commissary (Figure 98). Wide porches on both the first- and second-floor levels were a characteristic of the two-story hotel building. In Homestead, the Seminole Hotel building, originally Harry Tuttle's Airdome Theater, was moved from Miami in 1916 and renamed the Garden Theater, then the Seminole Theater. Later converted into a café, then a hotel, it is now the Landmark Hotel on Flagler Avenue. The present-day Seminole Theater on Krome Avenue was opened by James English in 1921. It burned down in 1939 and was rebuilt in 1940 with a design by the renowned theater architect Roy Benjamin. The Seminole Theater that joined the hotel was opened later, and was also in a building moved from Miami. The hotel, now renamed the Landmark Hotel, still operates in the original building, whereas the theater building was moved to Krome Avenue.

chapter 8

Historic-Style Public Buildings

T HE architecturally significant public buildings in the various communities of Greater Miami vary in type of use from the commercial, community, cultural, educational, entertainment, government, to the religious. Each locale has its own particular mix of public building types, some with many types and others with very few. This chapter, in line with the previous one on historic-style private buildings, is organized by community. The historic-style public buildings described in each locale are the most notable structures constructed during the first half of the twentieth century. Generally, each community has a dominant architectural style for its public buildings, differing from one community to another. In downtown Miami, the vernacular style prevailed among early buildings, whereas the Moderne and Renaissance styles were generally dominant in the later buildings, many of which still survive today. In contrast, the Moderne style predominates in the commercial buildings of Miami Beach, and the Mediterranean style rules in the downtown buildings of Coral Gables.

Downtown Miami and Peripheral Areas

Commercial Buildings. It is no surprise that the largest collection of commercial buildings in Greater Miami, including some of the most prominent ones, is located in downtown Miami. Early commercial buildings were one or two stories high with arcades and porches for climatic protection. The Chaille block (1914) is a fine surviving example of this type with its covered walkway, shops that opened directly onto the street, and upstairs rented rooms and balcony. Many buildings erected in the 1920s were inclined toward Beaux Arts massing. Facades are divided vertically into three parts—a base, the main body of the building, and an imposing top—with Renaissance detailing. Other buildings have a Moderne massing but also with Renaissance features.

The stone-faced facades of the Ingraham Building (1927) are reminiscent of a fifteenth-century Florentine palace. On the first floor there is heavy rusticated stone, graduating to a smooth surface on the upper floors. Architects for the building were Schultze and Weaver. The whole edifice is crowned by an ornate cornice. Other features of note are the bronze entrance doors, the double-arched windows, and the wrought iron decorations (Figure 99). In the interior, the lobby has a splendid vaulted ceiling decorated with rosettes and a gold-leaf border. Henry Flagler housed the real estate division of his Florida East Coast Company, the Model Land Company in the Ingraham Building. It was named after the president of the Land Company from 1910 to 1924, James E. Ingraham. Another building with a marvelous lobby is the Langford Building (1927), now renamed the Miami National Bank Building (Figure 100). It was designed by Hampton and Ehmann with classical decoration, including gilded elevator doors. The facade has a central arched portico with Corinthian pilasters that support a broad lintel with the building's name. Decoration on the entablature of the building is in the form of emblems and seals from early United States coins. The custom of beautifully embellished lobbies can also be seen in the old United States Post Office and Courthouse building (Figure 101). Designed by Oscar Wenderoth and built in 1912, it was the first major federal building in Miami. In 1937, the building became the headquarters of the First Federal Savings and Loan of Miami, then later the Amerifirst Federal until 1992, and now Office Depot. The upper floor of the two-story Hahn Building (1925), by

99. Ingraham Building entrance, 25 S.E. 2nd Avenue, Miami. 1927. Architects, Leonard Schultze and S. Fullerton Weaver of New York.

George Pheiffer, has some choice Renaissance details in the pierced tile parapet rail, cornice, and wavelike frieze. A departure from the Italian Renaissance style is the French Second Empire neoclassical manner of the Security/Capital Building (1926), whose architect was Robert Greenfield. A most distinctive aspect of this structure is the curved copper-faced mansard roof with its decorated cornice and decorated parapet. Arched and small circular windows puncture the roof that contains the building's top floor. The roof is accentuated by a domed octagonal tower. Other motifs on the facades are an eaves cornice, a frieze, and bay windows flanked by pilasters.

101. Old United States Post Office and Courthouse, afterwards the First Federal Savings and Loan of Miami/then Amerifirst, now Office Depot Building, 100 N.E. 1st Avenue, Miami. 1912. Architect, Oscar Wenderoth; remodeling, Kiehnel and Elliott, 1937.

In downtown Miami there are notable buildings that are essentially Moderne in their massing but with Renaissance decorative elements. The Biscayne Building, for example, has neoclassical ornamentation and cornice above the top-floor arched windows. Originally five stories when built in 1925, the building was increased by eight stories a year later after a ten-story height restriction in the building code had been removed.[1] In the Dade Savings Building (1925), decorated arches are to be found on the first floor facade as well as lining the internal arcade, which also has mosaic floors and coffered ceilings (Figure 102). Architects for both buildings were Pfeiffer and O'Reilly. They, with Louis Kamper, were also the architects for the Huntington Building (1925). The otherwise austere facades of this thirteen-story building are relieved by oversized sculptured busts on the roofline and a decorative third-floor cornice (Figure 103). Another structure that was increased in height was the Seybold Building and Arcade, a Kiehnel and Elliott creation (Figure 104). It was originally a two-story building when constructed in 1921 with the remaining eight stories added in 1925. Neoclassical pilasters and a cornice with carved eagles are features of the facade of the Meyer-Kiser/Dade-Commonwealth Building (1925), designed by Henry La Pointe (Figure 105).

One other architectural style prevalent in the historic-style commercial buildings of downtown Miami is the true Moderne style. Streamline Moderne themes of a rounded corner, a horizontal band of windows, and Art Deco signs are conspicuous in the five-story

102

103

102. Dade Savings Building, arcade,
120–122 N.E. 1st Street, Miami. 1925.
Architects, Pfeiffer and O'Reilly.
103. Huntington Building, 168 S.E. 1st
Street, Miami. 1925. Architects, Louis
Kamper of Detroit with Pfeiffer and
O'Reilly.
104. Seybold Office Building, N.E.
First Street facade, 36 N.E. 1st
Street, Miami. 1921–1925. Architects,
Kiehnel and Elliott.
105. Dade Commonwealth Building,
139 N.E. 1st Street, Miami. 1925.
Architect, Henry La Pointe.
106. Walgreen's, 200 E. Flagler
Street, Miami. 1936. Architects,
Zimmerman Saxe and MacBride; and
Ehmann.

104

105

Walgreen Drug Store Building (1936 [Figure 106]). Architects were Zimmerman Saxe and MacBride, and Ehmann. The severity of the Depression Moderne style is evident in the facades of the Alfred I. Dupont Building (1938) by Marsh and Saxelbye (Figure 107) and the two Burdine's buildings (1936) on East Flagler Street. Decorative richness is confined to the interiors, particularly the Dupont building's second floor bank lobby. This splendid space has a coffered central ceiling and outer ceilings with wooden beams artistically painted with scenes from Florida's history. Brass eleva-

106

tor doors are adorned with palms, flamingos, and pelicans. Teller screens are elaborately wrought.

In 1923, James Cox purchased the *Miami Metropolis* newspaper and changed its name to the *Miami Daily News*. He also announced plans for a new building, the Miami Daily News Tower, which opened in July 1925 (Figure 108). This building is an architectural treasure, designed by the New York firm of Schultze and Weaver. Their work also included the Ingraham Building, the Miami-Biltmore Hotel in Coral Gables, and the Breakers Hotel in Palm Beach. For the Miami Daily News Tower, the architects conceived the design in three segments, a base in the form of a rectangular three-story building, a middle section that consists of a twelve-story Spanish Baroque tower, and an elaborate crown. The top five levels of the tower begin with a setback to form a terrace with a paneled and balustraded parapet and "guardhouses" at each corner. Another terrace is created in a similar manner at level fifteen with an encircling parapet distinguished by a row of sixteen finials.

107. Alfred I. Dupont Building, 169 E. Flagler Street, Miami. 1938. Architects, Marsh and Saxelby of Jacksonville, Florida. 108. The Miami Daily News/ Freedom Tower, 600 Biscayne Boulevard, Miami. 1925. Architects, Leonard Schultze and S. Fullerton Weaver of New York.

107

108

At this level the square tower is transformed into a hexagonally shaped ensemble, which in turn is topped by a smaller hexagonal tower and then a dome and a lantern. The building is also noted for its Baroque entry portal and oak doors, its baronial lobby, and its splendid banquet hall with groin vaults and mural.

After the *Miami Daily News* moved in 1957, the building remained vacant until April 1962. From this time on the United States General Services Administration used it as a Cuban refugee center until early 1974. The building became the best-known structure in downtown Miami in the 1960s. It was symbolically renamed the Freedom Tower when it came to house the center that processed the tens of thousands of refugees who fled Castro's Cuba. The building remained vacant from 1974 until 1987, when restoration work was undertaken by R. J. Heisenbottle Architects and completed in 1989.[2] The building is now listed on the National Register of Historic Places.

Outside the downtown area, the Biscayne Boulevard Company of the Phipps family intended to construct an attractive commercial section on the Boulevard. This was from N.E. 13th Street to N.E. 40th Street. Many fine low-rise structures were constructed, including the Sears, Roebuck Building (1929) designed by Nimmons Carr and Wright, with its splendid tower. The vertical emphasis of the seven-story octagonal tower dominates the corner of the four-story L-shaped building. This fine Moderne-style build-

ing symbolized a most important intersection in the city, Biscayne
Boulevard and downtown Miami with the County Causeway from
Miami Beach.

Community Buildings. The Alamo Building, built between 1915
and 1918 and designed by August Geiger, was the first structure
of the City of Miami Hospital (Figure 109). White stucco walls,
a red tile roof, an elegant lantern, and an arcade running across
the entire front of the Mediterranean-style edifice, are features
of the two story building. In 1976 plans to raze the small building led to a "Save the Alamo" campaign. By 1979, enough funds
were raised to move the building to its present location and restore it.[3] The building is now a visitor information center with a
medical museum, meeting rooms, and administrative offices for
the huge Jackson Memorial Hospital complex, named after the
city's first doctor, Dr. James M. Jackson. In the areas beyond downtown Miami, another notable community building, also designed
by August Geiger, is the four-story Miami Women's Club (originally Woman's Club, 1925). It was formerly the Flagler library,
on North Bayshore Drive. Three sides enclose a garden courtyard
in this Mediterranean-style U-shaped building. The front of the
building faces Biscayne Bay and features a porte cochere, elliptical arches and a balustered parapet, and arched windows on the
top floor.

109. The Alamo, 1611 N.W. 12th
Avenue, Miami. 1918. Architect,
August Geiger.

110. Miami Senior High School, front facade, 2450 S.W. 1st Street, Miami. 1927. Architects, Kiehnel and Elliott. (Photo dated 1938.)

Educational Buildings. The original Miami High, built in 1902, was a two-room wood structure. It was located behind the Miami Public School, a small elementary school at what is now 301 N.E. 1st Avenue. In 1911, the two structures were replaced by a larger three-story building called Central School. The present complex, the Miami Senior High School, was built in 1927 and opened on Valentine's Day, 1928 (Figure 110).[4] A Romanesque style was used in the design of the buildings of the school by the architects, Kiehnel and Elliott. The imposing long two-story facade is punctuated by two taller end pavilions. Dominating the facade is a central four-story pavilion that features an arcade and window openings of rounded arches. Other attributes of the complex are the four large courtyards, the many colonnades, the heavy oak entrance doors with wrought iron hinges, and red roof tiles. Inside the building there is a Denman Fink mural depicting famous American figures. The auditorium has a magnificent proscenium, which is framed in an elaborate frieze, and enormous chandeliers. Another school from the period of the late 1920s and early 1930s is Edison Middle School. A Moderne-style building designed by Pfeiffer and Robertson, it too has an outstanding auditorium. Interestingly, the original school building was designed in 1928 by H. Hastings Mundy in the "Prairie Style."[5]

The Cushman School, designed by Russell Pancoast and Russell Skiptin, is a two-story corner building in modified Mission style. This private elementary school has been in operation continuously since 1924.

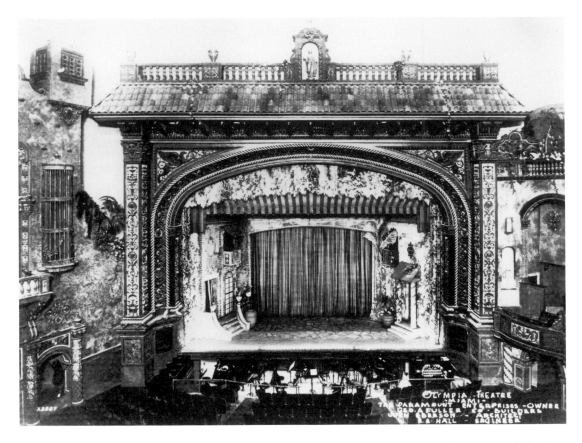

III. Original Olympia Theater proscenium/Maurice Gusman Center, 174 E. Flagler Street, Miami. 1925. Architect, John Eberson of Chicago.

Entertainment Buildings. The Lyric Theater (1910–1914) is the oldest theater in Miami and is now being restored.[6] It was built by a black developer, Geder Walker, with the primary function to show silent movies and present vaudeville performances. The most notable entertainment building in downtown Miami is the Olympia Theater and Office Building. It has been known as the Maurice Gusman Center since 1972, when Maurice Gusman donated the refurbished building to the City of Miami. The exterior of the ten-story building, designed by John Eberson, is a fine example of the application of the Mediterranean style to a high-rise commercial structure. Suggestive Venetian palazzo motifs on the top floor of the facades are continued in the theater's interior. The auditorium is meant to suggest an urban square with side walls representing enclosing palazzo facades. Despite the presence of large crystal chandeliers, the 246 twinkling ceiling lights and the artificial cloud machine manage to create for members of the audience the fantasy that they are seated outdoors in a Venetian square observing a glorious spectacle presented in front of them. The original proscenium had a richly decorated elliptical arch that supported a projecting balcony, on carved corbels, with a balustered parapet rail (Figure 111). Still flanking the stage area on both sides is a wall facade that resembles a bay from an ornate Venetian Gothic palace. The auditorium walls, the ceilings of the mezzanine, and loge balconies are embellished with paintings and ornate, painted plaster ornaments. It was one of the first theaters in the South, and the first building in Miami to be air-conditioned.[7] The movie shown at the grand opening of the Olympia Theater on 11 February 1926 was the silent *Grand Duchess and the Waiter*, starring Adolphe Menjou and Florence Vidor.

Government Buildings. Built in 1825, the longest-standing structure in Greater Miami is the sixty-five-foot-tall Cape Florida Lighthouse. It was rebuilt in 1846 after its destruction during an Indian raid. The design is not local; the standard lighthouse design was constructed of imported red brick. More typical of the vernacular buildings of the time was the Biscayne House of Refuge. It was constructed by the United States Coast Guard on Miami Beach near Indian Creek in 1875. The structure was raised off the ground, with a wraparound veranda and wood posts, steep-pitch hipped roof, and a row of dormer windows on both sides of the roof. Other notable government buildings that do not exist today were the Miami City Hall and adjacent Fire Station buildings on present-day Flagler Street. Both buildings were designed by Walter DeGarmo.

The original Dade County Courthouse (1899) was a two-story wood frame building that was built on the Miami River, just east of the old Miami Avenue bridge.[8] This structure was replaced in 1904 by a neoclassical-style building. An elegant Ionic column portico, a classical pediment, rusticated external walls, and a dome on top of an octagonal tower, are attributes of this building. A third building was constructed between 1925 and 1928 around the 1904 building. The new, tall Dade County Courthouse was for decades a landmark in Dade County, especially at night when the building was illuminated (Figure 112). The Courthouse building, designed by A. Ten Eyck Brown and August Geiger, shares the same design scheme as the Freedom Tower building. There is a tripartite form of facade organization in which the structure is divided vertically into three parts—a base, a tower, and a crown. The base is formed by a squat, three-story square building with cut-out corners and front faces of Doric half-columns. There are balustered parapet rails. The twelve-story square tower above is crowned with a five-story structure that has chamfered corners, with Corinthian pilasters, an encircling frieze, decorated pediments on each of the four facades, and a pyramidical roof. Ceiling mosaics and etched brass elevator doors decorate the lobby of the building. The predominant Beaux Arts–Renaissance style used in the design of the commercial build-

112. Dade County Courthouse
(built around the original 1904
building), 73 W. Flagler Street,
Miami. 1926. Architects, A. Ten
Eyck Brown of Atlanta and
August Geiger. (Photo dated
16 April 1933.)
113. Old United States
Courthouse, 300 N.E. 1st
Avenue, Miami. 1931. Architect,
Phineas Paist.
114. Gesu Church, 118–170 N.E.
2nd Street, Miami. 1922.
Architect, Orin T. Williams.

112

ings in downtown Miami applies also to the government buildings located there. Corinthian columns and pilasters, for example, are the major features in the frontages of the three-story former Miami Post Office and Courthouse (1931). Since 1978 the building has served as a United States Federal Courthouse (Figure 113). The entrance lobbies of this building are also decorated with coffered ceilings and brass postal fixtures. Phineas Paist, the architect, designed the building with an inner patio. This splendid colonnaded courtyard offers welcome shade and the cooling sound of gushing water from a fountain to counteract the heat of the South Florida summers. Denman Fink was responsible for the mural in the second-floor courtroom. A "pyramidical" composition is used for the mural. The figure of Justice is at the peak. Below, as the base of the invisible pyramid, is the evolution of Miami from a wilderness to a modern city, paralleling the theme of this book. Scenes still important to life in Miami are depicted in the design. On the left side of the mural are views of American Indian life; in the center, scenes of pioneer agricultural bustle; and on the right, a panorama of contemporary cultural endeavors in music, architecture, science, and the arts. Lush trees on the extreme left of the mural are replaced on the extreme right by buildings under construction. A bathing beauty under a swaying palm tree, with pleasure craft as a backdrop, is portrayed in the background on the far right.

113

Religious Buildings. The architect of the Gesu Catholic Church (1922) was Orin T. Williams (Figure 114). In this building he followed the typical Renaissance tripartite building composition, but in modified form. On the front facade the base of the edifice is a colonnade of three large arches. In the middle and set back is a short tower. Each of the four sides of this tower has small triple

114

115. Central Baptist Church, N.E. 4th Street portico, 500 N.E. 1st Avenue, Miami. 1927.
116. Mahi Shrine Temple/ Boulevard Shops, 1410 Biscayne Boulevard, Miami. 1930. Architect, Robert Law Weed.
117. Scottish Rite Temple, 471 N.W. 3rd Street, Miami. 1922. Architects, Kiehnel and Elliott. (Photo dated 1938.)

115

arches. Above at the crest of the front face of the tower there is a pediment. The top of the building is a square tower of two tiers, the crowning tier smaller than the one below it. A wide barrel-vaulted nave is lit by magnificent stained glass arched windows. Above the marble altar, below the curve of the barrel-shaped ceiling, is a painting that depicts a procession of pilgrims from various ancient and modern times. Another fine classical Renaissance-style building is the four-story Central Baptist Church (1927) with its symmetrically tripartite composed facades (Figure 115). Distinctive features are a projecting pedimented portico in the center of each of the two street-frontage facades, and the gilded cupola above the tiled roof dome. The lower-level windows of the social hall are stained glass.

Designed by Robert Law Weed, the Mahi Shrine Temple (1936), now the Boulevard Shops, is also an Early Moderne structure in the area (Figure 116). An even earlier Moderne-design building, preceding those in Miami Beach, is the Scottish Rite Temple (1922 [Figure 117]). The portico facade of the building is a prime example of Art Deco Moderne. Surface decorations are Egyptian-inspired. Four large two-headed eagles appear on the parapet. A distinctive feature is the ziggurat roof. The Scottish Rite Temple was designed by Kiehnel and Elliott, as were the Barclay Plaza and Carlyle hotels in Miami Beach. These architects are better known, however, for the exemplary Mediterranean style they used in the other buildings

116

they designed, including El Jardin and the Players State Theater in Coconut Grove, as well as the Elementary School and Congregational Church in Coral Gables. Richard Kiehnel was in charge of the firm's Miami office when it opened in 1917; he was thus instrumental in the establishment of the Mediterranean-style in Greater Miami.

A contrast in approach is the front facade of the Trinity Episcopal Church (1924), designed by H. Hastings Mundy. Romanesque concern for articulation and the use of decoration to emphasize architectural elements is displayed in the facade. Articulation is apparent in the division of the projecting porch into three bays, which reflects the interior separation of space. Also, turrets are used to accentuate the corners of both the porch and main building behind. Decoration is confined to the area around the three arched doorways and the semicircular mosaic panels above each door. In 1970, the church became the cathedral of the South Florida Episcopal Diocese.

117

Miami Beach

In Miami Beach the notable historic-style public buildings are located mainly on Washington Avenue and Lincoln Road. Buildings are chiefly in the Moderne style, mainly Depression Moderne.

Commercial Buildings. The Moderne-style buildings in Miami Beach tend to be of one story compared to the three stories common for hotels and two stories for apartment houses. Also, color is a distinguishing characteristic of the commercial buildings of Miami Beach. The Friedman's Bakery Building (1934) by E. L. Robertson, for example, is still noted for its confection of pink, blue, green, and white colors on its incised and fluted exterior walls and ziggurat roof (Figure 118). Dazzling images from the two sides of this corner building have been used in articles about the Art Deco District in architectural and other publications.[9] Nearby in the same street, there is another corner building where color is used in a similar manner. Conspicuous aspects of this latter building are the classical references in the stylized Corinthian capitals and acanthus friezes. In contrast to these two buildings is the two-story block-long Kress Company structure (1935), by T. H. Henderson, with its plain keystone facade. It was restored in 1982. The building has rounded corners with the three-story Cinema Theater edifice at the center.

118. Friedman's Bakery Building, 675 Washington Avenue, Miami Beach. 1934. Architect, E. L. Robertson.
119. Washington Storage, 1001 Washington Avenue, Miami Beach. 1927. Architects, Robertson and Patterson.
120. Chase Federal Savings and Loan Association Building, 1100 Lincoln Road, Miami Beach. 1947. Architect, August Geiger.

118

119

The Washington Storage Company Building (1927) is the only notable commercial building in South Beach not in the Moderne style (Figure 119). Robertson and Patterson, the architects, used instead Spanish Baroque motifs in the large cast applique in stucco above the entrance doors and in the two bands of friezes across the facade. As one would expect in a storage building, there are virtually no windows; but fenestration is alluded to in the pattern of blank recessed panels. The building was originally used to store the furniture of the seasonal visitors from the north. It has now been converted by the Wolfson Foundation to house a collection of twentieth-century art and books.

The Chase Federal Bank, formerly the Chase Federal Savings and Loan Association Building (1947), designed by August Geiger, is one of the last Moderne works in Miami Beach (Figure 120). The austere stepped-back frontage, faced in stone, is dominated by the stylized pediment and fluted pilasters that frame the entrance.

120

At the peak of the pediment is a relief of the American double-eagle symbol around the Chase company emblem. Entrance doors, decorated with chrome bosses, are framed by a vast tall glass panel.

Cultural and Educational Buildings. The Miami Beach Library and Art Center (1930) is another example of the Depression Moderne style (Figure 121). The Russell T. Pancoast design features symmetrically arranged cubic masses faced in keystone with few decorative elements. These elements, bas-reliefs by Gustav Bohland, are confined to three areas. First are the nature scenes set above each of the three entrance archways. Then there are the two wrought-iron sidelights on either side of the central archway. Finally, there are the three protruding seagulls at each of the chamfered corners of the parapet. When a new, larger library was built on Collins Avenue in 1962, the original library building became the home of the multimillion art collection donated by philanthropists John and Johanna Bass. The building was renamed the Bass Museum of Art and reopened in April 1964.[10] Arata Isozaki, the internationally famous architect, designed a visionary plan for the Museum property in 1993. He proposed an expansion of the museum building and the creation of a vast sculpture garden.

Entertainment Buildings. Hoffman's Cafeteria Building (1940), which later became the Warsaw Ballroom, was closed for many years before it was reopened in 1987 and occupied by various clubs (Figure 122). Henry Hohauser, the architect, created an admirable

121. Miami Beach Library and Art Center/Bass Museum of Art, 2121 Park Avenue, Miami Beach. 1930. Architect, Russell T. Pancoast.

122. Hoffman's Cafeteria, 1450
Collins Avenue, Miami Beach.
1940. Architect, Henry
Hohauser.

design solution for this corner building. Seen from a standpoint di-
agonally across Collins Avenue, each of the two side wings appears
to rise toward the striking corner structure by means of scalloped
parapets. A sequence of ever-larger concentric porthole symbols
provides accents. The structure commands the corner by means
of its geometrical form and two monumental round-edged pylons.
Between the pylons at the beveled corner are a pair of entrance
doors. Above these is a thin projecting horizontal slab that joins
the two pylons together. Above the slab is a large fluted cylinder
form backed by a circular tower. Smooth surfaces of the building's
exterior are relieved by various elements. These include the thin
raised horizontal bands above the windows, the narrow vertical
fluting below the windows, and the fluting at the top of the straight
parapets and the top of the tower. Each pylon has a central flagstaff
at the top.

The splendor of Moderne interior design is superbly displayed in
the French Casino supper club (1936), designed by R. E. Collins
and T. Lamb. After World War II, the building was converted to
the Cinema Theater. Following a renovation in the early 1980s, it
became a club again. In the lobby, glittering chandeliers, glowing
neon lighting, glistening metal trim, mirrored pillars, a pearly wall-
length bar, etched mirrors, and sweeping staircases challenge the
viewer's senses. In the auditorium, the cantilevered circular balconies and box seating are accentuated by their bands of color and
shiny chrome handrails. Matching colorful murals extend over the
entire large expanse of each of the two side walls. In the Cameo

123 124

Theatre (1938), also designed by R. E. Collins, the main Moderne characteristics of the front facade are confined to the large panel above the marquee (Figure 123). At the top of the panel is a large carved keystone frieze with foliage patterns around a central medallion of a female effigy. Between the frieze and marquee, there is a framed window of glass blocks. The Lincoln Theatre (1935), designed by T. Lamb, also has a carved and patterned keystone frieze on the facade, but it is smaller than the one in the Cameo (Figure 124).

Government Buildings. The first City Hall building (1927) was constructed on Washington Avenue after the devastating hurricane of September 1926. Martin L. Hampton, the architect of the building, designed it with Beaux Arts massing and Mediterranean details (Figure 125). A two-story horizontal structure forms the base for a nine-story tower that is placed at the center of the base structure. On either side of the entrance, large arched windows make up the facade of the first floor. The arch theme is repeated elsewhere on the exterior, both in the central windows of the penultimate floor of the tower and as blind arches on the facade of the pavilion that forms the top floor. Other prominent Mediterranean motifs are the red-tile hipped roofs and the Italian Renaissance balusters and urns. After the construction of the new City Hall building on Convention Center Drive, the old City Hall structure was renovated in 1987. It was used for a short time as the Miami Beach campus of the University of Miami.

An illustration of the sparse nature of the Depression Moderne facade style is the United States Post Office building, designed by Howard L. Cheney and completed in 1939 (Figure 126). It is an L-shaped building with the entrance at the corner of the L that is dominated by a rotunda. This circular structure is flanked on either side by lower rectangular masses. The smooth stucco surfaces of the building's geometrical masses are left unadorned. The roof of the rotunda is topped by a lantern. Dominating the internal

123. Cameo Theatre, 1443 Washington Avenue, Miami Beach. 1938. Architect, Robert E. Collins.
124. Lincoln Theatre, 555 Lincoln Road, Miami Beach. 1935. Architect, Thomas W. Lamb.
125. Old City Hall, 1130 Washington Avenue, Miami Beach. 1927. Architect, Martin L. Hampton.

125

wall of the rotunda is a large tripartite mural by Charles Hardman that was installed in 1941. The mural depicts three scenes from Florida's history, the meeting between Native Americans and Ponce de León, their battle with DeSoto, and their confrontation with American army commanders. The focal point of the circular ceiling, a sunburst around the geometrical light grille, is also by Hardman. The mailboxes and stamp tables are among other elements in the Moderne style. In 1977, the Post Office was the first building to be restored in the Art Deco District.[11]

Religious Buildings. A Spanish Colonial Revival style is exemplified in the Miami Beach Community Church (1921), designed by Walter DeGarmo. An elaborately decorated central feature and attached ornamentation around the entry overshadows the simple mass of the front facade. The wall finish is rough-textured stucco. In 1949, a Parish Hall designed by Russell Pancoast was added.

Coral Gables[12]

Commercial Buildings. All the notable historic-style commercial buildings in Coral Gables are located in the downtown area of the City, mainly along Ponce de León Boulevard. These buildings are virtually all in the Mediterranean style. Many were designed by Phineas Paist, with Denman Fink usually involved as artistic advisor.

Most impressive of the commercial buildings is the Colonnade (Figure 127). The building opened in 1926 and was intended to rehouse George Merrick's Coral Gables Sales Organization offices. The Organization never occupied the building, however. It was renamed the Colonnade in 1927 and became the home of the First National Bank of Coral Gables.[13] Over the years, the Colonnade has housed many operations, including a motion picture studio in 1940 and a training center for pilots during the Second World War. In 1988, the Colonnade was renovated and linked to a massive block-length, multistory Mediterranean Revival building behind it. The additional height of the new building over the thirteen-story zoning limit overpowers the historic Colonnade building; it was a bonus as part of the Mediterranean Ordinance referred to previously. The front facade of the Colonnade is distinguished by the commanding two-story Corinthian columns. These are placed on tall bases along the entire length of the building. A two-story arched and ornate Spanish Baroque portal in the center is another major feature. The architects, Phineas Paist in collaboration with Walter DeGarmo and Paul Chalfin, also designed a singular rotunda reminiscent of Roman models. Decorative panels ring the crown of the seventy-five-foot-high drum that has a Spanish tile roof topped by a circular lantern.

Other commercial buildings in downtown Coral Gables in Mediterranean style are small two- or three-story structures (see Figure 128). Originally, the first floor was typically devoted to retail use and the second floor (as well as the third floor, where there was one) to living quarters for the shopkeeper and his family. Paist was

127. Colonnade Building, 133–169 Coral Way (Miracle Mile), Coral Gables. 1925. Architects, Phineas Paist, Walter DeGarmo and Paul Chalfin. (Photo dated c. 1940.)

128

the architect for the H. N. Deitrich Commercial Building (1926), which is characterized by the large arched windows that run the full length of the first floor (Figure 129). He also designed the Coral Gables Bakery Building (1927), which features a second floor arcaded balcony and wrought ironwork balustrade and window grilles (Figure 130). He was responsible also for the Granada Shops (1925) and the Charade Restaurant (since 1960), noted for its patio, tile floor, and cypress ceiling. Phineas Paist made an exception to the Mediterranean style in his fine Renaissance-styled structure, the one-story Bank of Coral Gables Building (1924). This building housed a post office that was separated from the bank by a courtyard. The edifice is not recognizable today in the drastically

129

130

altered building that is now the Coral Gables First Presbyterian Church.

Phineas Paist and most of the other architects and artists who worked for George Merrick on the Coral Gables development, had their offices and studios in the three-story Art Center Building (Figure 131). This building was built in 1925 and designed by Paist. Since 1972, the architectural firm of Ferguson Glasgow and Schuster has occupied the building. The three-tiered entrance tower of the Art Center consists of a two-story hexagonal lower section, topped on the third level by a smaller multisided structure that features pilasters and blind arches. A small drum structure with a tiled roof crowns the whole. It was also in 1925 that another

131

132

architect, H. George Fink, the prolific designer of Mediterranean-
and Vernacular-style private buildings in Coral Gables, designed
his own office building. The small two-story building on Ponce de
León Boulevard is, oddly enough, in an interpretative Medieval
Revival manner. Of note are the delicate tracery of the three narrow Gothic arches, the leaded windows, and the arched pediment
above the first-floor balcony, on the facade.

In 1924 the John M. Stabile Building (Books and Books since
1982) was one of the earliest commercial structures in Coral Gables
(Figure 132). It set the tone for the Mediterranean style of architecture. The chamfered corner of the two-story building is dominated
by the ornate entrance with its wooden doors, decorated pilasters,
and elaborately carved pediment. On the Salzedo Street facade,
the second-floor wooden balcony is supported by four cypress
brackets. Its shed tiled roof, an extension of the main roof, is
bolstered by two turned and carved columns. J. P. Turner's First
National Bank Building (1926) on Ponce de León Boulevard is one
of the splendid Mediterranean-style small commercial structures
in downtown Coral Gables (Figure 133). The three-story building
has a symmetrical facade with a central two-story arch supported
on slender Corinthian columns. On top of the second floor is a
decorative entablature, while the third floor features a bas-relief.
The new Bank of Coral Gables Building is an excellent example of
the current Mediterranean Revival trend (Figure 134).

George Merrick planned his City Beautiful with several different
functional sections.[14] Between Red Road and Alhambra Circle and
between Coral Way and Anastasia Avenue was to be the original
Business Section. Commercial Entrance, on Douglas Road, was to
provide an impressive approach. Alhambra Circle was intended to

132. John M. Stabile Building, 296 Aragon Avenue, Coral Gables. 1924; 1928 addition, architect John Davis. (Photo dated 1924.)

133. First National Bank Building of Coral Gables, 2312 Ponce de Leon Boulevard. 1926. Architect, J. P. Turner.

134. New Bank of Coral Gables Building, 2701 Ponce de Leon Boulevard. 1985. Architect, David Case of Ferguson Glasgow and Schuster.

133

134

be the principal street. Instead, Sections K and L became the Business Section of the city. This is the area between Douglas Road and Le Jeune Road, and Coral Way and Alhambra Circle. Coral Way, renamed Miracle Mile by the local merchants, became the main business street after World War II.

In 1925, George Merrick purchased the Le Jeune Plantation to the west to open the Biltmore Section. This area stretches from Le Jeune Road to Anderson Road, and from Coral Way to Altamari Avenue. This new section was centered on Biltmore Way, a boulevard that linked the business area and the Miami-Biltmore Hotel. Merrick intended this to be a "New Fifth Avenue." He also opened the Craft Section, south of Coral Way/Miracle Mile, centered on Ponce de León Boulevard. His aim was to provide craftspersons, who were to furnish and embellish the buildings of Coral Gables, with workshops and showrooms on the Boulevard. This goal was never realized. Ponce de León Circle was to be the focal point of the Craft Section. It was also to have an exposition building to display artistic wares created in the various shops in the section. The small homes on the east side of Ponce de León were intended for the artisans and shopkeepers who chose not to live above their workshops or stores. The Granada Shops building, designed by Phineas Paist, was originally the successful furniture store and workshop of the brothers Ralph and Leland Wilkins. Leland also owned another store on Ponce de León Boulevard that he ran with his parents. The Leland Wilkins Shop (1925), by R. F. Ware, is typical of the Craft Section shops. It is small with a simple asymmetrical stucco facade, arched first-floor openings, a second-floor wrought-iron balcony, and tiled roof.

Community Buildings. On Aragon Avenue is the Medical Center Building (1927), which originally housed doctors' offices (Figure 135). It served patients as far north as Stuart and as far south as Key West. Many came from Cuba and other countries in South

135. Coral Gables Medical Center Building, 265 Aragon Avenue. 1927. Architect, Lee Wade.

136. Coral Gables Elementary
School, 105 Minorca Avenue.
1923–1926. Architect, Richard
Kiehnel.

America. The one-story symmetrical building, designed by Lee
Wade, has two identical wings connected by a recessed central arcade. In each wing, all three openings are arched. Behind the arcade
is a secluded courtyard. Mediterranean-style features continue in
the stucco finish of the exterior walls and the tiled parapet. The
one-story Coral Gables Women's Club on Ponce de León Boulevard
was constructed in the mid–1930s. It has a simple style with exposed cut oolitic limestone and tiled gable roofs. The building, the
first to be constructed by the federal Works Progress Administration in Coral Gables, housed an enlarged city library facility. The
library was formerly located in the Douglas Entrance and managed
by the Coral Gables Women's Club.

Educational Buildings. Three blocks north of Alhambra Circle on
Ponce de León Boulevard is what must surely be one of the finest
Mediterranean-style school buildings in Greater Miami. The Coral
Gables Elementary School, one of the first public structures in the
City of Coral Gables, was designed by Richard Kiehnel (Figure
136). It was built in three phases between 1923 and 1926. The 900-
seat auditorium that fronts onto the Boulevard has an imposing
entrance, consisting of a portico of three semicircular arches on
the first floor with a five-bay arcaded, gabled porch on the second
floor directly above. On either side of the portico are staircases
that provide access to the porch. A diagonal element in the symmetrical composition of the facade is provided by the walls of the
staircase. The classroom building to the east of the auditorium on
Minorca Way contains the main and original 1923 entrance to the
school. Climatic considerations are evident in the cross-ventilated

classrooms, and the arcaded loggias that shade these rooms from the sun. Mediterranean-style motifs are also visible in the two large courtyards, the stucco walls, and the tiled roofs.

University/Ponce de León High School (1925) was the second public school to be built in Coral Gables (Figure 137). The architect, H. George Fink, planned nine buildings clustered around a central commons. He designed the first three buildings in a severe Renaissance style. When the new Coral Gables High School was opened at the corner of Le Jeune and Bird Roads in 1950, Ponce became a junior high school.

George Fink was also responsible for the design of the Anastasia Hotel (Figure 138). The building was partially finished when it was leased by the newly chartered University of Miami. Its own facilities were not yet completed, and it needed the building so that it could offer the first classes on 18 October 1926. The epithet "Cardboard College" came about as temporary walls were constructed to create the classroom spaces. Arched openings on the first floor and the corner Renaissance-style tower characterized the three-story L-shaped building, completed only in 1942. The building was purchased by the University in 1936. By the time the original Classroom Building was demolished in 1968, the University had built many new buildings on its own campus. This was a tract of 160 acres bounded by San Amaro Drive, Campo Sano Avenue, University Drive, and South Dixie Highway, donated by George Merrick. Later the campus was expanded to its current size of 240 acres.

The original campus plan was prepared under instructions from Merrick. There were to be twenty buildings in Italian Renaissance style. The first edifice to be constructed was the administrative building, donated by George Merrick as a memorial for his father

137. University/Ponce De León High School, 1000 Augusto Avenue, Coral Gables. 1925. Architect, H. George Fink.
138. Anastasia Hotel/University of Miami Classroom Building, 515 University Drive, Coral Gables. 1926; Tower completed 1942. Architect, H. George Fink. (Building later demolished.)
139. Original Administration Building (only structural skeleton built), University of Miami, northeast of School of Business Building, Coral Gables Campus. 1926. Architect, Phineas Paist. Rendering by Denman Fink.

137

138

(Figure 139). After the 1926 hurricane, the collapse of the land boom, and the stock market crash, the skeleton of the building stood uncompleted for over twenty years. In the meantime, the university operated at its temporary facility in the converted Anastasia Hotel. The end of World War II brought a flood of students, former soldiers under the G.I. Bill. Revival of the abandoned building program became necessary. Temporary wooden structures were first erected, followed by the completion of the Memorial Classroom Building, the unfinished Merrick Building, twenty-seven apartment buildings for the students, and the Student Club. Phineas Paist's Mediterranean design for the Merrick Building (the uncompleted original administration building) was abandoned. All the buildings subsequently were in the prevailing Modern style of architecture.

139

140

Entertainment Buildings. What could be more Spanish than the Dream Theatre (1926), an outdoor movie house on Ponce de León Boulevard? It was designed by John and Coulton Skinner to resemble a bull ring. Bougainvillea and tropical vines covered the curved wall that enclosed the open-air seating area where patrons watched their Hollywood stars flicker silently across the large screen. The building has been remodeled, and the seating area is now a parking lot for Consolidated Bank.

A. Ten Eyck Brown's neoclassical-style Coliseum on Douglas Road was originally planned as a 7,500-seat cultural center (Figure 140). After completion, in 1927, the building never served its purpose owing to the poor financial conditions of the late 1920s and early 1930s. Subsequently, the structure was devoted mainly to entertainment uses, such as a World War II pilot training center, an ice skating rink and bowling alley, and a health club. It was demolished in 1993 to make way for a merchandise mart.

The Country Club of Coral Gables was built in the heart of the residential area (Figure 141). Its purpose was to entertain prospective land buyers. Growing demand led to the addition of a two-story structure only a year after the clubhouse was built in 1923.

140. The Coliseum, 1500 Douglas Road, Coral Gables. 1927. (Building demolished July 1993.) Rendering by architect A. Ten Eyck Brown.
141. Country Club addition, 997 North Greenway Drive, Coral Gables. 1985. Architect, David Harum. (Original 1923–1924 building destroyed in a 1983 fire. Architects, Hampton and Reimert.)
142. Venetian Pool and Casino, 2701 De Soto Boulevard, Coral Gables. 1923–1924. Architects, Denman Fink and Phineas Paist.

141

The focal point of the building, designed by Hampton and Reimert, was the three-stage tower that incorporated the main entrance to the clubhouse. A six-bay arcaded loggia enabled diners to watch play on the adjoining Granada Golf Course. Up to five hundred diners could be seated in the large dining room. The original out-door terrazzo dance floor later became the swimming pool and main lounge. A fire in 1983 destroyed almost all of the original building.[15]

The Venetian Pool has maintained its original and popular use as a unique swimming pool (Figure 142). It was initially a quarry pit for the oolitic limestone used in many early buildings and roads in Coral Gables. Concern about the eyesore led to the pit's conversion into a recreational facility in 1924. The designers of the Venetian Pool, Denman Fink and Phineas Paist, created an ir-regularly shaped pool about 300 feet by 200 feet. Their deliberate organic approach led to a natural-looking pool with rock outcrop-pings to provide cliffs. One of these was made into a diving plat-form. Underwater caves and cascades of falling water were other features. The whole complex was lushly landscaped. To create a feeling of old-world charm, the designers incorporated Venetian features: lamp posts and a bridge linking a small palm island to the Casino. The three-story tower buildings of the Casino were to pro-vide entertainment areas (excluding gambling) to take advantage of the poolside, and mundane functions such as dressing rooms and lockers. Between the square towers were a pergola, under which

142

outdoor meals and refreshments were served, and a terrazzo dance floor. There was also a loggia and a Spanish fountain with dazzling colored ceramic tiles. Until the water crisis of the mid-1980s, the Venetian Pool was drained every night during the summer months and was refilled with 800,000 gallons of unchlorinated water from artesian wells. In the past also, the pool has been drained and used as an amphitheater for orchestra concerts and opera performances. The audience was seated on bleachers supported by scaffolding especially built for the occasion. In 1989, a substantial restoration of the complex was completed. This work included digging of two deep wells into the Biscayne Aquifer. Water was now to be discharged and returned to the aquifer to prevent wastage, as required by the South Florida Water Management Board.

Government Buildings. The original City Hall Building (1922) on Alhambra Circle (now the Coral Gables American Legion Post) was replaced in 1927–1928. Its successor is the most imposing of the notable public buildings in Coral Gables, the new City Hall on Biltmore Way (Figure 143). Phineas Paist and Harold Steward were the designers. The western end of the visual axis of Coral Way/Miracle Mile terminates at Le Jeune Road in the monumental semicircular wing of the City Hall. The semicircle consists of a colonnade of twelve Corinthian columns and an entablature topped by a series

143. Coral Gables City Hall, 405 Biltmore Way. 1927–1928. Architects, Phineas Paist and Harold Steward with Denman Fink, artistic advisor.

144. Old Fire House and Police Station, 285 Aragon Avenue, Coral Gables. 1939. Architect, Phineas Paist.

of stone balusters. At the center, providing the focus of the balustrade is a large Baroque panel. It contains the coat of arms of Coral Gables, designed by Denman Fink as a shield with the emblems of a crocodile, a fish, and a lion. On either side of the shield are the symbolic figures of art and labor; the back of the shield portrays the Venetian Pool Casino. Behind the colonnade is a loggia associated with the Commission Council Chamber that sits in the semicircular wing. The three-story rectangular building that forms the remainder of the City Hall is crowned by a three-tiered clock and bell tower. Various departmental offices and the mayor's suite are housed in this part of the building. Inside the tower is a mural, painted by Denman Fink, which depicts the four seasons in radiant colors.

At the end of the 1930s, the two-story Old Fire House and Police Station was built (Figure 144). Like the Women's Club, it was designed in Depression Moderne style with oolitic limestone; but the architect, Phineas Paist, blended in Mediterranean details such as the arched second-floor windows and arched openings in the three-story tower on the northwest corner of the building. On the first floor of the tower was the firefighters' recreation room. The top of the tower was originally intended for hose drying but was later used to hold the water tank. Firefighters used the rest of the tower for training. Entrance to the Police Station was on Aragon Avenue. It was marked by carved stone pelicans perched above the first floor. Until 1975, the building was in use as both fire and police stations. Then the stations moved to larger quarters further south on Salzedo Road.

145. Alhambra Water Tower, Alhambra Circle, Greenway Court, and Ferdinand Street. 1924. Concept by Denman Fink. (Under restoration in August 1993.)

In 1924, Denman Fink conceived of a pair of water towers, each to resemble a lighthouse, for the City of Coral Gables. Only the Alhambra Water Tower remains; the second tower, at Indian Mound Trail and Valencia Avenue, was damaged in the 1926 hurricane and never rebuilt. The Alhambra Water Tower consists of a square base, and an octagonal tower topped by a dome and finial (Figure 145). Stucco surfaces were originally relieved by slender arched openings, a decorative balustrade on curved brackets between the base and tower, and a sundial. The City of Coral Gables is restoring the water tower, which was in service until 1931, when Coral Gables began to obtain water from the City of Miami.

Religious Buildings. Coral Gables Congregational Church, opposite the Miami-Biltmore Hotel, was the first church built in the City (Figure 146). When it was dedicated on Palm Sunday, 1925, the church was among the first public buildings built in Coral Gables. It was used by many organizations as a meeting place. The architects, Kiehnel and Elliott, who also designed the Coral Gables Elementary School, created a flamboyant Spanish Baroque portal for the entrance to the church. Less ornate in appearance is the campanile. Also with an ornate Baroque portal is the Saint Theresa Catholic Church of the Little Flower, designed by Barry and Kay in 1951 to replace the original 1927 building, which is now the Parish Hall (Figure 147). The two-story First/Central Christian Church

Three Coral Gables Churches
146. Coral Gables
Congregational Church, 3010 De
Soto Boulevard. 1923–1924.
Architects, Kiehnel and Elliott.
147. Saint Theresa Catholic
Church of the Little Flower, 1265
Anastasia Avenue, Coral Gables.
1951. (Original 1927 church
replaced and converted into the
Parish Hall.) Architects, G. M.
Barry and F. O. Kay.
148. First Church of Christ,
Scientist, 419 Andalusia Avenue,
Coral Gables. 1941. Architect,
Phineas Paist. (Built around the
1934 original building.)

146

147

148

(1927), designed by S. S. Hall, and the one-story First Methodist Church (1933), with Paist and Steward as architects, are both unadorned Mediterranean-style buildings. In contrast, the First Church of Christ, Scientist, Building (1941), designed by Phineas Paist, is neoclassical (Figure 148). More specifically, it is Palladian in its centralized plan and symmetrically composed exterior facades.

City Entrances. A special charm is lent to the City of Coral Gables by the entrance gateways that George Merrick envisioned as part of his overall architectural scheme. The formality of the gateways was intentional: they were to announce the entrance into the city from the already established banal developments surrounding his "City Beautiful." Merrick planned eight entrances, all designed by Denman Fink, but four were not completed—the Flagler, Coconut Grove, Gladeside, and Bayside entrances. Three of the four entrances completed are on the City's northern border of S.W. 8th Street.

At the northeast corner of the City is La Puerta de Sol (Gate of the Sun), that opened formally in 1927 (Figure 149). It is better known as the Douglas Entrance. The ten-acre area was originally intended to be an entire village centered on a square. Only the elliptical arched gateway; the imposing tower; two wings of shops, galleries, and apartments; and a ballroom on the uppermost floor

149

150

Four Coral Gables entrances.
149. La Puerta de Sol/Douglas Entrance, S.W. corner of Douglas Road and S.W. 8th Street, Coral Gables. 1925–1927. Architects, Walter DeGarmo and Phineas Paist.
150. Country Club Prado Entrance, Prado and S.W. 8th Street, Coral Gables. 1927. Architect, Denman Fink.
151. Granada Entrance, Granada Boulevard and S.W. 8th Street, Coral Gables. 1922. Architect, Denman Fink. (Photo dated 1993.)
152. Alhambra/Commercial Entrance, intersection of Alhambra Circle, Madeira Avenue, and Douglas Road, Coral Gables. 1923. Architect, Denman Fink.

151

152

were completed. The Mediterranean-style buildings were designed by Walter DeGarmo, Phineas Paist, and Denman Fink, who was also the artistic advisor for all the remaining completed entrances. In 1968, an application to tear down the Douglas Entrance buildings to make a supermarket parking lot generated strong protests from architects and preservationists. The City of Coral Gables was thus led to take its first historic preservation action.

At the northwest corner of the City is the Country Club Prado Entrance (Figure 150). It is more of an open space than anything else when compared to the more urban Douglas Road entrance. An elaborate, formal Italian Garden forms the end of a block-long 240-foot wide oak-lined parkway at the Prado Entrance. An enclosure in the garden is made up of twenty freestanding pillars of stucco, each topped by a classical urn. The pillars circle a reflecting pool that has pedestal fountains at each end.

The Granada Entrance, the first entrance to be built, is almost midway between the Douglas and Prado Entrances on S.W. 8th Street (Figure 151). It consists of a 340-foot-long wall at the center of which is a 40-foot-high arch spanning Granada Boulevard. Both wall and arch are constructed of rough-cast oolitic limestone. Alongside the walls are areas demarcated by floor tiles and wooden pergolas. There are also fountains and benches in various places.

The Alhambra/Commercial Entrance, the fourth completed entrance, is at the junction of Douglas Road, Alhambra Circle, and Madeira Avenue (Figure 152). It has an elliptical arched gateway and a 600-foot curved wall that follows the line of Alhambra Circle. The construction of the entrance follows the natural style of Granada Entrance in its rock wall, pergolas, trellises, and flowering vines. Recently the Coral Gables Garden Club initiated an "adopt-an-entrance" campaign. Their first effort was to complete the work at the Red Road and Coral Way intersection, Merrick's Gladeside Entrance.[16]

Plazas. George Merrick conceived his City Beautiful with both entrances and plazas. Both would be an integral part of the overall scheme. While he envisaged the entrances as the gateways to his city, the plazas were to lend architectural significance to the intersections of major boulevards and roads. Fourteen plazas were planned, all designed by Denman Fink with landscaping by Frank M. Button. Six of the plazas that were built proclaim the crossing of major north-south thoroughfares with Coral Way. From west to east there is, first, Augustine Plaza, where Coral Way meets the most spacious boulevard in the City, Country Club Prado. This boulevard is one and one-half miles long and 200 feet wide, with

153

154

Four Coral Gables plazas.
Architect, Denman Fink;
landscape designer, Frank M.
Button.
153. Ponce de León Plaza, Coral
Way and Granada Boulevard,
Coral Gables, as it was. 1921.
154. Segovia Plaza, Coral Way,
Segovia Street, and North
Greenway Drive, Coral Gables,
as it was. 1925.
155. Granada Plaza, Alhambra
Circle and Granada Boulevard,
Coral Gables, as it was. 1925.
156. De Soto Fountain and Plaza,
Sevilla Avenue, Granada and De
Soto Boulevards, Coral Gables.
1925. (Photo dated 1993.)

155

156

a central parkway. Next is Columbus Plaza at the intersection of Coral Way and Columbus Boulevard. Each corner of this Plaza has a different treatment. The materials used, however, are common. These include rough-cut coral rock, wrought iron, paving of cut oolitic limestone, and vegetation such as bougainvillea, royal poinciana, and sea grape. East of Columbus Plaza is Ponce de León Plaza, at the intersection of Coral Way and Granada Boulevard (Figure 153). The 600-foot-diameter plaza is bordered by fountains, pools, pergolas, and low stuccoed coral rock walls. Farther east along Coral Way, at South Greenway Drive, is Balboa Plaza, with a perimeter of 400 feet. Low walls are of rough-cut rock and these are combined with wrought iron fences, gates, and wooden pergolas. There are also three water fountains. The next plaza is Segovia Plaza at Coral Way and North Greenway Drive (Figure 154). The easternmost of the plazas on Coral Way is Le Jeune Plaza. Its semicircular shape and walls reflect the outline of the City Hall wing on the one side of the plaza.

Two other plazas of note are the Granada and the De Soto Plazas. Granada Plaza features wall fountains, inspired by Spanish models, reflecting pools with sitting ledges, and a pedestal fountain in the center underneath a pergola (Figure 155). A magnificent fountain is the central feature of the most resplendent plaza in Coral Gables, the De Soto Plaza (Figure 156). Two boulevards—De Soto and Granada—intersect with Sevilla Avenue to form a large European-type traffic circle with six approach roads and a central circular pool and fountain. There are three tiered pools, one smaller than the other. Water flows from an upper basin to each of the lower pools

157. Coconut Grove Bank, 3430 Main Highway. C. 1918. Architect, Walter DeGarmo.

158. Pan Am Dinner Key
Terminal/Miami City Hall, 3500
Pan American Drive, Coconut
Grove. 1931.

in turn. At the center of the upper basin is an hexagonal orna-
mented pedestal. It supports a composite column that serves as the
visual focal point of all the roads that converge on De Soto Plaza.

Coconut Grove

Commercial Buildings. Walter DeGarmo designed many public
structures in Coconut Grove. Two of his earlier buildings were the
Coconut Grove Bank (c. 1918 [Fig. 157]) and the Sunshine Building (1923). The architecture of the original buildings was Mission-
style, but both have been extensively altered. Also greatly modified
was the Anthony Arcade and Peacock Plaza Building (1925–1928).
The Plaza Building was noted for its Mediterranean features of
arched windows, balustrades, grillework, parapet, and planter in
the courtyard. The only commercial building whose exterior remains relatively unchanged until today is the Pan American Seaplane Base and Terminal at Dinner Key, built in 1931 (Figure 158).
The two-story Moderne building was purchased from Pan American Airlines by the City of Miami in 1946. It was converted into
the Miami City Hall in 1954.

Community Buildings. In addition to commercial buildings, Walter DeGarmo was also responsible for the design of a community
building. This was the Housekeeper's Club (1921), later renamed
the Women's Club of Coconut Grove. DeGarmo's idea for the building was for a simple one-story rectangular structure with a curvilinear gabled roof. Exterior walls are stuccoed. Oolitic limestone is
used for the wide porch that encircles the building on three sides.
The high ceilings and large arched wall openings allow cooling
breezes to circulate through the building.

Cultural and Educational Buildings. The oldest library in Dade County, the Coconut Grove Library, was founded in 1895. In 1901, the library was moved from its early location, on the second floor of Charles Peacock and Son General Store, to its own structure. The small one-story building, in early American vernacular, was incorporated into the present building in 1963.[17] Coconut Grove was the location of one of Dade County's first public schools. It was opened in 1887 in the home of Samuel Rhodes, but moved into a small wooden structure in 1889. The schoolhouse was sold and became the home of George Richardson in 1894. Ryder Systems bought the structure in 1970, completely restored it, and donated it to the Plymouth Congregational Church, near which it now stands (Figure 159). The two-story wooden buildings of the Adirondack-Florida School were similar in appearance to the Peacock Inn structure. Both had porches on both levels, steep gable roofs, and dormer windows. The Pagoda Building, so-called because of its roof shapes, has grouped windows and corner porches, and is externally faced with vertical boarding. Built in 1902, the building, designed by Greene and Wicks, is elevated off the ground on limestone piers. The structure is still in use as part of Ransom-Everglades School.

Entertainment Buildings. Coconut Grove Playhouse, a three-story building designed by Kiehnel and Elliott, has rich Spanish-style ornamentation, particularly in the elaborate frame around the entranceway (Figure 160). The Playhouse opened as a movie house on 1 January 1927. It was used as such until its conversion to a live theater in 1955.

159

159. Coconut Grove
Schoolhouse, presently located
on the grounds of the Plymouth
Congregational Church. 1889.
(Photo dated 1993.)
160. Coconut Grove Playhouse,
3500 Main Highway. 1926–1927.
Architects, Kiehnel and Elliott.

160

Religious Buildings. One of many Mission-style structures constructed in Dade County during the early part of this century was the original building of Saint Steven's Church (1912). The original church building is now the thrift shop in a complex that includes a large church and social hall, rectory and parsonage that were built during the 1950s. McKenzie based his design for the Plymouth Congregational Church (1917) on an old city Mission church in Mexico. All the stonework was done by a single skilled and dedicated mason. The most notable feature of the exposed stone exterior of the church is the large arched carved wooden front doors (Figure 161). These were brought from an old monastery in the Pyrenees Mountains. The building was paid for through the sale of four lots on the south side. As they were sold to four admirals, the area became known as Admirals' Row. In 1954, the church was enlarged by the addition of two transepts and a new chancel. The

161

162

William Jennings Bryan Memorial Church (1925–1926) is a complete contrast to the style of the Plymouth Congregational Church (Figure 162). Instead of stone it is a bright white geometrical mass. The Bryan Memorial Church is a two-story octagonal-shaped building notable for its arcades, loggias, and Byzantine columns. The roof is topped by a slender copper lantern.

163

North Dade

Community Buildings. There are two structures of unusual interest in North Dade. Both are in North Miami Beach, formerly the town of Fulford. The first structure is the Fulford-by-the-Sea monument built in 1924 to denote the entrance to Fulford (Figure 163). The monument consists of a triumphal arch structure set in the center of a circular fountain. It is a composite of architectural styles. There are Roman-style urns and Corinthian pilasters. There are four pediments with unicorns at each corner. Then there is a dome covered with gold ceramic tile. Finally, there is a fleur-de-lis at the crest. The second structure of unusual interest in North Dade is the Romanesque-style Spanish Monastery described later.

Educational Buildings. The Mediterranean-style William Jennings Bryan Elementary School (1930) in North Miami is a two-story building with arched openings (Figure 164). E. L. Robertson was the architect. On the front facade, there are bas-relief decorations. These consist of ornamentation in each of the three small arches above the second-floor entrance windows and nine carved stone shields at the crest of the entrance tower. Mediterranean features continue in the interior courtyard and arcade. In contrast, the Miami Shores Elementary School (c. 1929), by Robert Law Weed, is one of the earliest Moderne buildings in the Miami area (Figure 165).

164

164. William Jennings Bryan
Elementary School, 1200 N.E.
125th Street, North Miami. 1930.
Architect, E. L. Robertson.
165. Miami Shores Elementary
School, 10351 N.E. 5th Avenue.
C. 1929. Architect, Robert Law
Weed.
166. Old Pump House/
Community Church Chapel, 9823
N.E. 4th Avenue, Miami Shores.
1925.

Entertainment Buildings. Perhaps the most magnificent public structure in North Dade is the Mediterranean-style Hialeah Race Track building (1925). It was constructed initially as a venue for dog races and jai alai, and as a luxuriant landscaped amusement park. In 1932, the structure was rebuilt to offer horse racing and to serve as a tourist attraction.

The Miami Shores Theatre, by Harold Steward, is one of the last Moderne buildings to be built in Dade County. Scheduled to be constructed in 1942, it was delayed until 1946 on account of World War II. Apart from the two "Shores" signs on the marquee, there is no other ornamentation on this Streamline building.

Government Buildings. The Biscayne Park Village Hall (1933) is an exceptional example of log cabin architecture in Dade County. It was constructed under the Works Progress Administration program. Exterior walls are of saddle-notched logs and the roof is covered with wood shingles. Roof trusses are left exposed in the interior.

Built in 1925, the Old Pump House is the oldest building in Miami Shores (Figure 166). This modest and elegant structure was a fire station and waterworks until 1932. It was then used as a community center and now serves as a chapel.

In Opa-locka Glenn Curtiss, along with his architect Bernhardt Muller, fulfilled their Arabian fantasies. They developed the city's

165

downtown public buildings in their version of the Moorish style. The dominant building is the City Hall (1926) with its horseshoe, semicircular, and scalloped arches, horizontal red stripes, domes and minarets (Figure 167). Other structures in a similar style are the railroad station, with its multicolored glazed tiles framing horseshoe-shaped arched openings, the hotel, and former bank buildings. The City Hall and the hotel were restored during the 1980s. The Hunt Building, later the Opa-locka Hotel, also displays Moorish turrets, parapets, and domes.

Religious Buildings. The second structure of unusual interest in North Dade is, strangely, the oldest building in Florida, and one of the oldest in the country—the Romanesque-style Spanish Monastery (Figure 168). This seemingly paradoxical statement is explained by the fact that the structure was built in A.D. 1141 as a Cistercian monastery in Sacremenia, Spain. Political tumult during the 1800s led to the confiscation of the monastery; the building was sold to a farmer who used it for storage. William Randolph Hearst, the newspaper tycoon, bought the structure in 1925. He had it

166

167

carefully disassembled with the intention that it be reconstructed as a chapel on his estate, San Simeon in California. This never came to pass. Instead, developers purchased the crated stones and reassembled the building in its present location in 1953. The Monastery was purchased by the Episcopal Diocese of South Florida in 1964.[18]

South Dade

Commercial Buildings. There is at least one significant historic-style commercial building in each of South Dade's older communities. In South Miami, initially named Larkins, there are several structures. The Dorn Building was built by the brothers Robert and Harold Dorn in 1924–1925. They left Chicago in 1910 and began mango and avocado plantations in Larkins. Near their packing house on South Dixie Highway, across Sunset Drive, they built a three-building complex (Figure 169). First was the Dorn-Martin Drugstore. In the middle was a building designed as a bank but never used as such. On the end was a building leased out as the town's first post office. Each of these buildings has a different appearance. The rectangular two-story structure that faces on both Sunset Drive and S.W. 59th Avenue was the original "drugstore." It is a simple Mission-style building. The other two buildings face South Dixie Highway. The most splendid is the two-story "bank" building. It is noted for its semicircular arched openings that have stone frames with unusual pointed keystones, projecting stone quoins, and decorative parapet. The "post office" edifice is one story with a front facade divided into three segments, each with an arched opening. A pediment crowns the central segment. On South Dixie Highway, close to the packing house, the Dorn brothers built the Riviera Theater (1925). It was later converted

167. Opa-locka Administration Building, 490 Ali
Baba Avenue. 1926. Rendering by the architect,
Bernhardt E. Muller.
168. Spanish Monastery, 16711 West Dixie
Highway, North Miami Beach. Built in
Sacremenia, Spain, A.D. 1141; reassembled on its
present site, 1953.
169. Dorn Building, 5900 Sunset Drive, and
5900, 5904 South Dixie Highway, South Miami.
1924–1925.

168

169

170

170. Riviera Theater/Holsum
Bakery, 5750 Sunset Drive, South
Miami. 1925. (Building later
demolished.)
171. Cauley Square Cottage,
22400 Old Dixie Highway,
Goulds. 1920.
172. Anderson's Corner, 15700
Silver Palm Drive (S.W. 232nd
Street), Silver Palm. 1911–1912.

into the landmark Holsum Bakery (Figure 170). This building and the surrounding structures were demolished in the early 1980s. Their replacement, the economically and architecturally disastrous Bakery Center monolith, is itself scheduled to meet the same fate— to be torn down after a very brief existence.

Two general store buildings in South Dade are architecturally noteworthy. The two-story Cauley Square Building (1920) is Spanish in style but has a flat roof and oolitic limestone-faced accents (Figure 171).[19] Customers were originally farm laborers, railway hands, and farmers. The other, Anderson's Corner (1911–12), primarily served farmers in the Silver Palm area and workers in the lumber camps (Figure 172). It sold everything from "dynamite to lace."[20] The two-story building is the only known commercial structure in wood frame vernacular style that survives from the first two decades of this century. It also retains its original appear-

171

172

ance although it has changed uses and is now a country inn and restaurant.

Many railroad structures were built around 1904, attesting the importance of the railroad in the early development of Greater Miami. The Princeton Depot was typical of the F.E.C.R. building style, although smaller than most of the other depots. The structure was rectangular, one-story, with a gable roof and broad overhangs, supported by curved brackets, over the loading platforms on three sides. Exterior walls were faced with vertical boards. The Homestead Depot building was larger but similar in appearance except for the sash windows (Figure 173). The renovated Homestead Station agent's house is in characteristic wood vernacular style (Figure 174). It is a one-story structure raised slightly off the ground and finished with horizontal weather boarding. There is a front porch with curved brackets and simple supports. The roof is steep and hipped with a dormer window. What distinguished this house from other houses in the area was that the station agent's

173. Homestead Depot, Florida East Coast Railway, 826 Krome Avenue. C. 1904. Destroyed by Hurricane Andrew, it is to be reconstructed by the Florida Pioneer Museum on the basis of the original drawings.
174. Homestead Station agent's house, Florida East Coast Railway, 826 Krome Avenue. C. 1904.
175. Coco Plum Women's Club, 1375 Sunset Drive, Coral Gables. 1926. Architects, Howard and Early.
176. Redland Post Office and Steward Fruit and Candy Store.

home and all F.E.C. Railway buildings were painted a "Flagler Yellow" with white trim. The Perrine packinghouse is one of the few structures still at its original location. Around the station, originally, clustered houses for the station agent, the section supervisor, and workers. The only surviving structure has been greatly altered and has been used by various businesses. Overall, there was a consistency to the railway structures with their large hipped roofs, broad overhangs, simple and solid construction.

Community Buildings. The clubhouse of the Coco Plum Women's Club was built by George Merrick in 1926 in exchange for the Club's selling him four of its five acres of land, which he wished to add to his expanding Coral Gables project. The one-story building, designed by Howard and Early in an elegant Mediterranean style, has a two-story-square tower (Figure 175). At the top of the tower

175

176

a three-bay arcade encloses all four sides. The much earlier Pioneer Guild Hall (1912) in Redland, in contrast, is a one-story wood frame building with horizontal weather boarding, a front porch with shed roof, and a gable roof with a diamond-shaped wood-lattice attic ventilation opening. The Hall was the focal point of Redland community life, where civic, social, and church activities took place. The structure is now used as a grocery store. Similar in construction and appearance was the Redland Post Office and Steward Fruit and Candy Store (Figure 176).

177

177. Larkins/Sunset School (west facade), 5190 Sunset Drive, South Miami. 1915 (various buildings 1911/1924/1939).
178. Homestead Public School, 520 N.W. First Avenue, Homestead. 1914. Renamed the Neva King Cooper School in 1934. Architect, August Geiger.
179. Homestead business section. View south on Krome Avenue. (Photo dated 1939.)

Educational Buildings. Several of the old school buildings that have survived are notable both for their architectural interest and for their reflection of the importance that the pioneer families placed on education. Sunset School (Figure 177), originally Coco Plum and then Larkins School, dates from 1896—South Dade's first schoolhouse. When the one-room school became too small to accommodate the children, a one-story L-shaped frame building in vernacular style was built in 1911 on the present site at the corner of Sunset Drive and Schoolhouse Road. The building has been incorporated into the modern school complex, as was another building for high school students that was built at about the same time. The two-story rectangular main school building dates from 1915. It has a symmetrical front facade with an arcaded loggia on the first floor, and a parapet with three curved pediments. An additional two-story L-shaped wing was added in 1924 and connected to the main structure with arcades. An auditorium was added in 1939, and other buildings over the years.

Nearly as old as the Sunset School is the Silver Palm School, founded as a one-room log cabin schoolhouse in 1902. The present two-story building was built in 1904. Its first floor was devoted to classrooms, while the second floor included a large room for meetings and church services. The main external changes are in the frame vernacular structure, in the porch balustrades, and in the removal of the small rooftop bell tower.

In Redland the little one-story wood frame schoolhouse is used today as a classroom in the Fruit and Spice Park. Homestead Public School (1914), today the Neva King Cooper School, was designed

by August Geiger in the shape of an H (Figure 178). At the center of the H he placed an auditorium, which served the local community for meetings and social activities. Although Geiger described the building as Mission-style, it is truly more Mediterranean in character with its large windows, a shaded breezeway onto which all the classrooms open, and roof overhangs.

Government Buildings. In the Homestead Town Hall structure (1917), designed by Hastings Mundy, the first floor was used as a fire station and police station. On the second floor were the municipal offices and a town council chamber. The fire station and the police station were relocated in the 1950s, and the offices and chamber were moved to a new building in 1975. Two original wide segmented arch openings on the first floor at the front of the building were for the fire engines. The narrow arch opening was the

180. Redland Community
Methodist Church, 24000 S.W.
187th Avenue. 1913–1914.
Demolished by Hurricane
Andrew.

entrance to the second floor, where the offices and chamber were located. On the front facade, the gable end of the roof is hidden behind a pediment-shaped parapet that has an abstract design bas-relief.

Religious Buildings. The Methodist Church (1913–1914) in Redland was a fine example of a small wood frame structure (Figure 180). It had a plan in the shape of a cross. Decoration to the wood frame vernacular building was limited. There was a simple fan-shaped stick pattern at the peak of each gable, and Doric capitals adorned the plain and slender entrance columns.

c h a p t e r   9

Modern-Style Private Buildings

I N the previous two chapters it was apparent that particular historic styles characterize the major communities of Greater Miami. Modern-style buildings, both private and public, do not do so. By definition, the International Style avoids locational context. For this reason, the chapters on modern-style buildings are not organized by community but by building type. Striking private buildings in the modern style date from the late 1950s until the present time. The various modern styles, surprisingly, did not dominate the designs of these buildings. What could be called the "contemporary vernacular" style was used consistently by a small group of architects devoted to transforming the language of the area's vernacular architecture into contemporary terms.

Single-Family Houses

The first notable Early Modern houses in Greater Miami built after World War II were inspired by Californian models. The Ferendino Residence (1957), for example, by the architectural firm of Pancoast, Ferendino Skeels and Burnham, follows the Richard Neutra style (Figure 181). Outdoor spaces are extensions of the indoor areas. In this residence only sliding glass doors separate the loggia and terrace from the inside living areas. The few solid interior walls establish the privacy of the bedrooms.[1] On the other hand, the Russell T. Pancoast Residence (1959) in Miami, also by the same architectural firm, is a one-story steel-and-glass rectangular box. It is similar to the internationally famous glass house of Philip Johnson, floating above the water of two limestone anchorages.[2]

More international and Classic Modern in style is the Isabella Ambrosey Berczeli Residence (1972), designed by Bouterse Bor-

181. Ferendino Residence, Miami. 1957. Architects, Pancoast Ferendino Skeels and Burnham.
182. Isabella Ambrosey Berczeli Residence, Miami. 1972. Architects, Bouterse Borrelli and Albaisa.
183. Borroto Residence, Key Biscayne. 1976. Architects, Borroto and Lee.
184. Lew Residence, Miami Beach. 1980. Architects, Baldwin and Sackman.

181

relli and Albaisa (Figure 182). This award-winning dwelling was described by the architectural jury as a "crisp well-arranged and detailed residence. . . . [t]he materials, textures, colors, and, particularly, the interior furnishings and art work are outstanding."[3] "A clear, volumetric simple, straightforward building with the elements clearly expressed"[4] is the way the architectural jury perceived the Firestone Residence (1971), by Robert Whitton. In the Antoniadis Residence (1971), by Antoniadis Associates, the jury noted the square plan with the modernist predilection for free-flowing spaces. Other houses in the Classic Modern style include

182

183

184

the Lee Residence (1975) in Miami, by Borroto and Lee. The Klein Residence (1975), by Donald Singer, was considered by the jury as "possibly too austere from the exterior."[5] Another fine example of the Classic Modern style is the Borroto Residence (1976) on Key Biscayne, another design by Borroto and Lee (Figure 183).[6] Mention should be made of Baldwin and Sackman's Lew Residence (1980) in Miami Beach with its bayside glass walls (Figure 184).[7] A splendid modern exemplar is the Bouterse House (1981) in Coconut Grove, by Bouterse Perez and Fabregas. This house consists of classic white austere geometrical planes, some curved, together with glass areas and pipe railings. The architectural jury commented pointedly "The forms in this house are a quotation of international style associated with the 1920's and Le Corbusier, but they are well used on an apparently tight site."[8] Flood criteria and a narrow lot required lifting the house above the ground.

Two fine illustrations of Classic Modern houses interpreted for the 1980s suggest the continuation of the original modernist style. One is a residence (1983) with a pure geometrical white mass, designed by Roberto M. Martinez (Figure 185). The building was described as the "Florida version of the International Style with cool planes and curved glass walls" by Chicago architect Harry Weese.[9] The other is a Mateu Rizo Associates design, the Mateu Family Compound (1987), consisting of two houses on a long narrow corner lot (Figure 186). The front house is a compact vertical composition of flowing spaces, rendered in a contemporary vocabulary of modular grid systems, glass, metal, and stucco-covered concrete block. The back house is a horizontal single-story construction of sloping roofs and discrete rather than flowing spaces. Although the houses have disparate three-dimensional expression, they do have mirror-image floor distributions.[10] Modernist in style, the back house is a two-story glass box dominating the otherwise solid cube. Simple geometrical massing characterizes the front house. It has a white tile hipped roof and yellow colored stucco. A long narrow pool with terrace links the two houses.[11]

185. Residence, Dade County. 1983. Architect, Roberto M. Martinez.

186. Mateu Family Compound, Miami. 1987. Architects, Mateu Rizo Associates.

The High Modern style's departure from the Classic Modern is apparent in nearly all of a group of twenty illustrated single-family houses; illustrations of them appeared in an architectural journal, a special 1981 issue titled "Miami: Razzle-Dazzle Town."[12] One example of the High Modern style is the Phillip George House in Coconut Grove, by Spillis Candela and Partners. This house has very geometric masses, a few openings, and narrow recessed horizontal and vertical bands. These bands relieve the otherwise austere white planes of the walls.[13] A common theme among the High Modern style houses is the incorporation of the traditional courtyard, as in the Raul Rodriguez Residence (1978) by architect Raul Rodriguez (Figure 187). Other features in these houses are the extensive use of wood and large windows. A residence (1980) by Roney J. Mateu, of Baldwin and Sackman, remains the only house in the group of illustrations that portrays the classic lines of the modern style (Figure 188). The two double-story geometrical masses with their flat roofs and smooth surfaces contrast with the horizontal railings of the front balcony and the glass block wall of the other balcony.

Houses that have a modernist appearance but are made with traditional materials are variations from the Early Modern style. These houses span three decades from the 1960s onwards. The

187. Raul Rodriguez Residence, Dade County. 1978. Architect, Raul Rodriguez.

Larimore Residence (1961), by Pancoast Ferendino Skeels and Burnham, for example, is a wood structure with bleached, textured plywood sheathing on the exterior. This gives it a modern rather than a vernacular appearance.[14] Another illustration is the Sebastian Trovato Residence (1968). It has large geometric forms, but is finished in a rough stucco that provides a contrast with the diagonal wood siding on the remaining wall planes. The house was designed by Milton C. Harry for the owners, a painter and a sculptor.[15] The Alexander Residence (1982) in Coconut Grove, by Henry C. Alexander, Jr., is also modernistic in form but is sheathed in cypress wood that is stained (Figure 189). The three-story house is designed as a square within a circle plus another square on the diagonal, "a derivative of geometry."[16]

There are but a few single-family houses in other than the Early/Classic or High Modern styles. Nonetheless they are significant in the architecture of Greater Miami. One of these is the Blanco House (1986) in Miami, "a strong architectural statement meshing modern with elemental vernacular forms" (Figure 190).[17] The architects, Rodriguez Khuly and Quiroga, designed the main entrance to the house behind an arched opening in a brightly

189

colored stucco wall. In so doing, they extend classic modern principles of composition. Another Late Modern design is the Kassamali House (1990), by Harper Carreno and Mateu (Figure 191). The dwelling has a sculptural form bisected on its long axis by a ten-foot-wide skylight running the full length of the house. A curved walkway connects the detached garage with the house, which is a study in pure geometry.[18] The architectural jury commented, "It's minimalist, but at the same time very playful . . . ."[19] Progressive neoclassicism is recalled in the Hibiscus House (1980), designed by Andres Duany and Elizabeth Plater-Zyberk (Figure 192). Traditional compositional devices appear with unusual clarity, free of any ornament. A loggia facing the street forms one of three separate but well-juxtaposed buildings.[20] Duany and Plater-Zyberk's design for the Vilanova House (1983) on Key Biscayne is ". . . a rather grand, classically-inspired 'palazzo,'" prompted per-

190

191

192

193

192. Hibiscus House, Coconut
Grove. 1980. Architects, Andres
Duany and Elizabeth
Plater-Zyberk.
193. Vilanova House, Key
Biscayne. 1983. Architects,
Andres Duany and Elizabeth
Plater-Zyberk.

haps by small ancient Greek temples high up on a hilltop (Figure 193).[21] The entrance processional of their El Prado House (1990) in Cocoplum was praised by the architectural jury, which also commented on the skillful massing achieved by the grouping of pavilions around the raised courtyard.[22] The house is composed of two pavilions and an exterior courtyard, with a pool and pergola, on a podium. A sequence of entry spaces, pavilion, stepped garden, and foyer provides a transition from street level to the first floor, which is raised to meet flood prevention criteria. Mediterranean tradition is alluded to in the masonry and stucco construction, the terra cotta roof, and the coral stone courtyard floor.

Duany and Plater-Zyberk have become international figures in their advocacy and design of neotraditional communities. Characteristics of these communities include mixed land uses and convenient walking distances from homes to various local community facilities. Buildings and spaces are to a human scale, and local materials are used. One example of an application of their ideas in Greater Miami is the proposed Kendall Village Center on North Kendall Drive just west of the Florida Turnpike.

Contemporary Vernacular-Style Single-Family Houses

"Contemporary vernacular" may at first sight appear to be a contradiction. Works of three architects, though, represent the minor but persistent wood vernacular style reinterpreted with modern design motifs. The architects are Alfred Browning Parker, Charles Harrison Pawley, and George F. Reed. Other architects who used the style were Rufus Nims and Robert Bradford Browne.

Alfred Browning Parker is a significant figure; his wood vernacular designs established a presence among the modernistic design awards between 1959 and 1971. He had conceived of a distinctive approach to vernacular design much earlier, for example, in the McDermott House (1950) and the Linden R. Chandler House (1951). His own residence (1954) consists of two separate buildings, both made of wood. Exteriors are vertical siding, wood louver doors, with shingle hipped roofs.[23] Coconut Grove Residence, Woodsong (1971), also designed by Parker is constructed entirely of wood, except for the base slabs, which are made of concrete (Figure 194). The residence consists of three separate square-shaped pavilions, each two-story, linked together by a long, narrow covered walkway and a swimming pool.[24]

Charles Harrison Pawley's distinguished wood vernacular designs span two decades. His own residence, built in 1970, consists of four pavilions linked together by a central gallery and screened

194. Woodsong, Coconut Grove.
1971. Architect, Alfred Browning
Parker.
195. Pawley Residence, South
Dade. 1970. Architect, Charles
Harrison Pawley.
196. Walter Goodman Residence,
Miami. 1973. Architect, Charles
Harrison Pawley.
197. Carlos Solis Residence,
Miami. 1987. Architect, Charles
Harrison Pawley.

194

dining area (Figure 195). Exterior walls are of white stucco, windows are a clerestory ribbon, and the roof is a hipped type covered with shingles.[25] His Walter Goodman Residence (1973) is a one-story house with horizontal wood siding and sliding French windows, hipped shingle roof, and covered porch with wooden railings (Figure 196).[26] The Carlos Solis Residence (1987), similarly, has horizontal wood siding and sliding louvers, wood French doors, steep hipped shingle roofs, and a porch overhang (Figure 197). This design was described by the architectural jury as a "house (that) is very much one with nature. It maintains the pavilion theme throughout and is consistently well-detailed."[27] Another Pawley-designed house in a contemporary vernacular style is the Smith Residence (1989) in Coconut Grove. On the exterior there are deep overhangs. To allow for cross-ventilation, door and window openings are carefully positioned and a square cupola with clerestory

195

198

windows is also used. The building is sited to take advantage of
the prevailing offshore breezes. Except for the concrete framing,
the house is entirely of wood. There are exposed cedar beams and
terra cotta floor tiles.[28]

George F. Reed's notable wood vernacular houses begin with the
design for the Osman Residence (1967) on Key Biscayne (Figure
198). This dwelling has three separate houses or pavilions, each

199

200

raised slightly off the ground to allow cooling breezes to flow through and underneath. Pavilions, with their deep porches, are grouped around a long, central swimming pool and interconnected by an elevated walkway. The exteriors of the buildings have vertical siding, wood jalousie slats, and there are cedar shingles on the hipped roofs.[29] The Rudolph Residence (1969) in Miami consists of three building masses set in a grove of three hundred oak trees. Reed used natural building materials—cypress paneling, coral rock, and cedar on the pitched roofs—and a low stone retaining wall to integrate the separate masses with each other and their setting.[30] The two-story Gibbs Residence (1973) on Key Biscayne has a vernacular feeling, "rustic elegance" as the architectural jurors described it (Figure 199). It features vertical siding, a lookout tower, and a balcony supported by freestanding circular timber columns.[31] Reed followed the theme of pavilions in the design of the Aguilera Residence (1982) (Figure 200). This complex of four sheltering structures is set among existing oak trees. The structures are built with vernacular materials (wood and shingles).[32]

Multi-unit Buildings

Among the first Early Modern style multi-unit buildings were the post–World War II student apartment buildings on the University of Miami campus. These buildings are three-story. They were designed by Marion Manley, an associate architect with Robert Law Weed. In 1983, two of the buildings were remodeled to accommodate the newly created School of Architecture. The architect in charge of the project, Jan Hochstim, recreated the original ambience of the style, specifying that walls be painted white, windows

201

yellow, and railings red. Robert Bradford Browne's scheme for a public housing project, the George A. Smathers Plaza (1968) in Miami, is also in a Modern style. Browne also designed the one-story all-wood building Ratner Residence (1960) on Miami Beach in the contemporary vernacular style.[33] The public housing project was complimented by the architectural jury for the level of amenity it could provide under severe regulative and budget limitations. The jury also remarked on the exteriors of the buildings that are in poured concrete so that "structure, form and finish are com-

202

203

bined in a single building operation."[34] Another architect who is associated with contemporary wood vernacular, Charles Harrison Pawley, also produced a design in the Modern style, the Lemontree Village Condominium complex (1972) in Coconut Grove (Figure 201). The complex consists of ten duplex units exhibiting varied stucco geometrical planes and flat roofs.[35]

There are other developments that are fine examples of the Classic Modern style. These include the Apogee Townhouses (1976), by Sieger Arden and Altman, which have exceptional open interiors, as well as the three-unit Banyon Manor complex (1983) in Coconut Grove by Architeknics (Figure 202). The design of the Banyon Manor complex is noted for its cubic masses, freestanding columns, and use of primary colors—all very much in the International style.[36] Another illustration, Oakgrove (1983) by Osvaldo J. Perez, was portrayed by a juror as "A fine example of Bauhaus modern adapted to Florida and done in the tradition of minimalism" (Figure 203).[37] An urban renewal project (1971) in Miami, by Borroto and Lee, features buildings with rainwater spouts in the style of Le Corbusier. This project consists of six two-story structures with buildings that have an austere, simple, geometrical mass with flat roofs and large rectangular window openings (Figure 204).[38] Elegant compositions are evident in the design of two other complexes. One is the Key Biscayne Condominium

Apartments (1985) by Charles Sieger, considered to be of "textbook quality" with a very geometric and boxy mass broken only by the diagonals of the sloped awnings.[39] The other is the four-story Lew Apartments (1990) in Miami, by Baldwin Sackman and Carrington.[40] This warm yellow stucco apartment building was judged to be "compositionally very elegant."[41] The José Martí Plaza housing complex for the elderly (1985) in Miami, by the architectural firm of Fraga and Feito, also has its roots "in the early geometries of modern architecture" (Figure 205).[42] The complex is five stories with severe geometric forms that are softened by the rounding of the end staircase enclosures.[43]

Apartment buildings in other than Classic Modern style can be identified. The High Modern style Biltmore II Condominium Building (1976) on Biltmore Way in Coral Gables by architects Filer Hammond and Cruz Associates, is one example (Figure 206). The use of rounded corners on the concrete balcony walls and parapets of the facade of the building softens the conventional angular appearance of the Modern style. The effect is strengthened by the cream-colored textured stucco, bronze ceramic tile, and bronze tinted glass. The themes from the facade are recalled in the thirteen-story atrium, lit through a skylight glass roof, in the central core of the building.[44]

Arquitectonica has given the architecture of Miami international recognition. Their approach has been to find a new place *in* architectural history rather than finding a place *from* history.[45] One of the firm's earliest finished works is the Babylon (1981), located across South Bayshore Drive from Biscayne Bay (Figure 207).[46]

204

205

206

204. Urban Renewal Project,
Miami. 1971. Architects, Borroto
and Lee.
205. José Martí Plaza Housing for
the Elderly, Miami. 1985.
Architects, Fraga and Feito.
206. Biltmore II Condominiums,
Coral Gables. 1976. Architects,
Filer Hammond Cruz Associates.

207. Babylon, Miami. 1981.
Architect, Arquitectonica.

Designed originally as an apartment structure, it became a casu-
alty of the building glut of the early 1980s and the owners converted it to offices. The pyramid-shaped building with rooftop pool
and stepped bayview balconies has historical allusions and nautical
imagery. Colors are a brick red with trim in white and gray.[47] The
other apartment buildings designed by Arquitectonica on Brickell
Avenue are also Late Modern in style, as is illustrated by the sym-
bolism of the red triangular roof perched atop the Atlantis (1982).
At the Imperial (1983), one is struck by the "dark-red masonry
wall on the north side that appears to float alongside the building in defiance of engineering logic and gravity" (Figure 208).[48]
A blue wave metaphor is apparent in an undulating wall on the
rooftop terrace. The narrow site and required setbacks meant that
the Atlantis Building had to be long and slender, 300 feet long and
only 37 feet wide (Figure 209).[49] This rectangular solid building
has a curved eastern end that faces the bay and a 37-foot cubic
void in the north facade. The eight apartments in the void share a
sky patio with a free-form jacuzzi and a palm tree. The "removed"
cube becomes a health club on the podium. Four triangular-shaped
balconies, colored yellow, project from the north side. A red triangular volume on the roof hides the cooling equipment. An oversized three-story blue frame masks the south face. The architectural jury liked "the reflective glass treatment and the overscaled

blue frame."[50] The Palace (1982) is a forty-two-story condominium apartment structure (Figure 210).[51] It consists of a taller glass slab building intersected by a smaller building that "takes the form of a giant stair rising up from the bay."[52] These two buildings sit on a podium that is lined with townhouses along the waterfront. The townhouses screen a two-story parking structure. The facade of the main building has an expressed two-story structural grid, painted white, and infill glass panels. A narrow seventeen-story stepped building projects at right angles from the main facade to add a three-dimensional quality to the whole. The stepped building, painted red, appears to pierce the taller structure from both sides. A long rectangular structure and a contrasting three-story glass-clad cube, which is a penthouse, accentuate the roofline.

208. The Imperial, Miami. 1983. Architect, Arquitectonica.

A departure from the Modern styles is the Williams Island Village complex on the Intracoastal Waterway. It is designed in Mediterranean Revival style. The second phase of the five-story condominiums Williams Island complex, designed by the firm of Sandy and Babcock Inc., was completed in 1989. Arched and segmental arches, red tile hipped roofs, and smooth stucco surfaces represent this Mediterranean Revival style.[53] The style appeared first in the design of private buildings, single and multi-unit dwellings, in the late 1980s and early 1990s.

Modern-Style Hotels

The Spillis and Candela design for the Hyatt Hotel (1982) is a "diligent and workmanlike building that ought to be one of Miami's most distinctive landmarks."[54] This hotel is on the north side of the Miami River and is part of the Knight Center in downtown Miami. Another downtown hotel with a prominent position is the Pavillon (1983), which is located on the bay. Its architecture also falls short. The exterior is troubling with its somber, too-dark stone.[55] Windows give the appearance of a gold mirror with bronze-colored trim. Henry Moore's sculpture *The Spindle*, located in the center of the lobby, provides an accent for the interior. The thirty-five-story, 660-room hotel was designed by Pietro Belluschi.

A successful Modern-style hotel is the Hotel Sofitel (1986), south of the Miami International Airport. It has a bold geometric mass

209. Atlantis, Miami. 1982. Architect, Arquitectonica.

210. The Palace, Miami. 1982.
Architect, Arquitectonica.

and rhythmic grid of windows that is softened by red, white, and blue colors.[56] The architect of this fifteen-story building was Martin Bolullo of Goleman and Rolfe of Houston. Very different in style is the fourteen-story pink Alhambra Hotel and Office complex (1987), one of the first buildings to be constructed in the new Mediterranean District of Coral Gables. The Mediterranean Revival–style buildings of the Alhambra complex have a first-floor arcade, setbacks in the upper stories, wrought-iron balconies, and multiple tiled roofs.[57]

Modern-Style Public Buildings

THE notable modern public buildings in Greater Miami span the period from the mid-1950s up to the present day. In architectural style the High Modern style is clearly dominant. A distinguishing characteristic of the city's modern public buildings is the number that have been designed by internationally renowned architects. As these buildings cluster downtown, the skyline of the business district has become a powerful image and a signature for the global city of Miami.

Commercial Buildings

The first modern commercial buildings in Greater Miami were in typical International style. An early example was the multi-story Dupont Plaza Center (1956) in downtown Miami, designed by architects Peterson and Shuflin.[1] Another Early Modern 1950s building was the two-story reinforced-concrete administrative headquarters of the Alliance Machine Company (1958), by Alfred Browning Parker (Figure 211).[2] The building, located in Coconut Grove facing Biscayne Bay, had an exterior skin of precast concrete units glazed with colored marine and hammered glass. Parker's other modern-style building is the Miami Bal Harbour Club (1956).[3] The building is raised off the ground with pilotis on the first floor and a glass wall and concrete columns on the second floor. Parker is more renowned, however, for his contemporary vernacular-style houses, described in Chapter 9.

Evidence of the persistence of the International Modern style is the use of bright primary colors in an industrial warehouse building (1981) in the foreign trade complex of the Miami Free Trade Zone.[4] At the beginning of the 1980s, the best Early Mod-

211

211. Alliance Machine Company,
Coconut Grove. 1958. (Building
later demolished.) Architect,
Alfred Browning Parker.
212. One Biscayne Tower, 2
South Biscayne Boulevard, Miami.
1973. Architects, Fraga and
Associates.

212

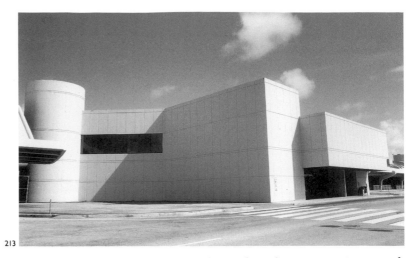

213

ern commercial buildings were located in downtown Miami and
downtown Coral Gables, according to a panel of well-known local
architects. The panel was assembled with the purpose of identifying the "newest and best of Miami's architectural palette."[5] Their
first choice in modern office buildings was One Biscayne Tower,
built in 1973 and designed by Fraga and Associates (Figure 212).
At forty stories, it was the tallest building in Greater Miami until
the 1980s. This building consists of a square glass office tower that
sits on a nine-story concrete parking structure. Also selected by
the panel were the "glass box" office structures in downtown Coral
Gables. Their height and glass curtain wall exteriors still have the
quality of reflecting the interesting cloud formations and blue sky
that prevail over Greater Miami.[6]

214

213. Passenger Terminal, Port of
Miami, 560 N.E. 2nd Avenue.
1970. Architect, John Andrews of
Toronto, Canada.
214. Concourse D Expansion,
Miami International Airport.
1984. Architects, Bouterse Perez
and Fabregas.
215. Luminaire Showroom and
Office, 2331 Ponce de Leon
Boulevard, Coral Gables. 1984.
Architects, Mateu Associates.

A fine example of a modernist-style building is a passenger terminal building (1970) in the port of Miami (Figure 213). The building consists of five "nodes" punctured by cylindrical towers through which passengers travel from car to ship. Four vaulted custom sheds connect the nodes in the design by the Toronto architect John Andrews. Clearly defined shapes reflect the separation of all the building's functions; it "becomes a machine in a formal expression of concrete massing while relating successfully to scales of humans, autos, and ships."[7] Another modernist transportation building is the Miami International Airport Concourse D Expansion (1984) by Bouterse Perez and Fabregas (Figure 214). These architects aimed to develop a strong sense of place for the visitor, as "skies may be friendly, but airports too often are not."[8] Interiors feature curved glass walls as well as staircases.

The Luminaire Showroom and Offices (1984) in Coral Gables is a building exemplifying the Classic Modern style (Figure 215). The design, by Mateu Associates, uses a fifty-inch module to regulate all the proportions of the structure as well as the facade. The austere geometry and the transparency of the building were meant to convey that good design is a way of life and, further, to showcase the philosophy of design for which Luminaire is so well known.[9]

High Modern style becomes apparent in some commercial buildings built in Greater Miami in the mid–1980s. In shopping complexes, there is the redesign of the first regional mall in South Florida, the Mall at N.E. 163rd Street. It was constructed in the

215

mid–1950s. This open-air center, with its empty three-level space (formerly a department store), was in desperate need of modernization. The solution of the architects, Wolfberg Alvarez Taracido and Associates, was to enclose both the mall and the three-level public atrium with a translucent fabric roof supported by a series of arches.[10] Another shopping mall is the Kendall Town and Country Specialty Center (1986), designed by Kober Belluschi Associates.[11] The idea for this mall is unusual. It consists of two separate and disparate masses separated by a surface parking area. On the east side of the parking area there is an enclosed U-shaped building. This building has a glass-roofed food court and rotunda and is centered on an artificial lake. On the other side of the parking lot is a shopping strip. High Modern office buildings include the Burger King Headquarters building (1989), which is located on a fifty-acre bayside tract on Old Cutler Road (Figure 216).[12] Hellmuth Obata and Kassabaum, an architectural firm from Saint Louis, planned the site with a campuslike atmosphere to save as many trees as possible. The exterior building materials are pink concrete with a grid and textured pattern. Accents are in aqua and pink marble. In complete contrast to anything else in Greater Miami is Bayside Marketplace (1989), designed as a festive waterfront place by the firm of Benjamin Thompson of Cambridge, Massachusetts, and the local firm of Spillis Candela and Partners (Figure 217).[13] On each side of an open market shed are two-story pavilions that use natural ventilation, exterior breezeways, and shaded open streets on

216. Burger King Headquarters, 17777 Old Cutler Road, Old Cutler. 1989. Architects, Hellmuth Obata and Kassabaum of St. Louis.

217. Bayside Marketplace, 401 Biscayne Boulevard, Miami. 1987. Architects, Benjamin Thompson of Cambridge, Massachusetts, with Spillis Candela and Partners.
218 (overleaf). Southeast Financial/First Union Center, 100 South Biscayne Boulevard, Miami. 1983. Architect, Edward Bassett of Skidmore Owings and Merrill of San Francisco.
219 (overleaf). CenTrust Tower/International Place, 100 S.E. 2nd Street, Miami. 1987.
Architects, I. M. Pei with Spillis Candela and Partners.

the first floor. In addition there are fountains, porches with fixed sun louvers, and Bahama-shuttered windows to reduce the effect of the heat.

In 1983, "downtown Miami's new skyline began to take shape."[14] Around Dupont Plaza, the Southeast Financial Center, the Ball Building, and the Pavillon Hotel buildings changed the silhouette of the city. That year, also, the Rouse Company was selected to create a bayside marketplace for Miami. Apart from the new United States District Courthouse, described as "dull-looking, with enormous expanses of concrete and vast, empty plazas,"[15] many distinctive office buildings were designed by internationally prominent architects.[16] The tall Southeast Financial Center (now renamed First Union) Building (1983), with its attached multistory garage structure, was designed by Charles E. Bassett of the San Francisco office of Skidmore Owings and Merrill (Figure 218). The stepped shape of the building and its silhouette against the sky reduce the visual impact of its large mass. Just the opposite effect is created by the massive form of the bayside Pavillon Hotel nearby. Between the Southeast Financial Center office building and garage structure is a courtyard. With its royal palm trees and high-level glass roof, it is a major contribution to the public realm in downtown Miami. CenTrust Tower (1987), renamed International Place, designed by I. M. Pei Associates with local architects Spillis Candela and Partners, also has a memorable shape (Figure 219). The building consists of a quarter-circle-shaped tower in three layers, each gradually stepping back. Imaginative lighting from the base of the building bathes the entire structure in colors to reflect special

220

occasions—orange and turquoise during Dolphin football games, for example, or red, white, and blue on the Fourth of July.[17] The firm of Spillis Candela and Partners was also responsible for the Museum Tower (1986) whose glass facade mirrors the shimmering images of surrounding buildings (Figure 220).[18] The architectural jury described the Museum Tower as a ". . . well-designed building . . . packaged in a most elegant skin."[19] Although it is a government edifice, the Metro Administration Building (1985) is included here as it is primarily an office building. It was designed by a renowned architectural firm, Hugh Stubbins Associates of Cambridge, Massachusetts. The thirty-story stone-faced office tower, with its bands of narrow dark-glass windows, has an octagonal commission chamber structure at its foot. These government buildings are an "austere, sober work of architecture [with two ends that] are simply bleak-looking—sheer, overpowering, monolithic slabs of stone."[20] (See Figure 243.)

Besides the Classic Modern Luminaire building, Mateu Associates were also responsible for a "Modern Moderne" style building. The 2424 South Dixie Highway Office Building (1985) uses Streamline Moderne style features without the decoration (Figure 221). The building is characterized by a rounded corner at the narrow end of the long building. Roundness is further expressed in the circular balcony and pipe railings and the circular glass block wall. The horizontal lines of the long side of the building are accentuated by the ribbon windows and raised stucco bands or stripes.[21]

221

The firm of Arquitectonica, which designed several Late Modern apartment buildings, also designed a few public buildings in the same style. The Overseas Tower (1980), a medium-rise suburban office building, was described as a "most extravagant core of glass wall . . ." (Figure 222).[22] The building consists essentially of two contrasting masses. One is an open office space in a semicircular curtain wall structure. The other contains circulation and support spaces in a rectangular masonry slab structure. This backs onto the semicircular structure. A two-story square perforation in the facade of rectangular slab forms a sky terrace. Another Arquitectonica building is the Miracle Center (1988), which is a multilevel mixed-use urban development (Figure 223).[23] On the facade of the building, a block long and seven stories high, are three super-scaled trapezoidal panels that float aslant like clouds above each of the three entryways. The panels are painted black and white with artificial veins to appear marbleized and to contrast with the blue background of the building mass. The panels were repainted without the veins in 1992. Undoubtedly, among the most striking Late Modern–style commercial buildings in Greater Miami were the Best Products Showrooms in Cutler Ridge and Hialeah. They were two of eight bold showrooms designed by the avant-garde New York architecture firm of SITE.[24] The "fractured facades" or jagged pieces of the Cutler Ridge showroom were like a jigsaw

222. Overseas Tower, 9600 N.W. 25th St., Miami. 1980. Architect, Arquitectonica.

223. Miracle Center, 3301 Coral
Way, Miami. 1988. (Artificial
marble veins on panels were
subsequently painted over.)
Architect, Arquitectonica.

puzzle. They represented the Late Modern predilection for the non-ordinary and the unexpected, and a building that was fun and an object of amusement. The Hialeah showroom has been demolished and the Cutler Ridge showroom closed.

The modernist office towers of Brickell Avenue make for an undistinguished streetscape. Each sits on a podium that is inimical to pedestrians. Mostly, these towers have bland images. One exception is the One Brickell Square/Tishman-Speyer Building (1985), designed by Raul DeArmas of the New York office of Skidmore Owings and Merrill (Figure 224). The street-level trellis, pierced with palm trees, sets the stage for an elaborate ziggurat crown, "28 stories of bottle-green glass and precast concrete *brise-soleils*."[25]

Contemporary Vernacular-Style Commercial Buildings

As was mentioned in chapter 9, notable contemporary vernacular-style private buildings continued to receive architectural awards and accolades during the past few decades in spite of the dominance of the International Modern style. The same applies to public buildings, but to a lesser extent. Alfred Browning Parker, for example, used the contemporary vernacular style in the conversion of a fruit-packing plant into his own architectural office. This sixty-year-old plant building was located on a site that was heavily wooded. The aged stone walls and columns were reused, the Dade County pine re-milled, and the old brick floors ground to a level, clean surface.[26] Another illustration, on a larger scale, is the Miami Lakes Town Center Phase B (1986).[27] It was designed by Baldwin Sackman and Associates to recapture the feeling of vernacular

224. One Brickell Square/
Tishman-Speyer Building, 801
Brickell Avenue, Miami. 1985.
Architect, Raul De Armas of
Skidmore Owings and Merrill,
New York.

town centers or hometown Main Streets of the past. The three-story complex of shops and boutiques on the ground floor and varied one- or two-story residential units above, are interconnected by arcades and brick walkways. The reddish color of the barrel tile hipped roofs complements the brick pavers. An exhilarating design for a new commercial building in vernacular style is the Caribbean Marketplace (1989) by Charles Harrison Pawley (Figure 225).[28] The building, the first time one in Miami has received a national American Institute of Architects honor award, is a remodeled warehouse on a tightly constrained inner-city site.[29] It recreates the original ambience and excitement of a "Little Haiti" marketplace. The festive and colorful building uses traditional Haitian motifs.

Most novel of Greater Miami's commercial buildings are the Mayfair in the Grove and Mayfair Place by Treister and Cantillo

Architects.[30] These were built during the mid- to the late 1980s. The buildings take up two blocks on the northern end of the Coconut Grove business area. Two separate but interrelated complexes contain a mix of luxury stores, boutiques, restaurants, and the Mayfair House Hotel (Figure 226). The organic shapes that pervade the free-form public spaces and the applied decorations are reminiscent of the Art Nouveau style of the Spanish architect, Antonio Gaudí. The hotel furniture, on the other hand, recalls the style of the Scottish architect Charles Rennie Mackintosh.

One of the few Progressive Fusionist buildings in Greater Miami is the 550 Biltmore Building (1988) on Biltmore Way in Coral Gables, undertaken as a joint venture between Thomas A. Spain and O. K. Houston (Figure 227).[31] On the first floor, shops, galleries, and restaurants generate activity at the sidewalk level. Connections to the urban texture of Coral Gables are made through

225. Caribbean Marketplace, N.E. 59th Terrace and N.E. 2nd Avenue, Miami. 1989. Architect, Charles Harrison Pawley.

226. Mayfair House Hotel, 3000 Florida Avenue, Coconut Grove. 1986. Architects, Treister and Cantilo.

fountains, two bronze lions that flank the main entrance, etched granite paving, travertine marble benches and planters, and a row of royal palms. The multistory office building takes a stepped form and has balconies and terraces, unusual features in a commercial building.

Community Buildings

The epitome of the International style, as practiced by the renowned architect Le Corbusier, is the Mailman Center for Child Development Building (1970 [Figure 228]). It is located on the University of Miami Medical Center Campus. The architects were Ferendino Grafton Pancoast and Watson Deutschman Kruse. A two-story structure is attached to the main edifice, an eight-story slab building that has curving, rising concrete fins on the facade to create a brise-soleil, a "concrete egg crate [that] acts as sun protection."[32] The external walls of the building are in exposed concrete in the Brutalist style made popular by the British architects Peter and Alison Smithson. Also in the Le Corbusian manner is the Opa-locka Neighborhood Service Center (1982), by Bouterse Perez and Fabregas. Like the Bouterse House, it is very much in the Classic Modern mode but with curved walls.[33] A Late Modern style building is the Recreational Facility (1985) at Bird Road Park for Metro Dade County Parks and Recreation Department, by Tomas

Lopez-Gottardi. The Facility consists of a complex of stucco park buildings, painted pale yellow and peach, which resemble an Italian village in miniature.[34]

Cultural and Entertainment Buildings

The Interama complex that was to have been constructed in North Dade was a special and unusual project (Figure 229). The idea of South Florida as a center for cultural and trade interests of the Americas had been a recurring dream since 1915.[35] In the late 1940s, William H. Walker, founder of America's first federal savings and loan association, spearheaded an effort that eventually led the Florida legislature to establish the Inter-American Center Authority. The Authority's first proposal for an Interama project, to be located in Miami, was announced in 1956 but was shelved owing to difficulties in acquisition of the proposed site. This project was revived in 1962 when the City of Miami finally deeded the 1,700-acre Graves Tract to the Authority. The Interama planning team was headed by architect Robert Bradford Browne. Working with him were Milton Harry, George Reed, Hernando Acosta, and others. Instead of having the design staff of the Authority control architectural design, full freedom of choice was to be given to the architects of individual buildings. Illustrative sketches by James Bingham, however, showed that the Cultural Area and the Industrial Development Area might have futuristic tentlike and spherical structures that depicted progress. These sketches also conveyed the

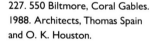

227. 550 Biltmore, Coral Gables. 1988. Architects, Thomas Spain and O. K. Houston.

228. Mailman Center for Child Development, 1601 N.W. 12th Avenue, Miami. 1970. Architects, Ferendino Grafton and Pancoast with Watson Deutschman and Kruse.
229. Proposed Interama Theme Center (now Florida International University North Campus), North Dade. 1956. (Drawing by Hugh Ferris.)

229

impression that the International Area would have various countries of the Americas produce their own indigenous art and architecture. The Board was to approve all the designs that were to be done by outside architects.[36] Members of the Interama Board of Design included the nationally distinguished architects Pietro Belluschi, Paul Rudolph, and Hugh Ferriss, and traffic engineer Wilbur Smith. Eero Saarinen, famous for his expressive designs for the Kennedy and the Dulles airports, was to be a consultant. In the end, the project was abandoned, and the tract became the north campus of Florida International University.

In complete contrast to the futuristic Interama buildings was the new Coconut Grove library building in contemporary vernacular style. The old structure was found in the mid–1960s to be weather-beaten, termite-infested, and a fire hazard. The new building (1964), designed by T. Trip Russell and Associates around the old structure, rises from a base of oolitic limestone and laminated-pine structural timber arches. These support the high-gabled, deep-overhung planked roof. A wide veranda, with a redwood rail, extends around three sides of the building; the old portico was reused.[37]

Philip Johnson, with John Burgee, created a stir in unveiling the design for the Metro-Dade Cultural Center on Flagler Street in downtown Miami. It was not in the expected International Modern style, for which Johnson was famous, but a "multi-dimensioned image of its [Miami's] cumulative character that will stand up (and for) next year, next decade, and next century."[38] The design for the "little cultural Acropolis" was published in 1978, and the Center was opened to the public in April 1983. Occupying a full city block, the Cultural Center consists of the Miami-Dade Library, the South Florida Historical Museum, and the Center for the Fine Arts. Each is housed in a substantial building grouped around a large open-air tiled plaza. The Center for Fine Arts building is a simple building, as is the larger Historical Museum. Dominating the plaza is the arcaded Library building (Figure 230). This latter edifice is "a formal, almost ceremonial building with grand proportions and a demure demeanor. It is an essay in pale lavender and apricot. . . . Arches abound inside and outside the building. The flat-topped rotunda in the entrance hall is rather flat, rotundas are meant to have domes."[39] The Mediterranean Revival buildings have Spanish tile roofs, wrought-iron balustrades, and walls with few openings. The whole complex is mounted on a one-story base with battered native coral rock walls. The fortresslike palazzo concept has been controversial as the plaza is elevated one story off street level without any visual access from the street. "The idea is peculiar in that the European Plaza draws the city in, rather than turning its back on the city. The plaza is a beautiful, though spartan space."[40] The design is not a slavish copy of the Mediterranean style but a modern synthesis of remembrances of the past.

Another Mediterranean Revival building was the proposed Archives of Caribbean Culture (1986) by José Gelabert-Navia. The structure was intended to have a primary axis and entry court that would allow the complex to be more closely associated with its neighbor, Vizcaya. Use of a porch structure and arcades added to

230. Miami-Dade Public Library in the Metro-Dade Cultural Center, 101 W. Flagler, Miami. 1983. Architects, Philip Johnson and John Burgee.

231. Homestead Baseball
Stadium, 1601 S.E. 28th Avenue.
1981. Architects, Hellmuth Obata
and Kassabaum of St. Louis.

this association.[41] One of the few Progressive-style public buildings is the New Biscayne College Library (1982), by architect
Raul Rodriguez, which shows a concern for classicism.[42] The new
Homestead Baseball Stadium (1991) is reminiscent of a Roman
amphitheater with its unadorned Tuscan columns, arches, and
entrance pediments (Figure 231).[43] The design, attentive to detail,
was executed by the nationally known architecture firm of Hellmuth Obata and Kassabaum. This firm was also responsible for
two other Greater Miami structures, the Burger King Headquarters
building and the Joe Robbie Stadium.

Education Buildings

The opening of the south campus of Miami-Dade Community College in the mid–1960s provided the architects with the opportunity to display the attributes of the modernist style.[44] Spillis Candela and Partners (the name of the firm has undergone changes
since the 1960s) have served as architects for Miami-Dade Community College, having designed all their academic buildings and support facilities. They produced in addition the master plans for the
College's four campuses.[45] The New World Center campus downtown was completed in phases, the first in 1972 and the second in
1982. The first-phase three-story building has three wings around
a six-story central atrium capped at the top by a skylight (Figure
232). The exterior facade is of precast concrete panels. This building was commented upon favorably by architectural jurors as a
contribution to the urban area of the city. While they liked the idea
of the "see through" and "walk through" approach, they felt that
"the design solution somewhat overwhelmed the individual with
its monumental and architecturally forced shapes."[46] Ferendino
Grafton Spillis and Candela, the architects, admitted that the mod-

232. Mitchell Wolfson New World Center Campus, Miami-Dade Community College, 300 N.E. 2nd Avenue, Miami. 1974. Architects, Ferendino Grafton Spillis and Candela.

ernistic building needed to accommodate the prevailing breezes for cross-ventilation, to deflect direct sunlight, and to allow for natural light to permeate through the buildings.[47]

When the library building was added to the University of Miami Coral Gables Campus in 1957, it followed the Modern style of the other buildings on the campus.[48] The architects were Watson and Deutschman. Another modernist-style building, with "simple concrete forms and deep shadows,"[49] was the Institute of Information Science Building (1966), designed by Watson Deutschman and Kruse. Additional campus buildings constructed during the decades of the 1960s and 1970s also reflect the dominant influence of the Modern style. Even a recent addition to the campus, the George W. Jenkins School of Business Administration Building (1981), follows this International Modern style (Figure 233). It does so in a most elegant manner, however. The facade of this building has an interesting pattern created by the closely spaced vertical precast concrete louvers placed at an angle to the plane of the windows. This arrangement provides shade to the ribbons of glass behind. The sunscreen idea was considered by a juror, Hugh Stubbins, as "finely tuned."[50] Boerema Bermello Kurki and Vera, the architects, included another striking feature—the upper four floors are raised on columns above an open first floor that becomes a shaded courtyard.[51] In the jury's view, however, ". . . the classroom and teaching buildings should have more spaces where people can meet as characterized in old college quadrangles."[52]

The Rosenstiel School of Marine and Atmospheric Science Building (1985) on the Virginia Key campus of the University of Miami continued the modernist tradition. The building is essentially a two-story building with a colonnaded walkway around much of the first floor. The architects, Abramovitz Kingsland Schiff of New York, designed a white concrete building, with freestanding columns, curved roof and canopies, black windows, and red trim, with "[p]ipe rails and window mullions [that] break up the monotony."[53] A departure in style is evident in the new James L. Knight Physics Building (1991), which is "at once simple and elegant, a lean, pale concrete building with a wonderful sequence of vaulted spaces" (Figure 234).[54] The design, by Spillis Candela and Partners, sets a high standard for future buildings on the campus.

On the North Dade Campus of Florida International University, the first major academic facility was the Interamerican Trade Center and Exhibition Building (1976), now the Hospitality Management Building (Figure 235). The architects were Bouterse Borrelli and Albaisa. The structure, with its expressive structural frame, set the architectural theme for the buildings to follow in the use of free-standing supporting columns or pilotis. Academic One Classroom Building (1979), designed by Greenleaf-Telesca, varied the theme by using shorter pilotis that supported the floors rather than a flat roof (Figure 236). Until the early 1980s, the main campus

233. George W. Jenkins School of Business Administration, Stanford Drive Circle, University of Miami, Coral Gables. 1981. Architects, Bermello Kurki and Vera.

234

235

234. James L. Knight Physics Building, Campo Sano, University of Miami, Coral Gables. 1991. Architects, Spillis Candela and Partners.
235. Interamerican Trade Center and Exchange/Hospitality Management Building, Florida International University, N.E. 151st Street and Biscayne Boulevard, North Dade. 1976. Architects, Bouterse Borrelli and Albaisa.

236. Academic One Classroom Building, Florida International University, N.E. 151st Street and Biscayne Boulevard, North Dade. 1979. Architects, Greenleaf and Telesca.

237. Physical Sciences Building, Florida International University, S.W. 8th Street at S.W. 107th Avenue, West Dade. 1991. Architects, Perez and Perez with the Architects Collaborative of Cambridge, Massachusetts.

236

of Florida International University, overall, had uninspired architecture with plenty of gray concrete. A welcome new addition is the "no frills, very solid" Physical Sciences Building (1991) (Figure 237).[55] Architects for this building were Perez and Perez with the Architects Collaborative of Cambridge, Massachusetts.

School buildings in Greater Miami, in general, have not fared well architecturally. The buildings tend to be more like warehouses, designed for efficiency rather than any educational expression. The massive bulk of the Sunset Senior High School (1977)

237

in South Dade is an example.[56] Another case, the Miami Lakes Senior High School building (1968) in Hialeah, although massive in area, is compact to minimize circulation distances. While the jury found the Miami Lakes building to have "a successful vertical organization of assembly spaces and a well-contrived circulation system," it seriously questioned the wisdom of the Dade County School Board's policy of windowless air-conditioned structures.[57] The Sunset Senior High School, with its long facades, relieved by semicircular stairwells, is also windowless according to the policy. The issue is not new; nearly two decades earlier, in 1959, the question of air-conditioning schools had arisen. Architects attending a conference on schools were provided with arguments for including air-conditioning in future Florida schools—and by implication eliminating windows.[58] The "windowless" policy of the Dade County School Board persists despite the detrimental psychological aspects of such classrooms. Among these is the lack of contact students have with the outdoors and natural lighting.[59] A successful response to the problem of massiveness in high school buildings is to be found in the Homestead Senior High School Building (1977), designed by Edward M. Ghezzi. This school, which holds 2600 students from grades ten to twelve consists of an assembly of buildings of varying heights and refined facades (Figure 238). The complex has received the Outstanding High School Award of the American Association of School Administrators and the American

238. Homestead Senior High School, 2351 S.E. 12th Avenue. 1977. Architect, Edward M. Ghezzi.

239. Booker T. Washington Middle School, 1200 N.W. 6th Avenue, Miami. 1991. Architect, Robert Bradford Browne.

Institute of Architects. Despite this model, architectural problems persist in school design. The G. Holmes Braddock High School (1990) in South Dade is "a huge warehouse of a structure with unadorned walls rather sloppily painted blue and mauve. . . . Rows of louvered windows seem methodically punched into concrete walls. . . . [It is overall a] bland building."[60]

There are, fortunately, some exceptions that show the way to good architectural design, such as the Booker T. Washington Middle School Building (1991) in Overtown, by Robert Bradford Browne (Figure 239). Buildings are arranged around three courtyards with corridors and classrooms open to cooling breezes. The design draws on and adapts Mediterranean-style characteristics. Arches, for example, are squared off. In this building each classroom has windows—large ones overlooking a courtyard and clerestory ones above the colonnaded hallways, in contrast to other school designs.[61] Toussaint Louverture Elementary School (1990), designed by Bernard Zyscovich, also has a courtyard theme (Figure 240). The building is a two-story concrete-and-masonry structure that is brightly colored and organized around a central open courtyard.[62] It was intended by the architect "to make this school a part of and a reflection of the Haitian community it serves, thus the vivid pastel walls, bright and cheerful."[63] An exciting design for a school is one by a former member of the firm of Arquitectonica, Hervin Romney. His design of the Jane S. Roberts Elementary

240. Toussaint Louverture Elementary School, 120 N.E. 59th Street, Miami. 1990. Architect, Bernard Zyscovich, Inc.

241. Jane S. Roberts Elementary School, 14850 Cottonwood Circle, Miami. 1990. Architect, Hervin Romney.

242. City of Miami Police Headquarters Building, 400 N.W. 2nd Avenue, Miami. 1976. Architects, Pancoast Architects with Bouterse Borrelli and Albaisa.

240

241

242

School (1990) in Miami reflects Romney's trademarks: bold geometries, zigzag roofs, free-form curves and primary colors (Figure 241).[64] Miccosukee Indian patterns are recalled in the combination of colors and shapes. Also of note is the new front entrance to the Fulford Elementary School. The design, by Samuels-Richter Architects, Inc., with R. J. Heisenbottle, is Postmodern in style. It incorporates historical allusions with modern elements.

Government Buildings

The City of Miami Police Headquarters building, constructed in the mid–1970s, was the first in the future complex of government buildings in downtown Miami (Figure 242). This building, in a High Modern style of architecture, was designed by Pancoast Architects, with Bouterse Borrelli and Albaisa.[65] The four-story building departs from the traditional Modern-style architecture through its articulated massing and its use of an unusual material for the area—brick infill panels between concrete beams. Bouterse Borrelli and Albaisa used a similar approach to the massing of the Vanidades Continental office building on Le Jeune Road near the airport.[66]

The new Miami Beach City Hall (1977 [Figure 244]) and the new Miami Beach Judicial Center (1987 [Figure 245]) are both very modernistic in style. Architects for the Miami Beach Judicial Center were Borrelli Frankel and Blitstein. Borrelli was also one of

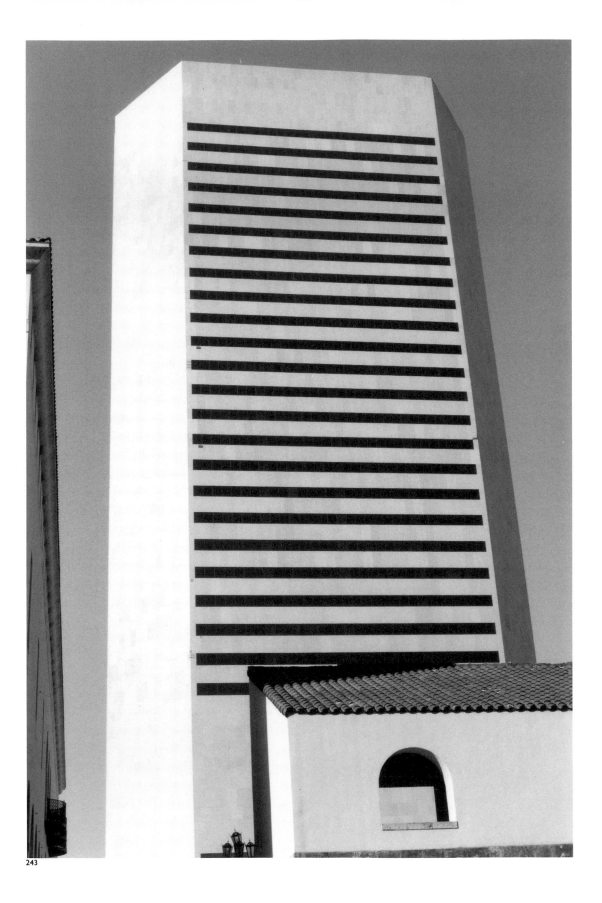

243

244

245

243. Dade County Administration Building, with Cultural Center in foreground, 111 N.W. 1st Street, Miami. 1985. Architect, Hugh Stubbins Associates of Cambridge, Massachusetts.

244. Miami Beach City Hall, 1700 Convention Center Drive. 1975. Architects, Bouterse Borrelli and Albaisa, then Bouterse Perez and Fabregas, with Grove and Hack.

245. Miami Beach Judicial Center, 1100 Washington Avenue. 1987. Architects, Borrelli, Frankel and Blitstein.

the architects for the Miami Beach City Hall that involved Grove/ Hack, and Bouterse Borrelli and Albaisa, then Bouterse Perez and Fabregas. The Judicial Center building is an attempt at a modern interpretation of the historical tropical Deco architecture in the use of curving facades, glass blocks, and the application of aqua color glazing and pipe railings.[67] This large four-level building, all in white, conflicts, however, with the old City Hall. Old and new are separated by a pedestrian plaza created by the partial closing of Drexel Avenue. Another modernist building with historical connotations is the maximum-security forensic hospital. It was completed in 1986 and is located in a residential area near downtown Miami. The building incorporates an old arch that originally marked the entrance to the Seaboard Coastline Railroad Station.[68] A more successful strategy in reinterpreting the Moderne tradition is the design of the PSB/UPH United States Coast Guard Base (1990) on Miami Beach by Harper Carreno and Mateu (Figure 246). The complex consists of very composed buildings with top floors that have exterior corridors and nautical imagery in the decks, railings, and shiplike massing. The architectural jury remarked, "We have seen a lot of these white, concrete, horizontal buildings, but this one really succeeds."[69] Another notable government building in High Modern style is the classroom structure of

246. PSB/UPH United States Coast Guard Base, 100 MacArthur Causeway, Miami Beach. 1990. Architects, Harper Carreno and Mateu.

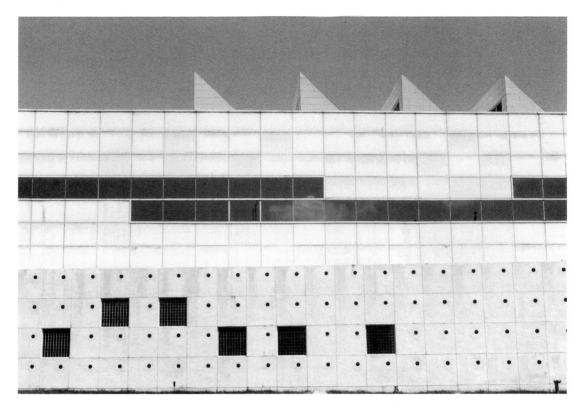

247. North Dade Justice Center, 15555 North Biscayne Boulevard. 1984. Architect, Arquitectonica.

the Metro-Dade Police Department Center (1988), by Mateu Rizo Associates and Baldwin Sackman and Associates. They designed the classroom building as an entry symbol to the complex so as to establish the image of the training aspects of the facility.[70] One reviewer, Hardy, praised both the United States Coast Guard base and the Metro-Dade classroom center for "breaking out of the typi-cal and minimal governmental 'box,' with buildings that were not in the slightest fortress-like."[71]

Another Harper Carreno and Mateu design is the Turner Guild-ford Knight Correctional Center (1989), a facility that attempts to emphasize the dignity and individuality of each inmate in as secure and normal an environment as possible. This Center is a "third-generation" detention facility using state-of-the-art concepts in correctional philosophy and technology. The exterior presents a noninstitutional appearance in the way the heights of the build-ing masses vary. The tallest building is nine stories. Spandrel glass panels function both to enforce security and to allow natural day-light into all inmate rooms.[72] The architectural jury admired "the stepping down and carving out of the masses [which] helped very much to scale down an enormous building to seem more humane."[73]

Arquitectonica's consistent Late Modern approach is evident in their design of the North Dade Justice Center (1984) (Figure 247).

This building consists of three intersecting structures, a parking area, a lobby, and the main building. Each has its own geometry.[74] In the center of the two-story curved main building, there is a linear pedestrian plaza that passes underneath an upper suspended volume. The distorted checkerboard pattern of the terrazzo floor is an indication that nothing is taken for granted in the building. The exterior of the main structure is clad in white spandrel glass and silver reflective glass, while vertical panels of pink marble and green glass cover the lobby building. A wall of green stucco and black tile encloses and protects the parking area. The skyline is dominated by a triangular clerestory structure encased in yellow tiles.

Hurricane Andrew

JUST before dawn on Monday, 24 August 1992, Hurricane Andrew made landfall in South Dade. The eye of the hurricane came ashore due east of Homestead Air Force Base at 4:55 a.m. With sustained winds of 145 miles per hour and gusts estimated as high as 175 mph, according to the National Hurricane Center, the storm blew westward.[1] The highest storm surge of 16.9 feet above sea level was measured at the Burger King Headquarters building at S.W. 184th Street.[2] This building suffered severe water and wind damage. The lowest point of the storm surge was at Morningside, in line with about N.E. 54th Street, at a height of 3.7 feet.

The loss of life owing to Hurricane Andrew was minimal. Population in the path of the hurricane had adequate warning time to board up or evacuate their homes. This was not the case with prior hurricanes this century, particularly before the "big blow" of 1926, when on the evening of 17 September, even though the local newspapers warned residents to prepare for a tropical storm, life continued as usual. When the category-4 hurricane (see Table 4) roared through Miami during the night, people were surprised. Some of those inhabitants who ventured outdoors at dawn were deceived by the calmness of the eye. They were stranded without shelter when the strong winds came from the opposite direction. After the storm abated late in the afternoon, the stunned population was able to view the destruction caused by the huge storm. In the Miami area, 113 people died in the hurricane and 854 people were hospitalized. Two thousand homes were destroyed and three thousand damaged. Coral Gables, with its well-constructed buildings, suffered the least, while the loss in Hialeah was staggering

Before 1992, "there was only one real hurricane. When South Floridians speak of 'the hurricane,' everyone knows which storm is meant—the infamous storm of 1926." Arva Moore Parks, Introduction to L. F. Reardon, *The Florida Hurricane and Disaster*, ii.

TABLE 4 Hurricane Activity in Dade County During the Twentieth Century

Year (grouped by decades)	Landfall Date	Name*	Category**	Eye over Dade County	Eye around Dade County
1904	October 17		1	•	
1906	June 16		2	•	
1906	October 17		2	•	
1909	October 11		3		•
1916	October 18		2		•
1924	September 15		1	•	
1926	July 28		2		•
1926	September 18		4	•	
1929	September 28		3		•
1935	September 3		5		•
1935	November 14		2	•	
1941	October 6		2	•	
1945	June 24		1	•	
1947	September 17		4		•
1947	October 11		1	•	
1948	October 5		2	•	
1950	October 17	King	3	•	
1960	September 9	Donna	4		•
1964	August 27	Cleo	2	•	
1965	September 8	Betsy	3		•
1966	October 4	Inez	1		•
1979	September 3	David	2		•
1987	October 13	Floyd	1		•
1992	August 24	Andrew	4	•	

Source: Adapted from Stephen K. Doig, "Storm Warnings."

*Storms were not named before 1950.

**Category 1 designates hurricanes with sustained wind speeds of 74–95 mph; category 2, those of 96–110 mph; category 3, those of 111–130 mph; category 4, those of 131–155 mph; and category 5, hurricanes packing winds in excess of 156 mph.

because of the poorly constructed homes. In Dade County as a whole, forty-seven thousand people were left homeless.

The 1992 and 1926 hurricanes are just two of fifty-six tropical storms that have battered Florida since the beginning of the twentieth century.[3] In this century the Dade County area has experi-

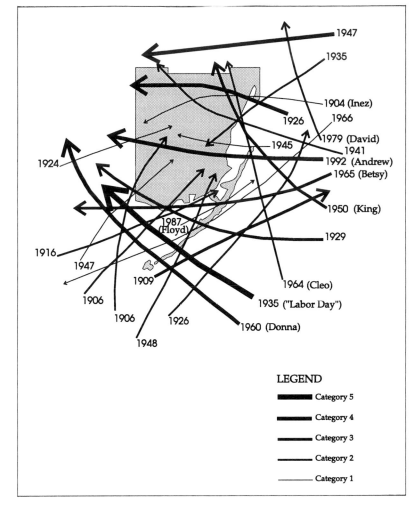

248. Hurricane activity in Dade County during the twentieth century.

1947
1935
1904 (Inez)
1966
1979 (David)
1941
1992 (Andrew)
1965 (Betsy)
1950 (King)
1929
1926
1945
1924
1987 (Floyd)
1916
1947
1909
1906
1906
1926
1948
1964 (Cleo)
1935 ("Labor Day")
1960 (Donna)

LEGEND
▬▬▬ Category 5
▬▬▬ Category 4
▬▬ Category 3
▬ Category 2
— Category 1

enced a total of twenty-four hurricanes, of which thirteen passed directly over and the remaining eleven around the area (Figure 248). Dade County has experienced at least one direct hurricane in seven of the ten decades this century (Table 4). Three-quarters of the twenty-four hurricanes occurred in the months of September and October. The strongest hurricane of the century raged through during the Labor Day holiday in 1935 and devastated the Keys. Four hundred eight people were drowned or crushed to death by debris left by a seventeen-foot tidal surge. Of those who died, 288 were World War I veterans working on Federal Emergency Relief projects. The fierce hurricane also destroyed the Florida East Coast Railway right-of-way to Key West.

Hurricane Andrew was the third category-4 tropical storm to strike the Greater Miami area in this century. Andrew was regarded as the country's worst natural disaster in terms of property damage until the Los Angeles earthquake of 1994. The most badly hit areas were Florida City, Redland, Homestead, Naranja, Princeton,

Goulds, Cutler Ridge, Perrine, and West Kendall, which all bore the brunt of the continuous high winds within the dangerous eye wall of the small, intensely violent storm. The outer edges of the eye wall extended from Kendall Drive in the north to just beyond the Ocean Reef Club in Key Largo to the south (Figure 249). Descriptions of the destructive force of the hurricane were a daily feature in the local communication media for weeks after the storm. In the *Miami Herald*, special articles on the devastation of the communities in South Dade included *For rebounding West Perrine, storm is a detour; Goulds: Dade's stepchild?; Naranja: Ignored, except by storm; In Redland, nature destroyed itself; Town 'nobody wanted' in ruins: Florida City demolished but not dead.* The community of Naranja Lakes, which once numbered three thousand five hundred people, was reduced to a virtual ghost town as residents abandoned their destroyed homes.[4] It is located west of the Florida Turnpike and north of S.W. 280th Street. Later property owners voted Naranja Lakes out of existence, and a community died. Besides the extensive damage to the built-up area, Hurricane Andrew also dam-

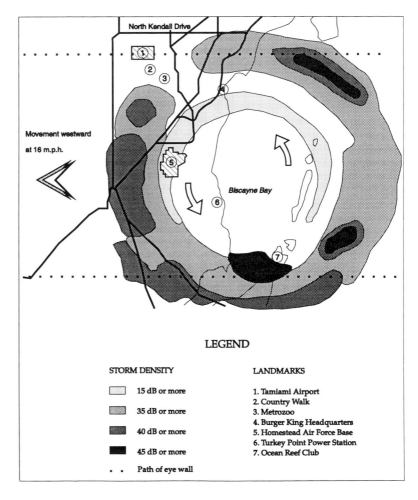

249. Hurricane Andrew's eye over South Dade at 4:55 a.m., Monday, 24 August 1992.

LEGEND

STORM DENSITY

15 dB or more

35 dB or more

40 dB or more

45 dB or more

· · Path of eye wall

LANDMARKS

1. Tamiami Airport
2. Country Walk
3. Metrozoo
4. Burger King Headquarters
5. Homestead Air Force Base
6. Turkey Point Power Station
7. Ocean Reef Club

aged Biscayne National Park and denuded or uprooted 50 percent or more of the mangroves in the Everglades National Park. This damage was classified as "catastrophic" by Tom Smith, a marine biologist with the Florida Department of Natural Resources.[5]

Each update of the awesome impact of the hurricane increased the extent of the damage caused. Fifteen deaths in Dade County were directly attributable to Hurricane Andrew. By the end of the year at least eighty-five more people had died for reasons related to the storm. One detailed report catalogued the damage to buildings, agriculture, and the environment. It estimated the total impact as exceeding $20 billion, with the insurance industry losses estimated at $7.3 billion.[6] The same report further assessed that one hundred sixty thousand people were left homeless, eighty-six thousand were out of work, and eighty-two thousand businesses were devastated or damaged. Of the over twenty-eight thousand dwellings destroyed, nearly one-third were mobile homes. Electrical supply and telephone service to a large section of South Dade were severely curtailed because of damage to lines and equipment. A computer analysis of census and property data revealed that had Hurricane Andrew hit farther north than it did, property damage would have been three times greater, and nearly five times as many people would have been rendered homeless.[7]

Many private and public organizations responded to the aftermath of the hurricane. The greatest priority was given to supplying food, water, sanitation, and shelter, and to treating people who needed medical attention, particularly in the hardest-hit areas of southern Dade County. The extent of the natural disaster made it necessary for the military to be deployed, with its impressive array of hardware and work force. When the military machine had gathered speed, it turned out to be the biggest rescue mission ever, surpassing that of Hurricane Hugo in 1991 and the task of helping Kurdish refugees after the end of Desert Storm in 1991. It also exceeded the riot assignments in Los Angeles in 1992 and in Washington, D.C., in 1968.[8] In addition, the largest federal relief package in the country's history—$8 billion—was approved to aid residents, small businesses, the agriculture industry, transportation, education, the public health service, and Homestead Air Force Base.[9] The government's effort was supported by the We Will Rebuild organization of more than a hundred of Dade County's influential residents. They raised nearly $18 million in cash and pledges in just a few weeks after Hurricane Andrew ravaged South Dade.

The most visible change to the physical environment of South Dade immediately after the hurricane was the devastated homes and downed trees. Soon there were also new sounds. Neighborhoods resounded to the buzz of portable generators and the drone of Huey, Black Hawk, and Chinook Army helicopters overhead. In the worst-hit areas these sounds were overlaid by the rumble of the Army's "Humvee" jeeps and trucks. Within days the din of the chain saw became pervasive in all neighborhoods, as did the sights of ever-increasing piles of tree debris at the wayside. Soon South Dade experienced perhaps the greatest gathering of dump trucks in American history. Hundreds of independent drivers from all over made their way south to haul away the debris. Rubble was piled high along virtually every street in the areas ravaged by the hurricane. Surveys showed another consequence of Hurricane Andrew: over ninety thousand residents expect to move from the area, and more than half of these will leave Dade County permanently.

Critical comments on building practices surfaced soon after the hurricane had passed through South Dade. The major finding of various professionals—engineers, architects, and wind experts— was that many roofs were inadequately designed and constructed. It was argued that the destruction to so many homes, beginning with the roof, would not have been as severe if dwellings had been better designed and constructed. There was also concern that federal mobile home regulations offered less protection against high winds than had been previously thought. Failed lessons from the past now haunted local government officials. Articles such "A refusal to learn from the past" and "Hard lessons of '60 storm go

250. Defran House, 18050 S.W. 216th Street, Goulds. 1920s. Listed as a historic building by Metro-Dade County, this structure shows a typical level of destruction caused by the hurricane.

251. Anderson's Corner, 15700 S.W. 232nd Street, Silver Palm. 1911–1912. Roof and structural damage from Hurricane Andrew is evident.

unheeded"[10] pointed out that the results of studies conducted after Hurricane Donna blew through the Lower Keys in 1960 and Hurricane Betsy through Dade County in 1965 were strikingly similar to the preliminary results after Hurricane Andrew. Unfortunately, the warnings concerning the need to correct building design and construction faults made after the two hurricanes of the 1960s were disregarded, possibly contributing to the destruction caused by Hurricane Andrew. Three studies found that not only was the South Florida Building Code vague but also it had eroded over many years.[11] The vagueness led to misinterpretation by architects, engineers, and contractors and was a factor in the lack of crucial roof supports. Had these supports been adequately provided, they would have prevented much of the destruction wrought by the hurricane. Beyond construction problems, some homeowners soon found themselves in another predicament. Laxity in flood rules for the past twenty years would require rebuilding homes at an elevated level, adding dramatically to construction costs.[12]

Damage to the historical buildings located in South Dade was generally severe (Figure 250). A report recorded that Hurricane Andrew destroyed fifteen of sixty-five recognized landmarks in the southern area of the county.[13] Examples of the damage to the private buildings described or illustrated earlier in this book include the severe damage to the Charles Deering Estate buildings and landscape, with partial demolition of the Richmond Inn. The Mobley Wood House and the Mindermann House both suffered the loss of the roof and some structural damage, requiring massive repair. Palm Lodge had repairable damage. As the Seminole/Landmark Hotel had lost most of its roof and part of the north wall, the structure would require complete rebuilding. The Redland Community Church building is a great loss to the Redland Historic District.

Damage to the public buildings of South Dade was even worse than that wrought on the private buildings. Several structures in the Cauley Square complex were demolished by the hurricane. There was severe damage to the second story of the Boulevard Building. At Anderson's Corner, the second floor was shifted by the intense winds, and the front gable end fell in so that the building may have to be completely reconstructed (Figure 251). At the old Homestead Town Hall building, most of the roof covering was lost during the storm and most of the truss system disappeared (Figure 252). The Homestead Depot, which had been part of the Florida Pioneer Museum, was demolished. The Redland Schoolhouse was leveled by the storm. Significant modern buildings that were severely damaged included the Burger King Headquarters building and the Cutler Ridge Mall; both were reopened a year later. Homestead Air Force Base is to be reopened as a joint military-civilian airport and as an International Technical Research and Aviation Center. Military use will be reduced to two Air Force Reserve units and the Florida National Guard.

Besides destroying historic buildings, Hurricane Andrew also devastated gardens and parks. At David Fairchild Tropical Garden, for example, 75 percent of the Garden's 5,000 species of trees and

252. Old Town Hall, 43 North Krome Avenue, Homestead. 1917. Roof and interior suffered damage from Hurricane Andrew.

253. Baldwin House, Stiltsville, Biscayne Bay, 1988. The house itself suffered little damage, but the docks were swept away by Hurricane Andrew.

shrubs was destroyed. At Matheson Hammock Park, the coral rock concession stand was virtually destroyed. The marina had to be closed on account of extensive damage to over a hundred boats docked there and to the marina piers.

Damage to historic landmarks just beyond the northern wall of the eye of the hurricane in Coral Gables, Coconut Grove, and downtown Miami was moderate (Figure 253). In Coral Gables, the major damage was to the Alhambra Water Tower. The Miami-Biltmore Hotel suffered shattered windows and some water damage, as did the Freedom Tower in downtown Miami. At Vizcaya, the basement flooded because of the storm surge, the stone barge in the bay was damaged, and the statues in the garden were overturned. Many trees, gates, and fences were blown down. The Cape Florida Lighthouse on the southern tip of Key Biscayne suffered only soil erosion at the foundation. Around the structure the 400-acre area of trees of the Cape Florida/Bill Baggs Recreation Area was razed by the hurricane. At the Barnacle in Coconut Grove the structure of the house remained intact although the front doors and back wall of the boathouse were blown out. The interior was damaged by wind and rain. There was extensive damage to the landscaping. It is marvelous that two of Dade County's oldest structures, the Cape Florida Lighthouse (1825) and the Barnacle (1891–1908), survived yet another hurricane.

a p p e n d i x   a

Human Interventions

Mosquito Control and Air-Conditioning

A S mentioned in Chapter 3, human intervention is needed in the Greater Miami to overcome two sources of discomfort in the area, mosquitoes and the heat and humidity. This Appendix covers these interventions in more detail.

Mosquito Control

After a dengue plague in Miami in the 1920s, the first concerted efforts were made to "get the bugs out" by spraying poison, stocking swamps with insect-eating fish, and cutting ditches throughout the swamps. In 1935, citizens voted to tax themselves to pay for mosquito control by approving the designation of Dade County as a Mosquito Control District. Under this program, drainage ditches were dug in low-lying areas to eliminate mosquito breeding grounds.

After World War II, spraying with DDT was introduced, ending in 1972, when the chemical was banned for environmental reasons. Malathion, used briefly thereafter, had to be discontinued on the same grounds. Its substitute, Baytex, is still in use today.

Metro-Dade County's Mosquito Control Division employs a systematic domestic inspection service, then sprays selected areas from an aircraft or trucks. Areas are selected based on residents' telephone calls, which can number many hundreds a day during the season from May to October.

Air-Conditioning

The use of air-conditioning in Greater Miami is best understood in the context of its development nationally. Willis Haviland Carrier, regarded as the father of air-conditioning, introduced the world's

287

first scientific air-conditioning system in 1902 and marked the first major advance with the centrifugal refrigeration machine in 1923.[1]

Before the introduction of this machine, air-conditioning was installed in industrial plants, but now a new market opened up in motion-picture and other theaters, including the Gusman that started in downtown Miami in 1926.

The first sale nationally of a small air-conditioning unit—the self-contained "Weathermaker" for small retail stores, restaurants, and office suites—was made two years later. The "Atmosphere Cabinet" as a room cooler and the use of the nontoxic "Freon-12" as the refrigerant were destined to revolutionize air-conditioning when they were placed on the market in 1932. The Conduit Weathermaster System for skyscraper office buildings was introduced in 1939. But it was only after World War II that air conditioners were produced in volume, when the "luxury label" attached to air-conditioning gave way to recognition of its practical value.

Governance

Municipal Charter Process and
Metropolitan Government

I N Chapter 4 reference was made to the municipal charter process in Florida and also to the establishment of metropolitan government in Dade County. As these topics are not widely documented, this appendix may prove useful for those with special interests in these areas.

Municipal Charter Process

Historically, there were two ways in which settlements in Florida could incorporate as municipalities. One means was through a special act of incorporation passed by the Territorial Legislative Council or, after 1845, the legislature of the State of Florida. The other way was through general law, specifically Section 8, Article VIII, of the Florida Constitution of 1885. Section 8 provided the legislature with power to establish or abolish municipalities. Most settlements were incorporated under this section. Section 2 provided for the establishment and abolishment of municipalities by general or special law, the powers of incorporated areas to conduct municipal government, and annexation by municipalities.[1] In 1956, a third way to incorporate was added: An amendment to the state constitution allowed for Home Rule, in which, under certain conditions, there is a transfer of powers from the state to a county. Under this provision,.metropolitan government was established in Dade County in 1957, transforming the entire structure of local governance in the Greater Miami area.

Besides the constitutional authority that allowed the state to establish municipalities, general law also allowed communities to incorporate themselves. The first general law of this kind was the Government of Cities and Towns, passed in 1868.[2] Of relevance is

Section 1. It provided for a minimum of 100 qualified male inhabitants of any hamlet or village in the state to incorporate themselves and establish municipal government. Qualified males were those who had paid their poll taxes, who had resided in the area for at least six months, and who were registered to vote. This general law was repealed in 1869. It was replaced in its entirety by a new law. The new law became the basic act for the incorporation of cities and towns and a uniform system of municipal government in the state.[3] In this law of 1869, the minimum number of male inhabitants of a settlement who could establish a municipal government was reduced to 50. This number was further reduced to 25 in 1875, when a new general act for municipal incorporation was passed.[4]

In 1941, when the new decimal system was inaugurated, Chapter 165, Organization and Dissolution of Municipalities, became the operative act. It was not until 1947 that this law was amended to allow female inhabitants to be included in the process.[5] Another amendment in 1951 increased the minimum number of male and female inhabitants who could establish municipal government from 25 to 150.[6] In 1967, this number was further increased to 1,000.[7] The basic act of 1875, with its subsequent amendments, was replaced by the general law of 1974.[8] Under this current law, the minimum number required to establish a municipality is 1,500 people for counties where the population is under 50,000. In counties with a population over 50,000 the minimum is 5,000 people.

Section 3 of the 1868 law, the Government of Cities and Towns, specified that a settlement with 300 or more inhabitants would be designated a city, while a settlement with fewer than 300 would be declared a town. This definition was retained in subsequent laws until the distinction between city and town was abandoned in the current act of 1974.

Metropolitan Government

The significance of the creation of metropolitan government in Dade County should be seen in its national context. Although several metropolitan efforts were initiated in the country during the 1920s, there was little public interest until the end of World War II. After 1947, of fifteen major proposals for the creation of metropolitan government in the country, only three were accepted by voters: Dade County in Florida, Baton Rouge in Louisiana, and Nashville in Tennessee.[9] The major proposals were the culmination of over a century of efforts to solve the problems of the rapid population growth, industrialization, and the outward spread of cities.[10]

The "metropolitan problem" was identified as the frictions generated by multiple local government, the lack of areawide planning, the decline of the central city and unchecked suburban sprawl, and the depletion of financial resources. In the 1920s, a model for the reform in the governing of cities and counties had been formulated. The most important features of the model were nonpartisan local elections, the integration of local governments in urban areas to overcome the problem of fragmentation, home rule, and a council-manager form of government. The charter adopted by Dade County in 1957 included all these major reform proposals.

Functional Consolidations. Before the attempts to merge the cities in Greater Miami, there were several functional consolidations of areawide services. These involved a transfer of local power to one central agency.[11] Before any public agencies were consolidated, a private corporation, the Greater Miami Traffic Association, was organized in 1939 to coordinate a wide range of public transportation services and utilities. In the public sector, the Dade County Health Unit was established in 1943. Also in 1943, the Greater Miami Port Authority was created (to be replaced by the Dade County Port Authority in 1945) to acquire and manage harbor and airport facilities. In 1945, Mayor Leonard K. Thomson of Miami proposed that the city be consolidated with Dade County into a single entity, but voters rejected the proposal. The County Commission, led by Charles Crandon, did take over many areawide responsibilities, however, to begin the process of consolidation. The County took over the sewer system and Jackson Memorial Hospital, created a unified county school system out of ten districts, established the Port Authority, and created the site for the Miami International Airport from the Pan American Field and the Army Air Transport Field.

Recognition of the multiplicity and obsolescence of the building codes came to a head in 1947 when the Miami Builders Exchange formed a group called the "Building Officials of South Florida." After two years of work, the group prepared a uniform building code that was adopted only by the City of Miami and the County, for the unincorporated areas. This group persisted in its efforts, and in December 1957 its South Florida Building Code was adopted and became effective in Dade County. For the most part, the county government did not play a dominant role in many of these arrangements. Leaders of the consolidation movement were hardly satisfied by the services provided by these various consolidations. These activities, however, helped to inform the voters of the needs and issues in governing the county and prepared the way for governmental reform in Greater Miami.

The urban area of Dade County, much of which was administered by various municipalities, thus began to emerge as the city of Greater Miami. The creation of Metro-Dade County in 1957 was a compromise; existing cities and towns retained certain local duties. The County became responsible for certain areawide functions for the whole area and also for local issues in the unincorporated areas.

City-County Consolidation Proposals. The establishment of metropolitan government in Dade County did not occur overnight. Among the first proposals were those made by the University of Miami's Commission on Post-War Planning in 1943. It was the powerful business interests within the City of Miami, however, that were largely responsible for the consolidation attempts from 1944 to 1953. The Miami Chamber of Commerce Committee on Planning and Industry proposed the establishment of a county Co-ordinating and Planning Committee. This Committee was set up by the County Commission in 1944 with the assistance of Dr. Bowman F. Ashe, founder and president of the University of Miami. The Committee was replaced by a Planning Board in 1945, but the Board operated with only nominal effectiveness.[12] In 1945, a constitutional amendment was proposed by the Mayor of the City of Miami, Leonard K. Thomson. His purpose was to consolidate all existing governments in Dade County into a single municipality to be called the City and County of Miami. The proposal was not submitted for a vote by the Dade delegation in the state legislature. This radical proposal was modified in a measure passed by the legislature in 1947, but defeated by Dade voters in 1948. The modification was to amend the constitution to allow Dade County voters to. adopt a home rule charter for a new County of Miami, with limited consolidation—the City of Miami, four small municipalities, and Dade County. There were many arguments for and against consolidation to solve the problem of too many governmental units, conflict among them, and duplication of functions.[13] A proposed constitutional amendment to offer home rule to Florida counties was submitted to the state's electorate in 1952. The proposed amendment was carried in Dade County but was defeated statewide. The next year a special June referendum to abolish and consolidate the City of Miami into the government of Dade County was rejected by under a thousand votes (50.8 percent against abolition as opposed to 49.2 percent for it in a large turnout of city voters.[14]

In the same year, 1953, the City Commission of Miami, in reaction to the close call in the vote for abolition, created the Metropolitan Miami Municipal (3M) Board. The Board was to study municipal and county governmental operations and to draft a plan for either consolidation, merger, federation, or reorganization of local governments. In turn, the Board engaged the Department of Government at the University of Miami and a firm of Chicago governmental consultants, Public Administration Services, to carry out the project. In January 1955, the Board unanimously adopted the recommendations presented to it and voted to obtain the required legislation. The Florida legislature approved amending Article VIII, Section 11, of the Constitution of Florida to authorize home rule government for Dade County. In the November 1956 election, the voters of the state ratified the amendment in a 70–30 split. In Dade County the vote was similar to the statewide one, with 72 percent in favor of Dade home rule as compared to 28 percent against it.[15] The proposed amendment had survived a challenge when the Florida Supreme Court upheld its constitutionality in September. In 1955, the legislature also created the Metropolitan Charter Board to prepare a home rule charter for submission to the county electorate.[16] In a special countywide election in May 1956, the charter was adopted by the voters by only a small margin—51 percent for compared to 49 percent against—in a small turnout (26 percent).[17] It would appear that the public had become confused because of the anticharter campaign mounted by municipal officials, employees, and their organizations.[18] Metropolitan government was launched officially on 21 July 1957.

Metropolitan Government. In a home rule charter, a city or county may adopt its own charter and amend or repeal it at will. In other words, legislative consent is not needed for charter changes. The advantage of home rule is that local lawmaking power is transferred from the state capitol to the people of the city or county. It is a grant of local autonomy. The county and municipalities, therefore, are free from having to turn to the legislature for the enactment of local laws.

Besides Dade County, the only comparable system was the Toronto, Canada, federation formed in 1953. There were three basic characteristics of the original Metropolitan Dade County system of government.[19] The first was substantial home rule privileges, including power to create, merge, consolidate, and abolish municipal corporations, special taxing districts, boards, and other governmental offices. The second was a federated areawide government that both preserved the existing municipalities and created a new areawide government. The third was a council-manager system. In the November 1963 election, the charter was amended to adopt a weak-mayor and commissioner system.

Municipalities were to be left intact unless the services to their

"In summary the charter provides for a federated, two-tier government structure with the County having substantial area-wide powers and making it the exclusive local government for the unincorporated area. At the same time, the identity of the municipalities is protected, and the county and cities are to share responsibilities. Area-wide problems are thus addressed by an area-wide government while local problems are handled by local government."
Richard Langendorf, *Metropolitan Federalism*, 5–9, 10.

inhabitants failed to meet the minimum standards required by the metropolitan government of all municipalities. In that event, the metropolitan government could either supplement or assume the operation of such services. A municipality could not be abolished, however, without the affirmative vote of its inhabitants. The Home Rule amendment to the Florida constitution and the Metropolitan Charter provided Dade County with a strong areawide government while simultaneously preserving the municipalities as political jurisdictions. Also, the Charter did not mandate the distribution of areawide and local functions. Rather it created an arena for the continued discussion about the appropriate responsibilities and roles of the county and the municipalities. Richard Langendorf has analyzed in detail the distribution of functions, such as transportation, libraries, parks and recreation, welfare, health and hospitals, physical development, public safety, environmental services, and tax assessment and collection, that took place between the newly created two tiers of government in Dade County.[20]

The inauguration of metropolitan government in July 1957 has been described as "The Cities Declare War on Metro."[21] The negotiations that took place over the following year proved difficult in an atmosphere of conflict. The forces in favor of municipal autonomy, led by the City of Miami, were countered by the anti-autonomy groups, headed by the Miami-Dade Chamber of Commerce. In September 1958, the autonomy amendment to the Home Rule Charter was defeated at the polls. In Dade County, the autonomy amendment was defeated by a margin of 21 percent, with 39 percent of the votes for and 60 percent of the votes against the amendment.[22] Conflict continued over Metro ordinances concerning zoning and building, certificates of competency and licenses, traffic regulations, and public works. Metropolitan Dade County, however, did adopt a county urban renewal ordinance, create a county Water and Sewer Board, and establish a Transit Authority. Opposition to Dade County's home rule culminated in an amendment proposed by John McLeod, a former County Commissioner, which contained thirty-seven proposed changes to the charter. In October 1961, voters rejected the McLeod amendment by a bare 4 percent majority, 52 to 48 percent.[23] Approval would have constituted a new charter that would have deprived the metropolitan government of areawide functions, such as sewerage, water supply, transportation, traffic, and central planning. It would also have abolished the council-manager form of governance.

During the next two decades and more, there was relatively little turmoil. The election of 1972 is significant as the four candidates who believed growth should be brought under control were elected. Several reform proposals were introduced, including a sharp reduction in high-density zoning in unincorporated areas. In Key Biscayne, a building moratorium was instituted for a short while, and special waterfront development regulations were put in place.[24] Reports in 1978, 1981, and 1984 recommended altering the Dade County charter and changing the governmental structure, but these reports were not adopted.[25] In 1990, an attempt to increase the number of county commissioners, widen the geographical basis for their election, raise commissioners' salaries, and establish a stronger mayor, failed. In a small turnout of 17 percent, the voters rejected the charter revision by 78 to 22 percent.[26] Also, four attempts to change the name of Dade County did not succeed. The proposal to change the name to Miami County in 1950 lost by 69 to 31 percent. The proposal for Miami-Dade County did slightly better in the polls in 1976, losing 66 to 34 percent. There was a large loss for the name Miami-Dade again in 1984, when the vote was 73 to 27 percent. The proposal for Metropolitan Miami Dade County in 1990 lost by the largest margin of all, 87 to 13 percent.[27] It is unlikely that reform proposals to alter either the county charter or the Metro system, which has been in place since 1963, will emerge in the near future.

Notes

1. Camp to Cosmopolis

1. Fernald, *History of Florida: Atlas of Florida*, 122.

2. Tebeau, *History of Florida*, 12.

3. Bingham, "Miami: A Study in Urban Geography," 92.

4. Chardon, "Cape Florida Society of 1773," 40.

5. True, "Freducci Map of 1514–15," 50.

6. Andrews, "Florida Indians in the Seventeenth Century," 36; Kersey, *Pelts, Plumes and Hides*, 8.

7. Parks, *Miami: "The Magic City,"* 13; Kleinberg, "Ponce de León's Landings in Chequescha (Miami), Fla.," 11A.

8. Muir, *Miami, U.S.A.*, 31.

9. Marks, "Earliest Land Grants in the Miami Area," 16–18.

10. Marks, "Forgotten Spanish Land Grant in South Florida," 51–56.

11. Chardon, "Cape Florida Society of 1773," 40.

12. Frazier, "Samuel Touchett's Florida Plantation, 1771," 78.

13. Parks, "Miami in 1876," 89.

14. Dodd, "Jacob Housman of Indian Key," 3.

15. Warnke, *Ghost Towns of Florida*, 42.

16. Spanish Land Grants in Florida, vol. 3; Cash, *Story of Florida*, 2:781ff.

17. Hudson, "Beginnings in Dade County," 32.

18. Parks, "Miami in 1876," 92.

19. Black, "Richard Fitzpatrick's South Florida, 1822–1840: Part II," 45.

20. Black, "Richard Fitzpatrick's South Florida, 1822–1840: Part I," 48.

21. Acts of the Governor and Legislative Council of the Territory of Florida: Passed at the Fourteenth Session, Chapter 937 (no. XXVI), *An Act to Organize a County to be Called Dade County* (Tallahassee, Fla.: William Wilson, 1836), 19.

22. Chapter 1592, 62.

23. Peters, *Biscayne Country*, 32; Hudson, "Beginnings in Dade County," 34; Muir, *Miami, U.S.A.*, 99.

24. Grantham, "Archaeological Sites in Dade," 26.

25. Mohl, "Miami," Table 3-1, 64.

26. Kenzie, "Response to Urban Development," 17–19.

27. Heenan, "Global Cities of Tomorrow," 79–92.

28. Development Department, City of Coral Gables, "List of Multinational Companies," May 1991.

29. Whited, "Film Industry Is Basking in *Vice's* Glow," 4B.

30. Filkins, "Center for Arts Approved," 1A; Meadows, "Arts Hall: Now the Real Work Begins," 1I; Dolen et al., "Critics Assess Planned Art Center," *Miami Herald*, 18 July 1993, 8I.

31. Kohen, "Art in Public Places," 1I.

32. Garcia, "New Owner Rechristens CenTrust Tower," 1C.

2. Mosaic of Communities

1. Chapter 25758 (Number 762).

2. Rowe, "Islandia," 12.

3. Wragg, "Local Government, Key Biscayne Style," 2C; Faiola, "Conte to Head Key Biscayne," 2B, "Key Biscayne Voters," 1B, and "Metro Approves," 1B.

4. Burkhardt, " 'Starch Making': A Pioneer Florida Industry," 49.

5. Ammidown, "Wagner Family: Pioneer Life on the Miami River," 5.

6. Black, "Richard Fitzpatrick's South Florida, 1822–1840: Part I," 64.

7. Hudson, "Beginnings in Dade County," 29.

8. Parks, "Miami in 1876," 129.

9. Shappee, "Flagler's Undertakings in Miami in 1897," 3–13.

10. Sewell, *Miami Memoirs*, 5.

11. Sewell, ix.

12. Peters, *"Biscayne Country,"* 14.

13. Tebeau, *History of Florida*, 305.

14. George, "Traffic Control in Early Miami," 3.

15. Wolff, *Miami Metro: The Road to Urban Unity*, 43.

16. Huber, "Can Brickell Beat the Blues?" 24–26.

17. Kleinberg, *Miami: The Way We Were*, 96.

18. Rene Rodriguez, "Private Funds Built Boulevard," 18.

19. Parks, "History of Coconut Grove," 9.

20. Parks, "History," 21ff.

21. Parks, "History," 19.

22. Tanfani, "Grove Voters Pick Council, Support Secession from City," 3B.

23. Dietrich, "Arch Creek: Prehistory to Public Park," 55.

24. Historic Preservation Division, Metro-Dade County, *From Wilderness to Metropolis*, 111.

25. Parks, "Miami in 1876," 122.

26. Rene Rodriguez, "Ojus Neighborhood Began as a Short-lived Little Town," 25.

27. Taylor, *Villages of South Dade*, 37.

28. Taylor, 160.

29. Carson, "Forty Years of Miami Beach," 6.

30. Carson, 3.

31. Muir, *Miami, U.S.A.*, 140.

32. Root, *Miami Beach Art Deco Guide*, 9.

33. Department of Historic Preservation and Urban Design, Miami Beach, "Miami Beach Historic Data Base" (Miami Beach: City of Miami Beach, June 1991), a list of 871 standing buildings identified as "historic."

34. Introduction to *Portfolio*, edited by Capitman, 2.

35. Professor Aristides J. Millas called the new zoning ordinance "outrageous"; quoted in Gage, "South Beach Observed," 15. See also Warren, "Will Success Kill the Deco District?" 21–24.

36. Fred Tasker, "South Beach: Can It Win the Future Without Losing the Past?" 1D.

37. Curtis, "Lament for an Art Deco Landmark," 40–47; Tomb, "Extinct in the '80s," 2C.

38. Joaquin Roy, quoted in Biddulph, "Merrick's Idea for Street Names Confounds Author," 3.

39. Dunlop, "How Hialeah Happened," 1J.

40. Historic Preservation Division, Metro-Dade County, *From Wilderness to Metropolis*, 105.

41. Robertson, "Tales of Old Lie Within Area's Sprawl," 1G.

42. Taylor, *Villages of South Dade*, 17.

43. Peters, *Lemon City*, 3.

44. Mesa, "Kendall's Past," 28.

45. Taylor, *Villages of South Dade*, 50.

46. Hart, "Garald Parker: Glades' Great Discoverer," 2E.

47. Anderson, "Bush Signs Law to Expand Glades," 1A.

48. Rene Rodriguez, "Rock Pit Operator Namesake of Park," 19.

49. Historic Preservation Division, Metro-Dade County, *From Wilderness to Metropolis*, 150.

50. Georgia Tasker, "Parks' Designer Helped Shape Dade," 11H.

3. Factors of Growth

1. Parks, *Forgotten Frontier*, 41.

2. Wolff, "Recent Economic Trends in South Florida," 48.

3. Mohl, "Miami," 73ff.

4. Fred Tasker, "Greetings from Florida," 1J. See also graph in "Tourism Rebounds," *Miami Herald*, 10 November 1991, 4J.

5. Personal communication, John Benimeli, Dade County Public Works Department, Mosquito Control Division, 2 February 1990.

6. Ingels, *Willis Haviland Carrier: The Father of Air Conditioning*, 61.

7. Personal communication, Ted Olssen, professor emeritus, Department of Mechanical Engineering, University of Miami, 7 February 1990.

8. Bramson, "Railroad Stations in Dade County," 73–78.

9. Historic Preservation Division, Metro-Dade County, *From Wilderness to Metropolis*, 24.

10. *From Wilderness to Metropolis*, 45.

11. Baird, "Trailing the Barefoot Mailman," 46.

12. Hopkins, "Development of the Overseas Highway," 56.

13. Davis, "Development of the Major Commercial Airlines in Dade County," 4.

14. Reed et al., "The Bitter End: Pan Am Closes," 1A; "Pan Am's Storied History," 20A.

15. Adams, "Some Pre-Boom Developers of Dade County," 36.

16. George, "Brokers, Binders, and Builders," 46.

17. Mohl, "Miami," 59.

18. Allman, *Miami: City of the Future*, 225.

19. Sessa, "Miami on the Eve of the Boom: 1923," 11.

20. Tebeau, *History of Florida*, 384:

Assessed value of property: from $63,800,000 to $421,101,367 (a 560 percent increase).

Mileage of paved streets: from 32 to 420 (a 1212 percent increase).

Value of building permits: from $4,478,044 to $58,647,656 (a 1210 percent increase).

In Miami 7,500 real estate licenses were issued in 1925.

Countywide 971 subdivisions were platted; 174,530 deeds were filed; and 481 apartments and hotels were constructed.

21. Muir, *Miami, U.S.A.*, 165.

22. Muir, 167.

23. Tebeau, *History of Florida*, 434.

24. *Miami Herald*, Monday, 3 February 1986, 2B. See also "The Most Influential People in South Florida History," *Miami Herald*, 7 February 1993, 4J.

4. Framework of Development

1. Dade County Research Foundation, "Truth about City-County Consolidation," 21.

2. Sofen, *Metropolitan Experiment*, 12.

3. Lotz, *Metropolitan Dade County*, 11.

4. Sofen, *Metropolitan Experiment*, 211ff.

5. Langendorf, *Metropolitan Federalism*, Table 32, 12-4.

6. Wolff, *Miami Metro*, vi.

7. Glendening, "Metropolitan Dade County Government," 96.

8. Mohl, "Miami Metro Charter Revisions and the Politics of the Eighties."

9. Chapter 19539, renumbered Chapter 176 in 1941 when the decimal system was introduced.

10. Coral Gables (1925); City of Miami Beach (zoning code, 1930; building code, 1941); City of Miami (zoning code, 1934; building code, 1936); Dade County—unincorporated areas (1938).

11. Chapter 163, Part II, County and Municipal Planning for Future Development (sections 163.160 to 163.3211).

12. O'Connell, "Legislating 'Quality Planning,'" 3.

13. Rhodes, "Growth Management in Florida 1985 and Beyond," 1.

14. Chapter 163, Part II, was retitled the Local Government Comprehensive Planning Act (75–257).

15. Sadowski, "Growth Management," 1.

16. Dunlop, "Projects Threaten Biscayne Bay's Beauty," 2I.

17. Chapter 186, Florida State Comprehensive Planning Act of 1972, as amended in 1980 (1980–315).

18. Chapter 163, amended in 1982 (1982–180).

19. Chapter 163 was amended in 1987 (1987–243) to include Title IV, Neighborhood Improvement Districts, the Safe Neighborhood Act.

20. DeGrove, "Historical Development of Growth Management in Florida," 1.

21. Chapter 163, Part II, Florida Statutes, was amended in 1985. Section 9J–5, Florida Administrative Code, was adopted in 1986.

22. DeGrove, "Historical Development of Growth Management in Florida," 2.

23. Strouse, "300,000 Moved to West Dade in '80s," 1B.

24. Haas, "Shaping the Future," 1H.

25. Land and Water Management, Chapter 380: Part I, the Environmental Land and Water Management Act; Part II, the Florida Coastal Management Act of 1978; Part III, Florida Communities Trust Act of 1989.

26. The Water Resources Act of 1972, Chapter 373: Part I, State Water Resource Plan; Part II, Permitting of Consumptive Uses of Water; Part III, Regulation of Wells; Part IV, Management of Storage of Surface Waters; Part V, Finance and Taxation; Part VI, Miscellaneous Provisions.

27. The Land Conservation Act of 1972, Chapter 259.

28. Florida Statutes, Title XXVIII Natural Resources: Conservation, Reclamation—Chapter 376, Pollutant Discharge Prevention and Removal (1970–244); Chapter 377, Energy Resources (1974–186); Chapter 378, Land Reclamation (78–136).

29. So and Getzels, eds., *Practice of Local Government Planning*, 121 ff.

30. Anderson, "Bush Signs Law," 1A; Dewar and Zaldivar, "Congress Approves Bill," 30A.

31. Whited, "West Dade at Crossroads Over Growth," 1B.

32. "Environmentally Sensitive Lands Tax," *Miami Herald*, 9 May 1990, 1B.

5. Political, Social, and Economic Backdrop

1. Tebeau, *History of Florida*, 320.
2. Tebeau, 417.
3. Muir, *Miami, U.S.A.*, 232.
4. Carney, "Population Growth in Miami and Dade County," 51.
5. Buchanan, "Miami's Bootleg Boom," 13.
6. Tebeau, *History of Florida*, 394.
7. Muir, *Miami, U.S.A.*, 179.
8. Tebeau, *History of Florida*, 406.
9. Mohl, "Miami," 62.
10. Didion, *Miami*, 14.
11. Mohl, "Settlement of Blacks in South Florida," 124.
12. Boswell, Sheskin, and Truss, "Attitudes, Causes, and Perceptions," 1–15.
13. Cartano, "Drug Industry in South Florida," 109.
14. *Miami Herald*, 25 January 1990, 12A.
15. Gugliotta, "1980–1989: Decade in Review," 69.
16. "1987," *South Florida*, January 1990, 92.
17. Morgenthau et al., "Miami: America's Casablanca," 22.
18. Viewpoint Special, *Miami Herald*, 31 December 1989, M.
19. Mohl, "Settlement of Blacks in South Florida," 112.
20. Wallace, "South Florida Grows to a Latin Beat," 1A; Faiola, "Hispanics Rise to 42% in Gables, Black Numbers Fall," 6; Wallace, "South Florida's Evolving Ethnic Diversity," 1C.
21. Goldfarb, "Prejudice Felt by Latin Blacks," 1B.
22. Lopez, "Florida Fact," 6B.
23. Goldfarb, "Immigrants Change East Little Havana," 1B.
24. George, "Colored Town: Miami's Black Community, 1896–1930," 435; Strouse, "Rebirth of Overtown," 1A; and "Inner City," 1A; Swarns, "Exodus," 1A.
25. Mohl, "Settlement of Blacks in South Florida," 123.
26. Chapman, "History of South Florida," 41.
27. Boswell and Curtis, "Hispanization of Metropolitan Miami," 145.
28. Alvarez, "Thousands of Cuban Tourists Staying," 1B; "Cuban Rafter Tally (486) Tops Mark for all of '90," *Miami Herald*, 2 May 1991, 1B; Whitefield, "Raft Trips to U.S. Become Obsession," 1A; Viglucci and Bellido, "Waves of Cubans," 1B.
29. Boswell and Curtis, "Hispanization of Metropolitan Miami," 141.
30. Strouse, "Non-Cuban Hispanic Census Count Rising," 1B.
31. Sheskin, "Jews of South Florida," 163.
32. Sheskin, "South Florida—650,000 Jews!!"
33. Longino and McNeal, "Elderly Population of South Florida," 183.
34. Taylor, *Villages of South Dade*, 48.
35. Wilson, "Miami: From Frontier to Metropolis," 30.
36. Stronge, "Southeast Florida Economy," 85.
37. Chapter 663 (Chapter 77–157) Banking Code: International Banking, State of Florida.
38. *Miami Herald Business Magazine*, 21 May 1990, 13.
39. Parks, *Miami: "The Magic City,"* 167.
40. Ferdinand, "Bridge to Latin Markets," 6B; Birger, "Gateway for the Latin Trade," 24ff; Booth, "Capital of Latin America, Miami," 84.
41. Reed, "Running to Stay in Place," 1ff.
42. Strouse, "Picture Perfect," 30ff.; Dorschner, "Light Industry," 8ff.
43. Russell, "Business in Miami Is a Tale of Two Fortunes," 1C.

Part II

1. Milizia, *Principj di Archittetura Civile*.

6. Architectural Styles

1. Historic Preservation Division, Metro-Dade County, *From Wilderness to Metropolis*; Historic Preservation Division, Metro-Dade County, *Resourceful Rehab: A Guide for Historic Building in Dade County Miami*; Dunlop, "A Style of Our Own," 1I; Ducassi, "History Shaped Housing," 6–7HB; Vondracek, "Know Your Art Deco," 1G.
2. Gelabert-Navia, "Mediterranean Legacy," 49–51; Pancoast, "Miami Architecture So Far," 16.
3. LaRoue and Uguccioni, *Coral Gables in Postcards*, 9–10.
4. Ordinance 2665, adopted 13 January 1987, and Ordinance 2714, adopted 25 August 1987.
5. Cerwinske, *Tropical Deco*, 9.
6. Historic Preservation Division, Metro-Dade County, *From Wilderness to Metropolis*, 70–73.

7. Fletcher, *History of Architecture*, 1321.

8. Hitchcock and Johnson, *The International Style*.

9. Raeburn, *Architecture of the Western World*, 264.

10. Jencks, "Evolution and Mutation of Modern Architecture," 12–17.

11. McKean, "Twentieth Century," 262.

12. Penn, "Glass Buildings," 14.

13. Eagleton, "Awakening from Modernity," 194.

14. Greenwood, "Review Essay," 53–59.

15. Miami: Historic Preservation Division, Metro-Dade County, *From Wilderness to Metropolis*; Junior League of Miami, *Historic Downtown Miami: Self-Guided Tour*.

Miami Beach: Historic Preservation Division, Metro-Dade County, *From Wilderness to Metropolis*, Appendix—Selected List of Significant Sites; Olsen, *A Guide to the Architecture of Miami Beach*; Cerwinske, *Tropical Deco*; Capitman, *Deco Delights*.

Coral Gables: LaRoue and Uguccioni, *Coral Gables in Postcards*; Historic Preservation Division, Coral Gables, *Coral Gables: A Brief History*; Historic Preservation Committee, Junior League of Miami, *Historic Coral Gables: Self-Guided Tour*.

Coconut Grove: Historic Preservation Division, Metro-Dade County, *From Wilderness to Metropolis*; Historic Preservation Division, Junior League of Miami, *Historic Coconut Grove: Self-Guided Tour*.

North Dade: Historic Preservation Division, Metro-Dade County, *From Wilderness to Metropolis*; Junior League of Miami, *Historic Northeast Dade: Self-Guided Tour*.

South Dade: Historic Preservation Division, Metro-Dade County, *From Wilderness to Metropolis*; Junior League of Miami, *Historic South Dade: Self-Guided Tour*.

16. City of Coral Gables, *Master List. Coral Gables Register of Historic Landmarks*, May 1991 (65 properties listed); City of Miami, *City of Miami Historic Sites and Districts*, June 1991 (79 sites and districts listed); City of Miami Beach, *Miami Beach Historic Properties Data Base*, June 1991 (871 properties listed); Metro-Dade County, *Historic Sites Designated by the Metro-Dade Historic Preservation Board*, December 1990 (98 sites listed, including archaeological sites and zones).

17. Dunlop, "Readers' Opinions," 1E.

18. Dunlop, "Palette of the Past," 1L.

19. "Miami-Myomy," 25–30.

20. "Spy-Glass View of Architecture," 14–17.

21. Dunlop, "Shaping the 90s," 1I; Dunlop, "Tropical Blueprint," 1E.

22. Dunlop, "Architect Honored for Breadth of Work," 1G.

23. "Fiorentino Residence," *Florida Architect* 39, no. 5 (September/October 1992): 20.

7. Historic-Style Private Buildings

1. Robertson, "Tales of Old Lie Within Area's Sprawl," 1G.

2. Mesa, "Bungalows' Future Looks Grim," 4J; Wallace, "Little Havana Excursion Includes a History Lesson," 1B.

3. Historic Preservation Division, Metro-Dade County, *From Wilderness to Metropolis*, 40–43.

4. Strouse, "Plan to Preserve Overtown Spirit," 16.

5. Werne, "Morningside," 1J.

6. Olson, *Guide to the Architecture of Miami Beach*, MB–8.

7. Capitman, *Deco Delights*; Cerwinske, *Tropical Deco*; Olsen, *Guide to the Architecture of Miami Beach*.

8. Rene Rodriguez, "Luxury Miami Beach Resort Housed Mount Sinai Hospital," 28.

9. Millas, "South Miami Beach, Florida, U.S.A.," 1206.

10. Olsen, *Guide to the Architecture of Miami Beach*, MB–15.

11. Dunlop, "Glitter of Miami Beach Was Architect's Signature," 3G.

12. Coral Gables House Governing Board, *Coral Gables House*. (Coral Gables, Fla.: n.p., n.d.). The year 1978 is given in this pamphlet as the date of the beautiful cover drawing of the house by T. A. Spain.

13. Faiola, "Workshop Offers Loan Information," 6.

14. Historic Preservation Committee, Junior League of Miami, *Historic Coral Gables: Self-Guided Tour*.

15. LaRoue and Uguccioni, *Coral Gables in Postcards*, 13; Uguccioni, "Villages That Might Have Been," 16.

16. Georgia Tasker, "Expansion Plan Will Keep Kampong Flourishing," 1G.

17. Rene Rodriguez, "A Link to Vizcaya's Past," 36.

18. Rene Rodriguez, "Well-loved Grove Mansion Is Growing Old Gracefully," 25.

19. Dunlop, "Endangered Species: Before New Work, Deering Estate Needs Restoration of Old Structures," 1I.

8. Historic-Style Public Buildings

1. Historic Preservation Division, Metro-Dade County, *From Wilderness to Metropolis*, 118.

2. "Freedom Tower Restoration: A 1990 FA/AIA Award for Excellence in Architecture," *Florida Architect* 37, no. 4 (July/August 1990): 16–17.

3. Rene Rodriguez, "Miami's Alamo Was Hospital, Not Fort," 30.

4. Rene Rodriguez, "Miami High Building Is an Architectural Gem," 32; Fichtner, "The Palace of Higher Learning," 1E.

5. Dunlop, "Edison's Architecture Is Midwest-inspired Design," 3B.

6. Bernfeld, "Lyric Theater Is Focus of First Phase of Overtown's Historic Village Plan," 21.

7. Martin, "Alfred Weiss, Force Behind Olympia Theater," B4; Rene Rodriguez, "Gusman Center: Urban Oasis," 28.

8. Rene Rodriguez, "Dade County Courthouse Was Built Around the Old," 40.

9. "Revitalizing Miami," by architects Venturi, Rauch and Scott-Brown, *Urban Design International* 1, no. 2 (January/February 1980): 20–25; Capitman, *Deco Delights*, frontispiece and 61.

10. Rene Rodriguez, "Bass Museum Started as Library," 23.

11. Capitman, *Deco Delights*, 55.

12. Historic Preservation Committee, Junior League of Miami, *Historic Coral Gables: Self-Guided Tour*; LaRoue and Uguccioni, *Coral Gables in Postcards*; Historic Preservation Division, Coral Gables, *Coral Gables: A Brief History*.

13. Rene Rodriguez, "Gables' Colonnade Boasts a Rich Past," 24.

14. Millas and Patricios, eds., *Coral Gables Central Business District Study: Report No. 1*, II–2ff.

15. Rene Rodriguez, "Gables Club Was *the* Spot to Socialize in the 1920s," 30.

16. Moss, "Gates to the Gables," 1B; Rene Rodriguez, "Gates Enhance Gables' Charm," 28.

17. Rene Rodriguez, "Grove Library to Mark 96 Chapters of History," 8.

18. "The Oldest Church in the U.S.A.," 3–8.

19. Rene Rodriguez, "Cauley Square Started as Storm-proof Fortress," 32.

20. Junior League of Miami, *Historic South Dade: Self-Guided Tour*, 20.

9. Modern-Style Private Buildings

1. "Elegance—Here it Grew from Simplicity . . . ," *Florida Architect* 8, no. 1 (January 1958): 17–19.

2. "The 1960 AIA Convention Exhibit Awards," *Florida Architect* 10, no. 6 (June 1960): 15–17.

3. "The 1972 Architectural Awards," *Florida Architect* 22, no. 5 (September/October 1972): 50.

4. "The 1971 Architectural Awards," *Florida Architect* 21, no. 4 (July/October 1971): 30–31.

5. "The 1975 Architectural Design Awards," *Florida Architect* 25, no. 5 (September/October 1975): 21–22.

6. "The 1976 Architectural Design Awards," *Florida Architect* 26, no. 5 (September/October 1976): 29.

7. "The 1980 Awards for Excellence," *Florida Architect* 27, no. 1 (Fall 1980): 23; Markham, "Kaleidoscope," 1H.

8. "The 1981 FA/AIA Design Awards," *Florida Architect* 28, no. 4 (Fall 1981): 21.

9. Markham, "Open to the Great Outdoors," 1H.

10. Florida South American Institute of Architects File, 1986 Awards.

11. "The 1988 FA/AIA Awards for Excellence in Architecture," *Florida Architect* 35, no. 5 (September/October 1988): 28–29.

12. "Miami-Myomy," 25–30.

13. Florida South American Institute of Architects File, 1982 Awards.

14. "The 1961 FAA Honor Awards Program," *Florida Architect* 11, no. 12 (December 1961): 12–15.

15. "The 1968 FAAIA Awards Program," *Florida Architect* 18, no. 10 (October 1968): 48–49.

16. Werne, *Miami Herald*, 6 February 1983, 1H; 1982 FA/AIA Awards for Excellence in Architecture, *Florida Architect* 29, no. 5 (Fall 1982): 12.

17. Florida South American Institute of Architects File, 1986 Awards.

18. Dunlop, "FA/AIA Awards," 1J.

19. "The 1990 FA/AIA Awards for Excellence in Architecture," *Florida Architect* 37, no. 4 (July/August 1990): 14–15.

20. "The 1985 FA/AIA Awards of Excellence in Architecture," *Florida Architect* 32, no. 5 (September/October 1985): 33.

21. Dunlop, "AIA Winners Rooted in Geometry," H1, H12.

22. Florida South American Institute of Architects File, 1990 Awards.

23. "1—Merit Award, Custom-Built Category," *Florida Architect* 9, no. 11 (November 1959): 21–23.

24. "Woodsong . . . Winner of the 1971 Architectural Award," *Florida Architect* 21, no. 5 (September/October 1971): 4–7.

25. "Charles Harrison Pawley Residence," *Florida Architect* 20, no. 5 (September/October 1970): 56–57.

26. "The 1973 Architectural Awards," *Florida Architect* 23, no. 5 (September/October 1973): 27.

27. "The 1987 FA/AIA Awards for Excellence in Architecture," *Florida Architect* 34, no. 5 (September/October 1987): 25.

28. "Charles Harrison Pawley Architect," *Florida Architect* 36, no. 3 (May/June 1989): 31.

29. "The 1967 FA/AIA Architectural Exhibit— Honor Awards," *Florida Architect* 17, no. 11 (November 1967): 14–18.

30. "The 1969 Architectural Awards Program," *Florida Architect* 19, no. 10 (October 1969): 118–20.

31. "The 1973 Architectural Awards," *Florida Architect* 23, no. 5 (September/October 1973): 28.

32. "The 1982 FA/AIA Awards for Excellence in Architecture," *Florida Architect* 29, no. 5 (Fall 1982): 10.

33. "Merit Award—1960 FAA Convention . . . Residence for Nat Ratner, Miami Beach," *Florida Architect* 11, no. 1 (January 1961): 22–23.

34. "The 1968 FA/AIA Awards Program," *Florida Architect* 18, no. 10 (October 1968): 56.

35. "Lemontree Village," *Florida Architect* 22, no. 3 (May/June 1972): 23–25; The 1972 Architectural Awards, *Florida Architect* 22, no. 5 (September/October 1972): 47.

36. "The 1984 FA/AIA Awards for Excellence in Architecture," *Florida Architect* 31, no. 6 (November/December 1984): 15.

37. Nagel, "1983 FA/AIA Awards for Excellence in Architecture," 31.

38. "The 1971 Architectural Awards," *Florida Architect* 21, no. 4 (July/October 1971): 40–41.

39. Florida South American Institute of Architects File, 1985 Awards.

40. Florida South American Institute of Architects File, 1990 Awards.

41. Dunlop, "Miami Chapter AIA Awards," 1990, 1J.

42. Dunlop, "AIA Winners Rooted in Geometry," H1, H12.

43. "José Martí Plaza," *Florida Architect* 33, no. 4 (July/August 1986): 37.

44. "Miami-Myomy," 15.

45. Dunlop, *Arquitectonica*, ix.

46. Dunlop, *Arquitectonica*, 18–21.

47. Dunlop, "Spirit and Splendour," 1L; Rogers, "Miami (Brickell) Arquitectonica," 2.

48. Dunlop, *Arquitectonica*, 32.

49. Dunlop, *Arquitectonica*, 36–45.

50. Florida South American Institute of Architects File, 1982 Awards.

51. Dunlop, *Arquitectonica*, 22–29.

52. Florida South American Institute of Architects File, 1982 Awards.

53. "Architecture for the Good Life," *Florida Architect* 37, no. 2 (March/April 1990): 20–21.

54. Dunlop, "Knight Center: Review," 1L.

55. Dunlop, "Pavillon," 1L.

56. Dunlop, "Colorful, Geometric Sofitel," 8K.

57. Dunlop, "Alhambra Hotel," 1K.

10. Modern-Style Public Buildings

1. "No. One Miami," *Florida Architect* 6, no. 5 (May 1956): 6–8.

2. "The 1958 FAA Professional Awards Program," *Florida Architect* 9, no. 7 (July 1959): 19.

3. "Design Awards, 42nd FAA Convention," *Florida Architect* 7, no. 1 (January 1957): 18–19.

4. "The 1981 FA/AIA Design Awards," *Florida Architect* 28, no. 4 (Fall 1981): 18.

5. "Miami-Myomy," 12.

6. Nicholls Fullerton and Associates, architects of the Barnett Bank building on Douglas Road.

7. "Passenger Terminal/New Port of Miami," *Florida Architect* 20, no. 2 (March/April 1970): 6.

8. Florida South American Institute of Architects File, 1984 Awards.

9. "The 1984 FA/AIA Awards for Excellence in Architecture," *Florida Architect* 31, no. 6 (November/December 1984): 34.

10. Florida South American Institute of Architects File, 1984 Awards.

11. "The 1986 FA/AIA Awards for Excellence," *Florida Architect* 33, no. 5 (September/October 1986): 28–29.

12. "The 1989 FA/AIA Awards for Excellence in Architecture," *Florida Architect* 36, no. 5 (September/October 1989): 28–29.

13. "The 1989 FA/AIA Awards for Excellence in Architecture," *Florida Architect* 36, no. 5 (September/October 1989): 30–31.

14. Dunlop, "Building Up, Tearing Down," 7L.

15. Dunlop, "Miami's Newest Courthouse," 2L.

16. Ivan Rodriguez, "From Brickell Avenue to the Beach," 52–59.

17. Harper, "Power Skyline," 55–65.

18. Florida South American Institute of Architects File, 1987 Awards.

19. "The 1987 FA/AIA Awards for Excellence in Architecture," *Florida Architect* 34, no. 5 (September/October 1987): 20.

20. Dunlop, "Metro Administration Building," 1K.

21. "The 1985 FA/AIA Awards of Excellence in Architecture," *Florida Architect* 32, no. 5 (September/October 1985): 24–25.

22. Charles Gwathmey, a juror in the 1982 FA/AIA Awards for Excellence in Architecture, *Florida Architect* 29, no. 5 (Fall 1982): 11; Dunlop, *Arquitectonica*, 46–47.

23. "The 1989 FA/AIA Awards for Excellence in Architecture," *Florida Architect* 36, no. 5 (September/October 1989): 22–23; Dunlop, *Arquitectonica*, 118–21.

24. Dunlop, "Best Bet: Showroom Is Worth Preserving," 1I.

25. Harper, "Power Skyline," 57.

26. "Practice Profile: Alfred Browning Parker, FAIA," *Florida Architect* 21, no. 3 (May/June 1971): 23–28.

27. The 1986 FA/AIA Awards for Excellence, *Florida Architect* 33, no. 5 (September/October 1986): 16–17.

28. "The 1990 FA/AIA Awards for Excellence in Architecture," *Florida Architect* 37, no. 4 (July/August 1990): 22–23.

29. Dunlop, "First for Miami: Local Building Wins National Award," 7I.

30. Greer, "Marvelous, Magical, Mystical Mayfair," 24.

31. Lombard, "A Link in a Chain of Monuments," 24–25.

32. "Feature: Mailman Center for Child Development," *Florida Architect* 21, no. 1 (January/February 1971): 5–8.

33. Florida South American Institute of Architects File, 1982 Awards.

34. Dunlop, "AIA Winners Rooted in Geometry," H1, H12.

35. "Interama Gets the Green Light," *Florida Architect* 12, no. 8 (August 1962): 12–18.

36. "Progress Report—Interama," *Florida Architect* 6, no. 4 (April 1956): 11; "Interama," 6, no. 2 (February 1956): 2–5.

37. "The 1964 AIA Library Building Award," *Florida Architect* 14, no. 9 (September 1964): 16–17; "Architectural Exhibit Awards," *Florida Architect* 16, no. 11 (November 1966): 21.

38. Marlin, "Cultural Blueprint," 23.

39. Dunlop, "Cultural Center," 5L, and "Arches, Colors," 1C.

40. Ivan Rodriguez, "From Brickell Avenue to the Beach," 54.

41. Florida South American Institute of Architects File, 1986 Awards.

42. Garcia, "New Owner Rechristens CenTrust Tower," 1C.

43. Dunlop, "Homestead's Fine Ballpark Has Designs on Winning Fans Over," 1I.

44. The 1965 Architectural Exhibit Awards, *Florida Architect* 16, no. 1 (January 1966): 7.

45. Cruz, "Miami-Dade Community College," 18–19.

46. "The 1974 Architectural Design Awards," *Florida Architect* 24, no. 5 (September/October 1974): 23.

47. "Miami-Dade Community College Downtown Campus," *Florida Architect* 25, no. 3 (May/June 1975): 13–16.

48. "Design Awards, 42nd FAA Convention," *Florida Architect* 7, no. 1 (January 1957): 18–19.

49. "The 1966 Architectural Exhibit Awards," *Florida Architect* 16, no. 11 (November 1966): 21.

50. Markham, "Florida South AIA Awards," 5H.

51. "Miami-Myomy," 20.

52. "The 1981 FA/AIA Design Awards," *Florida Architect* 28, no. 4 (Fall 1981): 18.

53. Dunlop, "Rosenstiel School," 2K.

54. Dunlop, "First for Miami," 7I.

55. Dunlop, "FIU at Ten," 3L; Dunlop, "School Buildings Win Architecture Awards," 9G.

56. Dunlop, "School Design for Dade: Some 'Clunky,' Some Fine," 1E.

57. "The 1968 FA/AIA Awards Program," *Florida Architect* 18, no. 10 (October 1968): 54–55.

58. "Air Conditioning for Florida's Schools?" 27–28.

59. Patricios, "Comparisons of Post-occupancy Evaluations Between Users and Architects," 252–66.

60. Dunlop, "Two New Schools," 1I. The architects were Harper Carreno and Mateo.

61. Dunlop, "Return of Booker T. Washington," 1K.

62. "The 1990 FA/AIA Awards for Excellence in Architecture," *Florida Architect* 37, no. 4 (July/August 1990): 28–29.

63. Dunlop, "FA/AIA Awards," 1J.

64. Gude, "Follow the Yellow Brick Road," 24–25.

65. The 1976 Architectural Design Awards, *Florida Architect* 26, no. 5 (September/October 1976): 31.

66. "Coral Gables—The Vanidades Continental Building," *Florida Architect* 28, no. 2 (Spring 1981): 15.

67. "Pro Bono Publico in Miami Beach," *Florida Architect* 36, no. 1 (January/February 1989): 18–21.

68. "South Florida Evaluation and Treatment Center," *Florida Architect* 33, no. 6 (November/December 1986): 32–34.

69. "The 1990 FA/AIA Awards for Excellence in Architecture," *Florida Architect* 37, no. 4 (July/August 1990): 18–19.

70. Florida South American Institute of Architects File, 1987 Awards.

71. Beth Dunlop, "Miami Chapter AIA Awards," 1988, 1H.

72. Florida South American Institute of Architects File, 1989 Awards.

73. Dunlop, "Miami Chapter AIA Awards," 1989, 1H.

74. The 1989 FA/AIA Awards for Excellence in Architecture, *Florida Architect* 36, no. 5 (September/October 1989): 36–37; Beth Dunlop, *Miami Herald*, 21 February 1988, 4K; Dunlop, *Arquitectonica*, 90–95.

Epilogue. Hurricane Andrew

1. Markowitz, "145 mph: Andrew Whipped Gusts to 175 mph," 1A.

2. Markowitz, 14A; Doig, "The Ocean's Fury," 1D.

3. Doig, "Storm Warnings: 88 Years in Hurricane Alley," 2B.

4. *Miami Herald*, 8 September 1992, 2B; 30 August 1992, 24A; 2 September 1992, 21A; 3 September 1992, 23A; 29 August 1992, 16A; 26 September 1992, 1A; 25 October 1992, 1B.

5. "Andrew's Everglades Assault," *Miami Herald*, 8 September 1992, 15A; "Mangrove Loss Is 'Catastrophic'," 11 September 1992, 1A.

6. "Andrew's Awesome Impact," *Miami Herald*, 9 September 1992, 16A; "Andrew by the Numbers,"

Miami Herald, 24 September 1992, 24A; "Andrew," *Florida Planning* (November/December 1992), 16.

7. Doig, "Storm: A Wobble Away from Greater Disaster," 23A.

8. Slevin and Maass, "Military Machine Gathers Speed," 23A, 25A.

9. Anderson, "$8 Billion on Way to Florida," 1A.

10. Kleinberg, "Andrew's Legacies," 1M; Getter, "Donna's Lessons from 1960 Ignored," 1A.

11. Neal, "Building Code Cited in Failure of Roofs," 1A; Getter, "Building Code Eroded Over Years," 1A; Special Report "What Went Wrong," *Miami Herald*, 20 December 1992.

12. Finefrock, "Homeowners Pay for Dade Laxity on Flood Rules," 1A.

13. Dunlop, "Saving History," 1G; see also Faiola and Muhs, "Treasured Addresses," 20.

Appendix A

1. Ingels, *Willis Haviland Carrier*.

Appendix B

1. State constitution, 1968, Section 6 of Article VIII replaced the 1885 Article as a whole.

2. Chapter 1638 was a lengthy law with thirty-one sections.

3. Chapter 1688, approved 4 February 1869. This Act had thirty-two sections.

4. Chapter 2047 was enacted as an amendment to Chapter 1688.

5. Chapter 23656 (420), amended section 165.01.

6. Chapter 26913 (434).

7. Chapter 159.

8. Chapter 165, Formation of Municipalities Act (1974–92).

9. Glendening, "Metropolitan Dade County Government," 61ff.

10. Langendorf, *Metropolitan Federalism*.

11. Sofen, *Metropolitan Experiment*, 17ff.

12. Wolff, *Miami Metro*, 123.

13. Dade County Research Foundation, "Truth about City-County Consolidation."

14. Sofen, *Metropolitan Experiment*, Appendix D, 227.

15. Sofen, *Metropolitan Experiment*, Appendix D, 227–28.

16. Chapter 30686, Laws of Florida, Special Acts of 1955.

17. Sofen, *Metropolitan Experiment*, Appendix D, 228.

18. Parson, *Story of the First Metropolitan Government in the United States*, 6.

19. Glendening, "Metropolitan Dade County Government," 85ff.

20. Langendorf, *Metropolitan Federalism*, Tables 4, 5, 6, 9, and 14 in particular.

21. Sofen, *Metropolitan Experiment*, title of Chapter 10, 93ff.

22. Sofen, Appendix D, 228.

23. Sofen, Appendix D, 228.

24. Bennett, "Urban Growth and Metropolitan Planning," 163ff.

25. Touche Ross and Co., *Review of the Two-Tier Government in Miami/Dade County for the City of Miami*; Metropolitan Dade County Charter Review Commission Report, 1 January 1982, and "Charter Reviewers' Recommendations Aim to Make Metro More Responsive," *Miami Herald*, 4 January 1982; Hertz, *Governing Dade County*.

26. Goldfarb, "Voters Crush Charter Revamp," 1A, 1B.

27. Tomb, "Again on Ballot," 1B, and "Voters," 1B.

Bibliography

Adams, Adam G. "Some Pre-Boom Developers of Dade County." *Tequesta* 17 (1957): 31–46.

"Air Conditioning for Florida's Schools?" *Florida Architect* 9, no. 11 (November 1959): 27–28.

Allman, T. D. *Miami: City of the Future.* New York: Atlantic Monthly Press, 1987.

Alvarez, Lizette. "Thousands of Cuban Tourists Staying." *Miami Herald*, 31 May 1991, 1B.

Ammidown, Margot. "The Wagner Family: Pioneer Life on the Miami River." *Tequesta* 42 (1982): 5–38.

Anderson, Paul. "Bush Signs Law to Expand Glades." *Miami Herald*, 14 December 1989, 1A.

———. "$8 Billion on Way to Florida." *Miami Herald*, 19 September 1992, 1A.

Andrews, Charles M. "The Florida Indians in the Seventeenth Century." *Tequesta* 1 (1943): 36–48.

Associated Railway Land Department of Florida. *Sectional Map of Dade County, Florida.* Buffalo, N.Y.: Plant Investment Co., 1893.

Baird, Lisa. "Trailing the Barefoot Mailman." In *Mostly Sunny Days*, edited by Bob Kearney, 44–46. Miami, Fla.: Suniland Press, 1986.

Barbour, George M. *Florida for Tourists, Invalids and Settlers.* New York: D. Appleton, 1883.

Beckwith, J. P. *East Coast of Florida and the Florida East Coast Railway and Hotels.* Buffalo and New York: Matthews-Northrup Co., 1901.

Bennett, John W. "Urban Growth and Metropolitan Planning." Master's thesis in urban and regional planning, University of Miami, August 1979.

Berman, Marshall. *All That Is Solid Melts Into Air: The Experience of Modernity.* London: Verso, 1985.

Bernfeld, Linda Rodriguez. "Lyric Theater Is Focus of First Phase of Overtown's Historic Village Plan." *Miami Today*, 23 November 1989, 21.

Biddulph, Geoffrey. "Merrick's Idea for Street Names Confounds Author." *Miami Herald Neighbors*, 26 February 1989, 3.

Bingham, Millicent Todd. "Miami: A Study in Urban Geography." *Tequesta* 9 (1949): 92.

Birger, Larry. "A Gateway for the Latin Trade." *Miami Herald Business Monday*, 16 September 1991, 24.

Black, Hugo L., III. "Richard Fitzpatrick's South Florida, 1822–1840: Part I—Key West Phase." *Tequesta* 41 (1980): 47–78.

———. "Richard Fitzpatrick's South Florida, 1822–1840: Part II—Fitzpatrick's River Plantation." *Tequesta* 42 (1981): 34–53.

Blackman, E. V. *Miami and Dade County, Florida. Its Settlement, Progress, and Advancement.* Washington, D.C.: Victor Rainbolt, 1921.

Booth, Cathy. "The Capital City of Latin America, Miami." *Time* 142, no. 21 (Fall 1993): 82–85.

Boswell, Thomas D., and James R. Curtis. "The Hispanization of Metropolitan Miami." Chapter 11 in *South Florida: The Winds of Change*, edited by Thomas D. Boswell. Miami, Fla.: Annual Conference of the Association of American Geographers, April 1991.

Boswell, Thomas D., Ira Sheskin, and Carroll Truss. "Attitudes, Causes, and Perceptions: The 1980 Black Riot in Dade County (Miami) Florida." *The Florida Geographer* 20 (October 1986): 1–15.

Bramson, Seth. "Railroad Stations in Dade County." *Tequesta* 45 (1985): 73–78.

Buchanan, Patricia. "Miami's Bootleg Boom." *Tequesta* 30 (1970): 13–31.

Burkhardt, Mrs. Henry J. "'Starch Making': A Pioneer Florida Industry." *Tequesta* 12 (1952): 47–54.

Capitman, Barbara Baer. *Deco Delights: Preserving the Beauty and Joy of Miami Beach Architecture.* New York: E. P. Dutton, 1988.

———, ed. *Portfolio.* Miami Beach, Fla.: Miami Design Preservation League, 1979.

Carney, James J. "Population Growth in Miami and Dade County, Florida." *Tequesta* 7 (1947): 50–55.

Carson, Ruby Leach. "Forty Years of Miami Beach." *Tequesta* 15 (1955): 3–28.

Cartano, David G. "The Drug Industry in South Florida." Chapter 9 in *South Florida: The Winds of Change*, edited by Thomas D. Boswell. Miami, Fla.: Annual Conference of the Association of American Geographers, April 1991.

Cash, William T. *The Story of Florida.* 2 vols. New York: American Historical Society, 1938.

Cerwinske, Laura. *Tropical Deco: The Architecture and Design of Old Miami Beach.* New York: Rizzoli International Publications, 1981.

———, and Steven Brooke. *Miami Hot and Cool.* New York: Clarkson N. Potter, 1990.

Chapman, Arthur E. "History of South Florida." Chapter 3 in *South Florida: The Winds of Change*, edited by Thomas D. Boswell. Miami, Fla.: Annual Conference of the Association of American Geographers, April 1991.

Chardon, Roland E. "The Cape Florida Society of 1773." *Tequesta* 35 (1975): 37–74.

Committee of the Florida South Chapter, American Institute of Architects, *A Guide to the Architecture of Miami.* Miami, Fla.: Florida South Chapter, American Institute of Architects, 1963.

Cruz, Jesus. "Miami-Dade Community College: New World Center Campus Phase II." *Florida Architect* 32, no. 1 (January/February 1985): 18–19.

Culot, Maurice, and Jean-François Lejeune. *Miami: Architecture of the Tropics.* Brussels: Editions Archives d'Architecture Moderne, [1992].

Curtis, James R. "Lament for an Art Deco Landmark." *Landscape* 27, no. 1 (1983): 40–47.

Dade County Research Foundation. "The Truth about City-County Consolidation." Miami, Fla.: Dade County Research Foundation, 1948.

Davis, Aurora E. "The Development of the Major

Commercial Airlines in Dade County, Florida: 1945–1970." *Tequesta* 32 (1972): 3–16.

De George, Gail, and Antonio Fins, with Irene Recio. "Latin America's Newest Capital City: Miami." *Business Week*, 30 September 1991, 120–22.

DeGrove, John M. "The Historical Development of Growth Management in Florida." *Florida Environmental and Urban Issues* 13, no. 1 (October 1985): 1–2.

Department of Historic Preservation and Urban Design, Miami Beach. "Miami Beach Historic Data Base." Miami Beach: City of Miami Beach, 1991.

Dewar, Heather, and R. A. Zaldivar. "Congress Approves Bill to Expand Everglades Park in Dade County." *Miami Herald*, 23 November 1989, 30A.

Didion, Joan. *Miami.* New York: Pocket Books, 1987.

Dietrich, Emily Perry. "Arch Creek: Prehistory to Public Park." *Tequesta* 47 (1987): 49–66.

Dodd, Dorothy. "Jacob Housman of Indian Key." *Tequesta* 8 (1948): 3–20.

Doig, Stephen K. "The Ocean's Fury." *Miami Herald*, 1 October 1992, 1D.

———. "Storm: A Wobble Away from Greater Disaster." *Miami Herald*, 6 September 1992, 23A.

———. "Storm Warnings: 88 Years in Hurricane Alley." *Miami Herald*, 5 September 1988, 2B.

Dolen, Christine Arnold, James Roos, and Laurie Horn. "Critics Assess Planned Arts Center." *Miami Herald*, 18 July 1993, 8I.

Dorschner, John. "Light Industry." *Miami Herald Tropic Magazine*, 2 June 1991, 8.

Ducassi, Blanca. "History Shaped Housing." *Miami Herald*, 3 November 1989, 6–7HB.

Dunlop, Beth. "AIA Winners Rooted in Geometry." *Miami Herald*, Home and Design, 15 December 1985, H1, H12.

———. "Alhambra Hotel: New Giant in the Gables." *Miami Herald*, 20 December 1987, 1K.

———. "Arches, Colors Make Library True Classic." *Miami Herald*, 19 July 1985, 1C.

———. "Architect Honored for Breadth of Work." *Miami Herald*, 27 September 1992, 1G.

———. *Arquitectonica.* Washington, D.C.: American Institute of Architects Press, 1991.

———. "Best Bet: Showroom Is Worth Preserving." *Miami Herald*, 7 July 1991, 1I.

———. "Building Up, Tearing Down South Florida." *Miami Herald*, 25 December 1983, 7L.

———. "Colorful, Geometric Sofitel Stands Out." *Miami Herald*, 19 October 1986, 8K.

———. "Cultural Center: A Building for Our Time." *Miami Herald*, 8 January 1984, 5L.

———. "Edison's Architecture Is Midwest-inspired Design." *Miami Herald*, 4 April 1992, 3B.

———. "Endangered Species: Before New Work, Deering Estate Needs Restoration of Old Structures." *Miami Herald*, 16 June 1991, 1I.

———. "FA/AIA Awards." *Miami Herald*, 29 July 1990, 1J.

———. "First for Miami: Local Building Wins National Award." *Miami Herald*, 29 December 1991, 7I.

———. "FIU at 10: A Concrete Situation." *Miami Herald*, 19 September 1982, 3L.

———. "Glitter of Miami Beach Was Architect's Signature." *Miami Herald*, 29 September 1991, 3G.

———. "Homestead's Fine Ballpark Has Designs on Winning Fans Over." *Miami Herald*, 30 June 1991, 1I.

———. "How Hialeah Happened." *Miami Herald*, 28 April 1991, 1J.

———. "Knight Center: Review." *Miami Herald*, 26 September 1982, 1L.

———. "Metro Administration Building: Purple Seat of Power." *Miami Herald*, 1 September 1985, 1K.

———. "Miami Chapter AIA Awards." *Miami Herald*, 4 December 1988, 1H.

———. "Miami Chapter AIA Awards." *Miami Herald*, 3 December 1989, 1H.

———. "Miami Chapter AIA Awards." *Miami Herald*, 23 December 1990, 1J.

———. "Miami's Newest Courthouse Lacks Sense of Power." *Miami Herald*, 18 December 1983, 2L.

———. "The Palette of the Past." *Miami Herald*, 5 September 1982, 1L.

———. "The Pavillon Makes a Bid for Grandeur." *Miami Herald*, 18 March 1983, 1L.

———. "Projects Threaten Biscayne Bay's Beauty." *Miami Herald*, 6 May 1990, 2I.

———. "Readers' Opinions on Best, Worst South Florida Buildings." *Miami Herald*, 18 March 1983, 1E.

———. "The Return of Booker T. Washington: The New School Is a Superior Work of Art." *Miami Herald*, 3 September 1989, 1K.

———. "Rosenstiel School Is Bold Step for UM." *Miami Herald*, 3 November 1985, 2K.

———. "Saving History." *Miami Herald*, 4 October 1992, 1G.

———. "School Buildings Win Architecture Awards." *Miami Herald*, 15 December 1991, 9G.

———. "School Design for Dade: Some 'Clunky,' Some Fine." *Miami Herald*, 6 March 1992, 1E.

———. "Shaping the 90s: A Bold New Generation of Architects Is Gradually Transforming South Florida." *Miami Herald*, 1 April 1990, 1I.

———. "South Florida's Best Buildings." *Miami Herald*, 6 December 1987, 1H.

———. "Spirit and Splendour of South Florida's Architecture." *Miami Herald*, 12 August 1984, 1L.

———. "A Style of Our Own." *Miami Herald*, 12 May 1991, 1I.

———. "Tropical Blueprint." *Miami Herald*, 19 December 1992, 1E.

———. "Two New Schools: Lessons in Design." *Miami Herald*, 30 September 1990, 1I.

———. "Verdict on Courthouse: Delightful." *Miami Herald*, 21 February 1988, 4K.

Eagleton, Terry. "Awakening from Modernity." *Times Literary Supplement*, 20 February 1987, 194.

Faiola, Anthony. "Conte to Head Key Biscayne." *Miami Herald*, 4 September 1991, 2B.

———. "Hispanics Rise to 42% in Gables, Black Numbers Fall." *Miami Herald Neighbors*, 14 March 1991, 6.

———. "Key Biscayne Voters to Decide on First Charter." *Miami Herald*, 16 June 1991, 1B.

———. "Metro Approves June 18 for Key's Charter Vote." *Miami Herald Neighbors*, 18 April 1991, 11.

———. "Workshop Offers Loan Information." *Miami Herald Neighbors*, 4 June 1991, 6.

———, and Angie Muhs. "Treasured Addresses." *Miami Herald Neighbors*, 8 October 1992, 20.

Ferdinand, Pamela. "A Bridge to Latin Markets." *Miami Herald*, 2 July 1991, 6B.

Fernald, Edward A. *A History of Florida: Atlas of Florida*. Tallahassee, Fla.: Florida State Foundation, 1981.

Fichtner, Margaria. "The Palace of Higher Learning." *Miami Herald*, 27 April 1991, 1E.

Filkins, Dexter. "Center for Arts Approved." *Miami Herald*, 14 July 1993, 1A.

Finefrock, Don. "Homeowners Pay for Dade Laxity on Flood Rules." *Miami Herald*, 8 November 1992, 1A.

Fletcher, Sir Banister. *A History of Architecture*. 19th ed. London: Butterworth Group, 1987.

Frazier, James C. "Samuel Touchett's Florida Plantation, 1771." *Tequesta* 35 (1975): 75–88.

Gage, Randy. "South Beach Observed: Who's Afraid of the Big Bad Wolf? Preservationists Fear He'll Blow Down the Deco District." *Antenna* 13 (4 June 1991): 15.

Gannon, Michael. *Florida: A Short History.* Gainesville: University Press of Florida, 1993.

Garcia, Beatrice E. "New Owner Rechristens CenTrust Tower." *Miami Herald,* 8 November 1991, 1C.

Gardiner, R. A. *A Guide to Florida, the Land of Flowers.* New York: Cushing, Barden and Co., 1872.

Gelabert-Navia, José. "The Mediterranean Legacy." *Florida Architect* 34, no. 5 (September/October 1987): 49–51.

George, Paul S. "Brokers, Binders, and Builders: Greater Miami's Boom of the Mid-1920s." *Florida Historical Quarterly* 65, no. 1 (July 1986): 27–51.

———. "Colored Town: Miami's Black Community, 1896–1930." *Florida Historical Quarterly* 56, no. 4 (April 1978): 432–47.

———. "Traffic Control in Early Miami." *Tequesta* 37 (1977): 3–18.

Getter, Lisa. "Building Code Eroded Over Years: Watered-Down Rules Meant Weaker Homes." *Miami Herald,* 11 October 1992, 1A.

———. "Donna's Lessons from 1960 Ignored." *Miami Herald,* 20 September 1992, 1A.

Glendening, Parris N. "Metropolitan Dade County Government: An Examination of Reform." Ph.D. dissertation, Florida State University, 1967.

Goldfarb, Carl. "Immigrants Change East Little Havana." *Miami Herald,* 24 June 1991, 1B.

———. "Prejudice Felt by Latin Blacks." *Miami Herald,* 30 June 1991, 1B.

———. "Voters Crush Charter Revamp." *Miami Herald,* 9 May 1990, 1B.

Grantham, Tiffany. "Archaeological Sites in Dade." *Miami Herald Neighbors,* 5 May 1991, 26.

Greenwood, John. "Review Essay." *Journal of Architectural Education* 43, no. 4 (Summer 1990): 53–59.

Greer, Diane D. "Marvelous, Magical, Mystical Mayfair." *Florida Architect* 33, no. 4 (July/August 1986): 24–26.

Gude, Vivian. "Follow the Yellow Brick Road." *Florida Architect* 38, no. 1 (January/February 1991): 24–25.

Gugliotta, Guy. "1980–1989: Decade in Review." *South Florida,* January 1990, 69.

Haas, Jane Glenn. "Shaping the Future: Architects Try a Different Slant for New Homes." *Miami Herald,* 18 September 1988, 1H.

Harper, Paula. "Power Skyline." *Art in America,* September 1985, 55–65.

Hart, Richard. "Garald Parker: Glades' Great Discoverer." *Miami Herald,* 7 April 1990, 2E.

Harvey, David. *The Condition of Postmodernity.* Cambridge, Mass.: Basil Blackwell, 1991.

Hatton, Hap. *Tropical Splendor: An Architectural History of Florida.* New York: Alfred A. Knopf, 1987.

Heenan, David A. "Global Cities of Tomorrow." *Harvard Business Review* 55, no. 3 (May–June 1977): 79–92.

Hemingway, Leicester. "Thoughts on the District . . ." In *Portfolio,* edited by Barbara Baer Capitman, 10. Miami Beach, Fla.: Miami Beach Preservation League, 1979.

Hertz, David B. *Governing Dade County: A Study of Alternative Structures.* Coral Gables, Fla.: University of Miami, 1984.

Historic Preservation Committee, Junior League of Miami, *Historic Coral Gables: Self-Guided Tour.* Miami, Fla.: Junior League of Miami, 1986.

Historic Preservation Division, Junior League of Miami, *Historic Coconut Grove: Self-Guided Tour.* Miami, Fla.: Junior League of Miami, 1988.

Historic Preservation Division, Coral Gables. *Coral Gables: A Brief History.* Coral Gables, Fla.: Planning Department, 1989.

Historic Preservation Division, Office of Community and Economic Development, Metropolitan Dade County. *From Wilderness to Metropolis: The History and Architecture of Dade County, Florida, 1825–1940.* Miami, Fla.: Metropolitan Dade County, 1982.

Historic Preservation Division, Office of Community and Economic Development, Metropolitan Dade County. *Resourceful Rehab: A Guide for Historic Building in Dade County.* Miami, Fla.: Metropolitan Dade County, 1987.

Hitchcock, Henry Russell, and Philip Johnson. *The International Style.* New York: Norton, 1932.

Hopkins, Alice. "The Development of the Overseas Highway." *Tequesta* 46 (1986): 48–56.

Huber, Michael. "Can Brickell Beat the Blues?" *Miami Herald Neighbors,* 29 April 1991, 24–26.

Hudson, F. M. "Beginnings in Dade County." *Tequesta* 1 (1943): 1–35.

Ingels, Margaret. *Willis Haviland Carrier: The Father of Air Conditioning*. Garden City, N.Y.: Country Life Press, 1952.

Jencks, Charles. "The Evolution and Mutation of Modern Architecture." In *Architecture Today*, edited by Charles Jencks and William Chaitkin, 12–17. New York: Harry N. Abrams, 1982.

Junior League of Miami. *Historic Downtown Miami: Self-Guided Tour*. Miami, Fla.: Junior League of Miami, 1985.

———. *Historic Northeast Dade: Self-Guided Tour*. Miami, Fla.: Junior League of Miami, 1990.

———. *Historic South Dade: Self-Guided Tour*. Miami, Fla.: Junior League of Miami, 1988.

Kearney, Bob, ed., *Mostly Sunny Days: A Miami Herald Salute to South Florida's Heritage*. Miami, Fla.: Suniland Press, 1986.

Kenzie, Roy. "A Response to Urban Development." *Florida Architect* 29, no. 1 (Winter 1982): 17–19.

Kersey, Harry, Jr. *Pelts, Plumes and Hides*. Gainesville: University Presses of Florida, 1975.

Kiehnel, Richard, and John M. Elliott. *A Monograph of the Florida Work of Kiehnel and Elliott*. Miami: n.p., 1938.

Kleinberg, Howard. "Andrew's Legacies: It Seems as if We Never Learned from Our Warnings." *Miami Herald*, 20 September 1992, 1M.

———. "Do Seminoles, Miccosukee Come from Same Tribe?" *Miami Herald*, 18 December 1990, 15A.

———. *Miami: The Way We Were*. Surfside, Fla.: Surfside Publishing, 1989.

———. "Ponce de León's Landings in Chequescha (Miami), Fla." *Miami Herald*, 20 March 1990, 11A.

———. "A Wistful Eye Back to Young Coconut Grove." *Miami Herald*, 6 March 1990, 15A.

Kohen, Helen L. "Art in Public Places." *Miami Herald*, 18 July 1993, 1I.

Langendorf, Richard. *Metropolitan Federalism: An Evaluation of the Dade Experiment in Governmental Reform*. Coral Gables, Fla.: NSF/RANN Research Project #GI–39599, May 1976.

Lanier, Sidney. *Florida: Its Scenery, Climate, and History*. Philadelphia: J. B. Lippincott, 1876.

LaRoue, Samuel D., Jr., and Ellen J. Uguccioni. *Coral Gables in Postcards: Scenes from Florida's Yesterday*. Miami, Fla.: Dade Heritage Trust, 1988.

Lombard, Joanna. "A Link in a Chain of Monuments." *Florida Architect* 35, no. 4 (July/August 1988): 24–25.

Longino, Charles, Jr., and Ralph B. McNeal. "The Elderly Population of South Florida." Chapter 13 in *South Florida: The Winds of Change*, edited by Thomas D. Boswell. Miami, Fla.: Annual Conference of the Association of American Geographers, April 1991.

Lopez, Juan. "Florida Fact." *Miami Herald*, 26 May 1991, 6B.

Lotz, Aileen R. *Metropolitan Dade County: Two-Tier Government in Action*. Boston: Allyn and Bacon, 1984.

McKean, Charles. "The Twentieth Century." In *Architecture of the Western World*, edited by Michael Raeburn, 245–89. New York: Rizzoli International Publications, 1980.

McKean, John Maule. "The First Industrial Age." In *Architecture of the Western World*, edited by Michael Raeburn, 201–44. New York: Rizzoli International Publications, 1980.

Markham, Wayne. "Florida South AIA Awards." *Miami Herald*, 24 January 1982, 5H.

———. "A Kaleidoscope of Concrete." *Miami Herald*, 26 December 1982, 1H.

———. "Open to the Great Outdoors." *Miami Herald*, 20 November 1983, 1H.

Markowitz, Arnold. "145 mph: Andrew Whipped Gusts to 175 mph." *Miami Herald*, 18 September 1992, 1A.

Marks, Henry S. "Earliest Land Grants in the Miami Area." *Tequesta* 18 (1958): 16–18.

———. "A Forgotten Spanish Land Grant in South Florida." *Tequesta* 20 (1960): 51–56.

Marlin, William. "Cultural Blueprint Mirrors Miami Heritage." *Christian Science Monitor*, 21 April 1978, 23.

Martin, Lydia. "Alfred Weiss, Force Behind Olympia Theater." *Miami Herald*, Obituary, 21 April 1991, B4.

Meadows, Gail. "Arts Hall: Now the Real Work Begins." *Miami Herald*, 18 July 1993, 1I.

Merrick, George E. "Announcing the Opening of the Country Club Section Part One, Coral Gables America's Finest Suburb." Brochure published in Miami, Fla.: *The Herald*, Miami, 23 February 1924.

Mesa, Blanca. "Bungalows' Future Looks Grim: Little Havana Homes Stand in the Way of Redevelopment." *Miami Herald*, 19 August 1990, 4J.

———. "Kendall's Past." *Miami Herald Neighbors*, 15 September 1991, 28.

"Miami-Myomy." *Florida Architect* 28, no. 2 (Spring 1981): 25–30. Special issue on "Miami: Razzle-Dazzle Town."

Milizia, Francesco. *Principj di Archittetura Civile*. Milan: Giovanni Antoloni, 1832; rpt., Milan: Gabrielle Mazzotta, 1972.

Millas, Aristides J. "Miami Architecture Today: Observations on a Retrospective of Seventy Years." In *Seventy Years of Miami Architecture*, 8–17. Catalogue of the exhibition. Miami Beach, Fla.: Bass Museum of Art, 1991.

———. "South Miami Beach, Florida, U.S.A.; And the First Twentieth Century Historic District." In *'Armos' Timitikos Tomos*, 1199–1215. Thessaloniki: Department of Architecture, Aristotle University of Thessaloniki, 1991.

———, and Nicholas N. Patricios, eds. *Coral Gables Central Business District Study: Report No. 1*. Coral Gables: University of Miami for the City of Coral Gables, 1983.

Mohl, Raymond. "Miami." In *Sunbelt Cities: Politics and Growth Since World War II*, edited by Richard M. Bernard and Bradley R. Rice, 58–99. Austin: University of Texas Press, 1983.

———. "Miami Metro Charter Revisions and the Politics of the Eighties." *Florida Environmental and Urban Issues* 10, no. 1 (October 1982): 9–13, 21–23.

———. "The Settlement of Blacks in South Florida." Chapter 10 in *South Florida: The Winds of Change*, edited by Thomas D. Boswell. Miami, Fla.: Annual Conference of the Association of American Geographers, April 1991.

Morganthau, Tom et al. "Miami: America's Casablanca." *Newsweek* 111, no. 4 (25 January 1988): 22–29.

Moss, Bea. "Gates to the Gables." *Miami Herald*, 27 March 1991, 1B.

Muir, Helen. *Miami, U.S.A.* 2d ed. Coconut Grove, Fla.: Hurricane House Publishers, 1963.

Muller, Peter. "The Urban Geography of South Florida." Chapter 5 in *South Florida: The Winds of Change*, edited by Thomas D. Boswell. Miami, Fla.: Annual Conference of the Association of American Geographers, April 1991.

Nagel, James. "1983 FA/AIA Awards for Excellence in Architecture." *Florida Architect* 30, no. 5 (Fall 1983): 31.

Neal, Terry, "Building Code Cited in Failure of Roofs." *Miami Herald*, 6 October 1992, 1A.

Newcomb, Rexford. *Mediterranean Domestic Architecture in the United States*. Cleveland, Ohio: J. H. Hansen, 1928.

O'Connell, Daniel W. "Legislating 'Quality Planning': The 1985 Local Government Comprehensive Planning and Land Development Regulation Act." *Florida Environmental and Urban Issues* 13, no. 1 (October 1985): 3–5.

"The Oldest Church in the U.S.A." *The Anglican Digest* (4th Quarter A.D. 1979): 3–8.

Olsen, Arlene R. *A Guide to the Architecture of Miami Beach*. Miami: Dade Heritage Trust, 1978.

"Pan Am's Storied History." *Miami Herald*, 5 December 1991, 20A.

Pancoast, Russell T. "Miami Architecture So Far." In *A Guide to the Architecture of Miami*, edited by a Committee of the Florida South Chapter, American Institute of Architects. Miami, Fla.: Florida South Chapter, American Institute of Architects, 1963.

Parks, Arva Moore. *The Forgotten Frontier: Florida Through the Lens of Ralph Middleton Munroe*. Miami, Fla.: Banyan Books, 1977.

———. "The History of Coconut Grove." M.A. thesis, University of Miami, 1971.

———. "Miami in 1876." *Tequesta* 35 (1975): 89–139.

———. *Miami: "The Magic City."* 2d ed. Miami, Fla.: Centennial Press, 1991.

———. "Storm & Sunshine." *City News*, 1, 15. Miami: Downtown Development Authority, Fall 1992.

Parson, Franklin. *The Story of the First Metropolitan Government in the United States*. Winter Park, Fla.: Center for Practical Politics, [1959].

Patricios, Nicholas. "Comparisons of Post-occupancy Evaluations Between Users and Architects." *Proceedings of the Association of Collegiate Schools of Architecture (ACSA), 67th Annual Meeting*, edited by Michael Bednar, 252–66. Washington, D.C.: ACSA, 1979.

Penn, Stanley W. "Glass Buildings: Is Fashion Over?" *Wall Street Journal*, 19 February 1964, 14.

———. *Lemon City: Pioneering on Biscayne Bay 1850–1925*. Miami, Fla.: Banyan Books, 1976.

Peters, Thelma. *Biscayne Country, 1870–1926*. Miami, Fla.: Banyan Books, 1981.

"Practice Profile: Alfred Browning Parker, FAIA." *Florida Architect* 21, no. 3 (May/June 1971): 23–28.

Raeburn, Michael, ed. *Architecture of the Western World*. New York: Rizzoli International Publications, 1980.

Reardon, L. F. *The Florida Hurricane and Disaster*. Miami, Fla.: Miami Publishing Co., 1926; rpt ed., Coral Gables, Fla.: Arva Parks and Company, 1986.

Reed, Ted. "Running to Stay in Place." *Miami Herald Business Monday*, 12 February 1990, 1ff.

———, et al., "The Bitter End: Pan Am Closes." *Miami Herald*, 5 December 1991, 1A.

Rhodes, Robert M. "Growth Management in Florida 1985 and Beyond." *Florida Environmental and Urban Issues* 13, no. 2 (January 1986): 1.

Robertson, William. "Tales of Old Lie within Area's Sprawl: Buena Vista East Weathers Change." *Miami Herald*, 28 April 1991, 1G.

Robinson, Karalyn W. "Introduction: Coming of Age . . . the Art Deco District." In *Portfolio*, edited by Barbara Baer Capitman, 2–3. Miami Beach, Fla.: Miami Design Preservation League, 1979.

Rodriguez, Ivan. "From Brickell Avenue to the Beach, It's Marvelous, Magical, My-o-my Miami." *Florida Architect* 34, no. 3 (May/June 1987): 52–59.

Rodriguez, Rene. "Bass Museum Started as Library." *Miami Herald Neighbors*, 27 May 1990, 23.

———. "Cauley Square Started as Storm-proof Fortress." *Miami Herald Neighbors*, 15 July 1990, 32.

———. "Dade County Courthouse was Built Around the Old." *Miami Herald Neighbors*, 26 August 1990, 40.

———. "Gables Club was *the* Spot to Socialize in the 1920s." *Miami Herald Neighbors*, 26 May 1991, 30.

———. "Gables' Colonnade Boasts a Rich Past." *Miami Herald Neighbors*, 20 May 1990, 24.

———. "Gates Enhance Gables' Charm." *Miami Herald Neighbors*, 22 April 1990, 28.

———. "Grove Library to Mark 96 Chapters of History." *Miami Herald Neighbors*, 14 April 1991, 8.

———. "Gusman Center: Urban Oasis." *Miami Herald Neighbors*, 24 June 1990, 28.

———. "A Link to Vizcaya's Past." *Miami Herald Neighbors*, 31 March 1991, 36.

———. "Luxury Miami Beach Resort Housed Mount Sinai Hospital." *Miami Herald Neighbors*, 6 January 1991, 28.

———. "Miami High Building Is an Architectural Gem." *Miami Herald Neighbors*, 22 July 1990, 32.

———. "Miami's Alamo Was Hospital, Not Fort." *Miami Herald Neighbors*, 13 May 1990, 30.

———. "Ojus Neighborhood Began as a Short-lived Little Town." *Miami Herald Neighbors*, 1 July 1990, 25.

———. "Private Funds Built Boulevard." *Miami Herald Neighbors*, 21 July 1991, 18.

———. "Rock Pit Operator Namesake of Park." *Miami Herald Neighbors*, 23 June 1991, 19.

———. "Well-loved Grove Mansion Is Growing Old Gracefully." *Miami Herald Neighbors*, 23 December 1990, 25.

Rogers, Peggy. "Miami (Brickell) Arquitectonica." *Miami Herald Neighbors*, 6 May 1990, 2.

Root, Keith. *Miami Beach Art Deco Guide*. Miami Beach, Fla.: Miami Design Preservation League, 1987.

Rowe, Sean. "Islandia." *Miami Herald Neighbors*, 1 March 1990, 12.

Russell, James. "Business in Miami Is a Tale of Two Fortunes." *Miami Herald*, 3 October 1991, 1C.

Sadowski, Bill. "Growth Management." *Florida Planning* 2, no. 12 (August 1991): 1.

Safdie, Moshe. "Skyscrapers Shouldn't Look Down on Humanity." *New York Times*, 29 May 1988, 30.

Sanchez, Robert. "It's Time to Appreciate One of Florida's Resources." *Miami Herald*, 7 April 1990, 26A.

Sessa, Frank B. "Miami on the Eve of the Boom: 1923." *Tequesta* 11 (1951): 3–26.

Seventy Years of Miami Architecture. Catalogue of the exhibition. Miami Beach, Fla.: Bass Museum of Art, 1988.

Sewell, John. *Miami Memoirs*. Miami: Arva Parks and Co., 1987.

Shappee, Nathan D. "Flagler's Undertakings in Miami in 1897." *Tequesta* 19 (1959): 3–13.

Sherman, Roger W., AIA. Introduction to *A Guide to the Architecture of Miami*, edited by a Committee of the Florida South Chapter of the American Institute of Architects. Miami, Fla.: Florida South Chapter, AIA, 1963.

Sheskin, Ira M. "South Florida—650,000 Jews!!" *Florida Jewish Demography* 2, no. 1 (1 December 1988): [1–4].

———. "The Jews of South Florida." Chapter 12 in *South Florida: The Winds of Change*, edited by Thomas D. Boswell. Miami, Fla.: Annual Conference of the Association of American Geographers, April 1991.

Slevin, Peter, and Harold Maass. "Military Machine

Gathers Speed." *Miami Herald*, 1 September 1992, 23A.

So, Frank S., and Judith Getzels, eds. *The Practice of Local Government Planning*. Washington, D.C.: International City Management Association, 1988.

Sofen, Edward. *The Metropolitan Experiment: A Metro Section Study*. Garden City, N.Y.: Anchor Books, 1966.

Spanish Land Grants in Florida: Confirmed Claims. Vol. 3: *D–J*. Tallahassee, Fla.: State Library Board, March 1941.

"A Spy-Glass View of Architecture: Interview with Alfred B. Parker and Lester C. Pancoast." *Florida Architect* 8, no. 6 (June 1958): 14–17.

Stronge, William. "The Southeast Florida Economy." Chapter 6 in *South Florida: The Winds of Change*, edited by Thomas D. Boswell. Miami, Fla.: Annual Conference of the Association of American Geographers, April 1991.

Strouse, Charles. "In Inner City, Success Sprouts Amid Frustration." *Miami Herald*, 8 September 1993, 1A.

———. "Non-Cuban Hispanic Census Count Rising." *Miami Herald*, 9 April 1992, 1B.

———. "Picture Perfect." *Miami Herald Neighbors*, 6 October 1991, 30.

———. "Plan to Preserve Overtown Spirit." *Miami Herald Neighbors*, 26 November 1989, 16.

———. "Rebirth of Overtown a Promise Unfulfilled." *Miami Herald*, 7 September 1993, 1A.

———. "300,000 Moved to West Dade in '80s." *Miami Herald*, 17 March 1991, 1B.

Swarns, Rachel L. "Exodus from the Inner City." *Miami Herald*, 5 September 1993, 1A.

Tanfani, Joe. "Grove Voters Pick Council, Support Secession from City." *Miami Herald*, 23 October 1991, 3B.

Tasker, Fred. "Greetings from Florida: The Wave of Crime Against Visitors Hasn't Hurt Tourism. More People Than Ever Wish They Were Here." *Miami Herald*, 10 November 1991, 1J.

———. "South Beach: Can It Win the Future Without Losing the Past?" *Miami Herald*, 13 June 1990, 1D.

Tasker, Georgia. "Expansion Plan Will Keep Kampong Flourishing." *Miami Herald*, 10 November 1991, 1G.

———. "Parks' Designer Helped Shape Dade." *Miami Herald*, 11 February 1990, 11H.

Taylor, Jean. *The Villages of South Dade*. St. Petersburg, Fla.: Byron Kennedy and Company, 1985.

Tebeau, Charles W. *A History of Florida*. Coral Gables, Fla.: University of Miami Press, 1980.

Tomb, Geoffrey. "Again on Ballot: Who We Are." *Miami Herald*, 3 May 1990, 1B.

———. "Extinction in the '80s, Endangered in the '90s." *Miami Herald*, 31 December 1989, 2C.

———. "Voters Spell It Out: Keep it D-A-D-E." *Miami Herald*, 9 May 1990, 1B.

Touche Ross and Co. *A Review of the Two-Tier Government in Miami/Dade County for the City of Miami*. N.p., 1978.

Townshend, F. Trench. *Wild Life in Florida with a Visit to Cuba*. London: Hurst and Blackett, 1875.

True, David O. "The Freducci Map of 1514–15: What It Discloses of Early Florida History." *Tequesta* 4 (1944): 50–55.

Uguccioni, Ellen. "Villages That Might Have Been." *Miami Herald Neighbors*, 23 February 1989, 16.

Varona, Esperanza B. *The Bernhardt E. Muller Collection, 1923–1960*. Coral Gables, Fla.: University of Miami Otto Richter Library Archives and Special Collections, 1987.

Viglucci, Andres. "Miami Is Reflection of World." *Miami Herald*, 29 March 1990, 1B.

———, and Susana Bellido. "Waves of Cubans Risk Rough Seas." *Miami Herald*, 23 November 1993, 1B.

Vondracek, Woody. "Know Your Art Deco." *Miami Herald*, 3 January 1993, 1G.

Wallace, Richard. "Little Havana Excursion Includes a History Lesson." *Miami Herald*, 28 April 1991, 1B.

———. "South Florida Grows to a Latin Beat." *Miami Herald*, 6 March 1991, 1A.

———. "South Florida's Evolving Ethnic Diversity." *Miami Herald*, 17 March 1991, 1C.

Ward, C. H. *The Lure of the Southland, Miami, and Miami Beach, Florida*. Miami, Fla.: n.p., 1915.

Warnke, James R. *Ghost Towns of Florida*. Boynton Beach, Fla.: Roving Photographers and Assoc., 1978.

Warren, Michael. "Will Success Kill the Deco District?" *Planning* 56, no. 2 (February 1990): 21–24.

Weed, Robert Law. *Robert Law Weed, A.I.A., Architect*. N.p., n.d.

Werne, Jo. "Morningside." *Miami Herald*, 3 June 1990, 1J.

Whited, Charles. "Film Industry Is Basking in *Vice's* Glow." *Miami Herald*, 29 April 1990, 4B.

————. "West Dade at Crossroads Over Growth." *Miami Herald*, 24 February 1990, 1B.

Whitefield, Mimi. "Raft Trips to U.S. Become Obsession." *Miami Herald*, 2 June 1991, 1A.

Wilson, F. Page. "Miami: From Frontier to Metropolis: An Appraisal." *Tequesta* 14 (1954): 25–49.

Wolff, Reinhold P. *Miami Metro: The Road to Urban Unity*. Area Development Series, no. 9. Coral Gables, Fla.: University of Miami, Bureau of Business and Economic Research, 1960.

————. "Recent Economic Trends in South Florida." *Tequesta* 4 (November 1944): 45–49.

Wragg, Joanna. "Local Government, Key Biscayne Style." *Miami Herald*, 30 June 1991, 2C.

Year Book Committee, Architectural League of Greater Miami and the Florida South Chapter AIA. *Year Book of Joint Exhibition*. Miami, Fla.: Florida South Chapter, AIA, 1930; 1931; 1932.

Index

Picture Credits

The photographs included in this volume have been provided courtesy of the following collections or persons:

Figures 1, 2, 3, 6, 7, 11, 26, 27, 29, 30, 31, 34, 83, 85, 86, 101, 104, 110, 113, 114, 116, 117, 119, 139, 143, 165, 167, 211: Archives and Special Collections Department, Otto G. Richter Library, University of Miami, Coral Gables, Florida.

Figures 5a, 8, 9, 10, 12, 13, 16, 23, 28, 35, 36, 84, 88, 94, 103, 112, 131, 162, 176, 177, 179: Romer Collection, Miami-Dade Public Library.

Figures 64, 65, 66, 68, 69, 70, 71, 72, 73, 127, 128, 129, 130, 132, 135, 136, 138, 140, 144, 149, 150, 152, 153, 154, 155: Historic Preservation Division, City of Coral Gables.

Figures 95, 96, 97, 98, 158, 161, 168, 171, 172, 173, 174, 178, 180: Junior League of Miami.

Figures 5b, 109: Michael Golden Photography.

Figures 24, 46: Dade Heritage Trust.

Figure 32: School of Architecture Slide Library, University of Miami. Photograph by Paul Buisson.

Figures 40, 53, 54: David J. Kaminsky.

Figures 67, 108: Samuel D. LaRoue, Jr.

Figures 75, 107: Historical Association of Southern Florida.

Figure 111: Gusman Center for the Performing Arts.

Figure 157: Coconut Grove Bank.

Figure 170: Fuchs Baking Company.

Figure 182: Jaime E. Borrelli, AIA.

Figures 183, 204: Mark Surloff.

Figure 184: Gail Baldwin, AIA.

Figure 185: Cuban Museum of Art and Culture.

Figures 186, 191: Carlos Domenech.

Figures 187, 188, 190, 192, 193, 200, 215: Steven Brooke.

Figures 189, 197: Dan Forer.

Figure 196: Charles Harrison Pawley, FAIA.

Figure 197: Dan Forer.

Figure 198: Ezra Stoller.

Figure 199: George F. Reed, FAIA.

Figure 202: Ramon G. Perez-Alonzo, AIA.

Figure 203: Osvaldo Perez, AIA.

Figure 214: Daniel Perez-Zarraga, AIA.

Figure 224: Downtown Development Authority, Miami.

Figure 246: Roney J. Mateu, AIA.

Figures 251, 252: Margot Ammidown, Director, Historical Preservation Division, Metro-Dade County.

Figure 250: Rocco Ceo.

Figure 253: Ira Victor.

All other photographs are by the author.

Maps and Drawings

Figures 14, 15, 17: Adapted from Metropolitan Dade County Planning Department maps.

Figure 19: Adapted from a map by Reginald Myers and Steve Doig, *Miami Herald*, 17 March 1991, 1C.

Figures 20, 21: Adapted from Historic Preservation Division, Metropolitan Dade County, *Resourceful Rehab*, 1987.

Figure 248: Adapted from *Water Resources Atlas of Florida*, edited by Edward A. Fernald and Donald J. Patton.

Figure 249: Adapted from a satellite photo from the National Hurricane Center and a map by Dan Clifford of the *Miami Herald*.

Maps and drawings of architectural styles are by Lana Patricios.